Early praise for *Software Design X-Rays*

Adam has made one of the most significant contributions to software engineering over the past years. Listen and ye shall learn.

➤ **John Lewis**
Consultant and Troubleshooter

Adam successfully teaches me *why* things are the way I have learned that they are during my 30 years in the software-development world. As if that wasn't enough, he also teaches me a whole slew of things I didn't know about! This is a must-read!

➤ **Jimmy Nilsson**
Author of *Applying Domain-Driven Design and Patterns*

I felt my brain was exploding with ideas and *aha*s all the way through my reading.

➤ **Giovanni Asproni**
Principal Consultant

Adam encapsulates the challenges of a technical lead for a product in a large shared codebase. His social code-analysis techniques turn a dry static codebase into a living, breathing ecosystem and chart its interactions over its lifetime, helping you to identify those areas worth refactoring.

➤ **Ivan Houston**
Principal Software Engineer

Adam takes you behind the scenes of pragmatic software analysis. He's bridging the gap between algorithms for mining software repositories and performing refactorings based on the gained insights. Definitely the right way to go in our industry!

➤ **Markus Harrer**
Software Development Analyst

Software systems age and erode like any other human-made structure. *Software Design X-Rays* provides immediately useable tools and approaches to spot the parts in most dire need of improvement and helps you manage your technical debt. Adam does a great job at explaining that this seemingly complex analysis is actually not that hard and that you can do it right now.

➤ **Michael Hunger**
    Head of Developer Relations Engineering, Neo4j

This book offers plenty of valuable psychological insights that are likely to surprise developers and managers alike. Tornhill's ability to apply heuristics like the "concept of surprise" to complex code systems reinforces the human element of software development and connects code to emotion.

➤ **Lauri Apple**
    Open Source Evangelist and Agile Coach, Zalando

An invaluable set of techniques to get a better understanding of your code, your team and your company.

➤ **Vicenç García Altés**
    IT Consultant, Craft Foster Ltd.

Software Design X-Rays

Fix Technical Debt with Behavioral Code Analysis

Adam Tornhill

The Pragmatic Bookshelf

Raleigh, North Carolina

Our Pragmatic books, screencasts, and audio books can help you and your team create better software and have more fun. Visit us at *https://pragprog.com*.

The team that produced this book includes:

Publisher: Andy Hunt
VP of Operations: Janet Furlow
Managing Editor: Brian MacDonald
Supervising Editor: Jacquelyn Carter
Development Editor: Adaobi Obi Tulton
Copy Editor: Candace Cunningham
Indexing: Potomac Indexing, LLC
Layout: Gilson Graphics

For sales, volume licensing, and support, please contact *support@pragprog.com*.

For international rights, please contact *rights@pragprog.com*.

ISBN-13: 978-1-68050-272-5

Book version: P1.0—March 2018

Contents

Part II — Work with Large Codebases and Organizations

Acknowledgments

Writing a book is a lot like programming in the sense that it's an iterative process where most of the work is rework. Since *Software Design X-Rays* is my fourth book I sort of knew the effort and time it would take. Or at least I thought I did, as it turned out to be so much harder than I initially expected. (Again a bit like programming, isn't it?) At the end it was worth every minute and I'm really proud of the book you're reading right now. That wouldn't have been possible without all the wonderful people who helped me make this book much better than what I could have done on my own.

I'd like to thank The Pragmatic Bookshelf for this opportunity. I also want to thank my editor, Adaobi Obi Tulton, for all her support, motivation, and great work in shaping the book.

Several people volunteered their time and expertise by reading early drafts of the book: Jimmy Nilsson, Giovanni Asproni, Ivan Houston, Markus Harrer, Michael Hunger, Lauri Apple, Per Rovegård, Joseph Fahey, Louis Hansen, Vicenç García Altés, Nascif Abousalh-Neto, Clare Macrae, Michael Keeling, Alberto Fernandez Reyes, Javier Collado, and Ian Sleigh. Thanks for all your helpful advice and constructive criticism.

Over the past years I've been contacted by people from all around the globe who've read my previous work or watched my presentations. Thanks to all of you—your feedback and friendly words are what motivates me to keep doing this. The same goes for my amazing colleagues at Empear and for my fantastic parents, Eva and Thorbjörn, who always encourage and support me.

Finally, I want to thank my family—Jenny, Morten, and Ebbe—for their endless love and support. You mean everything to me and I love you.

The World of Behavioral Code Analysis

Welcome, dear reader—I'm happy to have you here! Together we'll dive into the fascinating field of evolving software systems to learn how behavioral code analysis helps us make better decisions. This is important because our average software project is much less efficient than it could be.

The history of large-scale software systems is a tale of cost overruns, death marches, and heroic fights with legacy code monsters. One prominent reason is technical debt, which represents code that's more expensive to maintain than it should be. Repaying technical debt is hard due to the scale of modern software projects; with hundreds of developers and a multitude of technologies, no one has a holistic overview. We're about to change that.

In this book, you learn a set of techniques that gives you an easily accessible overview of your codebase, together with methods to prioritize improvements based on the expected return on investment. That means you'll be comfortable with picking up any large-scale codebase, analyzing it, and suggesting specific refactorings based on how the developers have worked with the code so far.

Good code is as much about social design as it is about technical concerns. We reflect that by learning to uncover organizational inefficiencies, resolve coordination bottlenecks among teams, and assess the consequences of knowledge loss in your organization.

Why You Should Read This Book

We can never reason efficiently about a complex system based on its code alone. In doing so we miss out on long-term trends and social data that are often more important than any property of the code itself. This means we need to understand how we—as an organization—interact with the code we build.

This book shows you how as you learn to do the following:

- Use data to prioritize technical debt and ensure your suggested improvements pay off.

- Identify communication and team-coordination bottlenecks in code.

- Use behavioral code analysis to ensure your architecture supports your organization.

- Supervise the technical sprawl and detect hidden dependencies in a microservice architecture.

- Detect code quality problems before they become maintenance issues.

- Drive refactorings guided by data from how your system evolves.

- Bridge the gap between developers and business-oriented people by highlighting the cost of technical debt and visualizing the effects of refactorings.

If all this sounds magical, I assure you it's not. Rather than magic—which is usually a dead end for software—this book relies on data science and human psychology. Since we're part of an opinionated industry, it's hard to know up front what works and what doesn't. So this book makes sure to include references to published research so that we know the techniques are effective before attempting them on our own systems.

We also make sure to discuss the limitations of the techniques, and suggest alternative approaches when applicable. As noted computer scientist Fred Brooks pointed out, there's no silver bullet. (See *No Silver Bullet—Essence and Accident in Software Engineering [Bro86]*.) Instead, view this book as a way of building a set of skills to complement your existing expertise and make decisions guided by data. The reward is a new perspective on software development that will change how you work with legacy systems.

Who Is This Book For?

To get the most out of this book you should be an experienced programmer, technical lead, or software architect. The most important thing is that you have worked on fairly large software projects and experienced the various pains and problems we try to solve in the book.

You don't have to be a programming expert, but you should be comfortable looking at small code samples. Most of our discussions are on a conceptual level and since the analyses are technology-neutral, the book will apply no matter what programming language you work with. This is an important aspect of the techniques you're about to learn, as most of today's systems are polyglot codebases.

You should also have experience with a version-control system. The practical examples assume you use Git, but the techniques themselves can be used with other version-control tools, such as Subversion, TFS, and Mercurial, by performing a temporary migration to Git.[1]

How Should You Read This Book?

The book progresses from smaller systems to large-scale codebases with millions of lines of code and thousands of developers. The early chapters lay the foundation for the more complex analyses by introducing fundamental concepts like hotspots and dependency analyses based on time and evolution of code. This means you'll want to read the first three chapters to build a solid toolset for tackling the more advanced material in Part II.

The last two chapters of Part I, Chapter 4, *Pay Off Your Technical Debt*, on page 51, and Chapter 5, *The Principles of Code Age*, on page 73, travel deeper into real code and are the most technical ones in the book. Feel free to skip them if you're more interested in maintaining a high-level strategic view of your codebase.

We'll touch on the social aspects of code early, but the full treatment is given in the first chapters of Part II. Modern software development is an increasingly collaborative and complex effort, so make sure you read Chapter 6, *Spot Your System's Tipping Point*, on page 93, and Chapter 7, *Beyond Conway's Law*, on page 117.

No analysis is better than the data it operates on, so whatever path you chose through the book, make sure to read *Know the Biases and Workarounds for Behavioral Code Analysis*, on page 205, which explains some special cases that you may come across in your work.

Most chapters also contain exercises that let you practice what you've learned and go deeper into different aspects of the analyses. If you get stuck, just turn to Appendix 4, *Hints and Solutions to the Exercises*, on page 227.

Access the Exercise URLs Online

 Most exercises contain links to interactive visualizations and graphs. If you're reading the printed version of this book you can access all those links from a document on my homepage instead of typing them out by hand.[2]

---

1.   https://git-scm.com/book/it/v2/Git-and-Other-Systems-Migrating-to-Git
2.   http://www.adamtornhill.com/code/xrayexercises.html

To Readers of *Your Code as a Crime Scene*

If you have read my previous book, *Your Code as a Crime Scene [Tor15]*, you should be aware that there is an overlap between the two books, and *Software Design X-Rays* expands upon the previous work. As a reader of my previous book you will get a head start since some topics in Part I, such as hotspots and temporal coupling, are familiar to you. However, you will still want to skim through those early chapters as they extend the techniques to work on the more detailed level of functions and methods. This is particularly important if you work in a codebase with large source-code files that are hard to maintain.

 Joe asks:
Who Am I?

Joe is a reading companion that shows up every now and then to question the arguments made in the main text. As such, Joe wants to make sure we leave no stone unturned as we travel the world of behavioral code analysis.

How Do I Get Behavioral Data for My Code?

The techniques in this book build on the behavioral patterns of all the programmers who contribute to your codebase. However, instead of starting to collect such data we want to apply our analyses to existing codebases. Fortunately, we already have all the data we need in our version-control system.

Historically, we've used version control as a complicated backup system that—with good fortune and somewhat empathic peers—allows several programmers to collaborate on code. Now we'll turn it inside out as we see how to read the story of our systems based on their historical records. The resulting information will give you insights that you cannot get from the code alone.

As you read through the book, you get to explore version-control data from real-world codebases; you'll learn to find duplicated code in the Linux kernel,[3] detect surprising hidden dependencies in Microsoft's ASP.NET Core MVC framework,[4] do some mental gymnastics as we look at a refactoring of Google's TensorFlow codebase,[5] and much more.

---

3. https://en.wikipedia.org/wiki/Linux_kernel
4. https://www.asp.net/mvc
5. https://www.tensorflow.org/

These codebases represent some of the best work we—as a software community—are able to produce. The idea is that if we're able to come up with productivity improvements in code like this, you'll be able to do the same in your own work.

All the case studies use open source projects hosted on GitHub, which means you don't have to install anything to follow along with the book. The case studies are chosen to reflect common issues that are found in many closed-source systems.

Time Stands Still

 The online analysis results represent the state of the codebases at the time of writing, and a snapshot of each repository is available on a dedicated GitHub account.[6] This is important since popular open source projects evolve at a rapid pace, which means the case studies would otherwise become outdated faster than this week's JavaScript framework.

Most case studies use the analysis tool *CodeScene* to illustrate the examples.[7] CodeScene is developed by Empear, the startup where I work, and is free to use for open source projects.

We won't spend any time learning CodeScene, but we'll use the tool as a portfolio —an interactive gallery. This saves you time as you don't have to focus on the mechanics of the analyses (unless you want to), and guarantees that you see the same results as we discuss in the book. The results are publicly accessible so you don't have to sign up with CodeScene to follow along.

I make sure to point out alternative tooling paths when they exist. Often we can go a long way with simple command-line tools, and we'll use them when feasible. I also point out third-party tools that complement the analyses and provide deeper information. Finally, there's another path to behavioral code analysis through the open source tool *Code Maat* that I developed to illustrate the implementation of the different algorithms. We cover Code Maat in Appendix 2, *Code Maat: An Open Source Analysis Engine*, on page 215.

Finally, think of tooling as the manifestation of ideas and a way to put them into practice. Consequently, our goal in this book is to understand how the analyses work behind the scenes and how they help solve specific problems.

---

6. https://github.com/SoftwareDesignXRays
7. https://codescene.io/

Online Resources

As mentioned earlier, the repositories for the case studies are available on a dedicated GitHub account. Additionally, this book has its own web page where you can find the community forum.[8] There you can ask questions, post comments, and submit errata.

With the tooling covered, we're ready to explore the fascinating field of evolving systems. Let's dig in and get a new perspective on our code!

@AdamTornhill

Malmö, Sweden, March 2018

---

8. https://pragprog.com/book/atevol

Part I

Prioritize and React to Technical Debt

In this part you'll learn to identify the aspects of your system that benefit the most from improvements, to detect organizational issues, and to ensure that the suggested improvements give you a real return on your investment.

Man seems to insist on ignoring the lessons available from history.

> ➤ *Norman Borlaug*

CHAPTER 1

Why Technical Debt Isn't Technical

Most organizations find it hard to prioritize and repay their technical debt because of the scale of their systems, with millions of lines of code and multiple development teams. In that context, no one has a holistic overview. So what if we could mine the collective intelligence of all contributing programmers and make decisions based on data from how the organization actually works with the code?

In this chapter you'll learn one such approach with the potential to change how we view software systems. This chapter gives you the foundation for the rest of the book as you see how behavioral code analysis fills an important gap in our ability to reason about systems. Let's jump right in and see what it's all about.

Questioning Technical Debt

Technical debt is a metaphor that lets developers explain the need for refactorings and communicate technical trade-offs to business people.[1] When we take on technical debt we choose to release our software faster but at the expense of future costs, as technical debt affects our ability to evolve a software system. Just like its financial counterpart, technical debt incurs interest payments.

Technical-debt decisions apply both at the micro level, where we may choose to hack in a new feature with the use of complex conditional logic, and at the macro level when we make architectural trade-offs to get the system through yet another release. In this sense technical debt is a strategic business decision rather than a technical one.

---

1. http://wiki.c2.com/?WardExplainsDebtMetaphor

Recently the technical debt metaphor has been extended to include *reckless debt*.[2] Reckless debt arises when our code violates basic design principles without even a short-term payoff. The amount of reckless debt in our codebase limits our ability to take on intentional debt and thus restricts our future options.[3]

In retrospect it's hard to distinguish between deliberate technical debt and reckless debt. Priorities change, projects rotate staff, and as time passes an organization may no longer possess the knowledge of why a particular decision was made. Yet it's important to uncover the root cause of problematic code since it gives you—as an organization—important feedback. For example, lots of reckless debt indicates the need for training and improved practices.

That said, this book uses both kinds of debt interchangeably. Sure, technical debt in its original sense is a deliberate trade-off whereas reckless debt doesn't offer any short-term gains. However, the resulting context is the same: we face code that isn't up to par and we need to do something about it. So our definition of technical debt is *code that's more expensive to maintain than it should be.* That is, we pay an interest rate on it.

Keep a Decision Log

 Human memory is fragile and cognitive biases are real, so a project decision log will be a tremendous help in keeping track of your rationale for accepting technical debt. Jotting down decisions on a wiki or shared document helps you maintain knowledge over time.

Technical debt is also frequently misused to describe *legacy code*. In fact, the two terms are often used interchangeably to describe code that

1. lacks quality, and

2. we didn't write ourselves.

Michael Feathers, in his groundbreaking book *Working Effectively with Legacy Code [Fea04]*, describes legacy code as code without tests. Technical debt, on the other hand, often occurs in the very test code intended to raise the quality of the overall system! You get plenty of opportunities to see that for yourself in the case studies throughout this book.

In addition, legacy code is an undesirable after-the-fact state, whereas technical debt may be a strategic choice. "Let's design a legacy system," said absolutely no one ever. Fortunately, the practical techniques you'll learn in

---

2.   https://martinfowler.com/bliki/TechnicalDebtQuadrant.html
3.   http://www.construx.com/10x_Software_Development/Technical_Debt/

this book work equally well to address both legacy code and technical debt. With that distinction covered, let's look into interest rate on code.

Interest Rate Is a Function of Time

Let's do a small thought experiment. Have a look at the following code snippet. What do you think of the quality of that code? Is it a solution you'd accept in a code review?

```
void displayProgressTask() {
    for (int i = 1; i < 6 ; i++) {
        switch (i) {
            case 1:
                setMark("<step 1");
                updateDisplay();
                break;
            case 2:
                setMark("<step 2");
                updateDisplay();
                break;
            case 3:
                setMark("<step 3");
                updateDisplay();
                break;
            case 4:
                setMark("<step 4");
                updateDisplay();
                break;
            case 5:
                setMark("<step 5");
                updateDisplay();
                break;
        }
    }
}
```

Of course not! We'd never write code like this ourselves. Never ever. Not only is the code the epitome of repetitive copy-paste; its accidental complexity obscures the method's responsibility. It's simply bad code. But is it a problem? Is it technical debt? Without more context we can't tell. Just because some code is bad doesn't mean it's technical debt. It's not technical debt unless we have to pay interest on it, and *interest rate is a function of time.*

This means we would need a time dimension on top of our code to reason about interest rate. We'd need to know how often we actually have to modify (and read) each piece of code to separate the debt that matters for our ability to maintain the system from code that may be subpar but doesn't impact us much.

You'll soon learn how you get that time dimension of code. Before we go there, let's consider large-scale systems to see why the distinction between actual technical debt and code that's just substandard matters.

The Perils of Quantifying Technical Debt

Last year I visited an organization to help prioritize its technical debt. Prior to my arrival the team had evaluated a tool capable of quantifying technical debt. The tool measured a number of attributes such as the ratio of code comments and unit test coverage, and estimated how much effort would be needed to bring the codebase to a perfect score on all these implied quality dimensions. The organization threw this tool at its 15-year-old codebase, and the tool reported that they had accumulated 4,000 years of technical debt!

Of course, those estimated years of technical debt aren't linear (see the following figure), as much debt had been created in parallel by the multitude of programmers working on the code. Those 4,000 years of technical debt may have been an accurate estimate, but that doesn't mean it's particularly useful. Given 4,000 years of technical debt, where do you start if you want to pay it back? Is all debt equally important? And does it really matter if a particular piece of code lacks unit-test coverage or exhibits few code comments?

With 4,000 years of technical debt, your debt started to accumulate from the time Moses parted the Red Sea.

In fact, if we uncritically start to fix such reported quality issues to achieve a "better" score, we may find that we make the code worse. Even with a more balanced approach there's no way of knowing if the reported issues actually affect our ability to maintain the code. In addition, it's a mistake to quantify technical debt from code alone because much technical debt isn't even technical. Let's explore a common fallacy to see why.

Why We Mistake Organizational Problems for Technical Issues

Have you ever joined a new organization and been told, "Oh, that part of the codebase is really hard to understand"? Or perhaps you notice that some code attracts more bugs than a sugar cube covered with syrup on a sunny road. If that doesn't sound familiar, maybe you've heard, "We have a hard time merging our different branches—we need to buy a better merge tool." While these claims are likely to be correct in principle, the root cause is often social and organizational problems. Let's see why.

Several years ago I joined a project that was late before it even started. Management had tried to compress the original schedule from the estimated one year down to a mere three months. How do you do that? Easy, they thought: just throw four times as many developers on it.

As those three months passed there was, to great dismay, no completion in sight. As I joined I spent my first days talking to the developers and managers, trying to get the big picture. It turned out to be a gloomy one. Defects were detected at a higher rate than they could be fixed. Critical features were still missing. And morale was low since the code was so hard to understand.

As I dove into the code I was pleasantly surprised. Sure, the code wasn't exactly a work of art. It wasn't beautiful in the sense a painting by Monet is, but the application was by no means particularly hard to understand. I've seen worse. Much worse. So why did the project members struggle with it? To answer that question we need to take a brief detour into the land of cognitive psychology to learn how we build our understanding of code and how organizational factors may hinder it.

Your Mental Models of Code

One of the most challenging aspects of programming is that we need to serve two audiences. The first, the machine that executes our programs, doesn't care much about style but is annoyingly pedantic about content and pretty bad at filling in the gaps. Our second audience, the programmers maintaining our code, has much more elaborate mental processes and needs our guidance to use those processes efficiently. That's why we focus on writing expressive and well-organized code. After all, that poor maintenance programmer may well be our future self.

We use the same mental processes to understand code as those we use in everyday life beyond our keyboards (evolution wasn't kind enough to equip our brains with a coding center). As we learn a topic we build mental representations of that domain. Psychologists refer to such mental models as *schemas*. A schema is a theoretical construct used to describe the way we organize knowledge in our memory and how we use that knowledge for a particular event. You can think of a schema as a mental script implemented in neurons rather than code.

Understanding code also builds on schemas. You have general schemas for syntactic and semantic knowledge, like knowing the construction order of a class hierarchy in C++ or how to interpret Haskell. These schemas are fairly stable and translate across different applications you work on. You also have specific schemas to represent the mental model of a particular system or module. These schemas represent your domain expertise. Building expertise means evolving better and more efficient mental models. (See *Software Design: Cognitive Aspects [DB02]* for a summary of the research on schemas in program comprehension and *Cognitive Psychology [BG05]* for a pure psychological view of expertise.)

Building efficient schemas takes time and it's hard cognitive work for everything but the simplest programs. That task gets significantly harder when applied to a moving target like code under heavy development. In the project that tried to compress its time line from one year to three months by adding more people, the developers found the code hard to understand because code they wrote one day looked different three days later after being worked on by five other developers. Excess parallel work leads to *development congestion*, which is intrinsically at odds with mastery of the code.

Readable Code Is Economical Code

 There's an economic argument to be made for readable code, too. We developers spend the majority of our time making modifications to existing code and most of that time is spent trying to understand what the code we intend to change does in the first place. Unless we plan for short-lived code, like prototypes or quick experiments, optimizing code for understanding is one of the most important choices we can make as an organization.

This project is an extreme case, but the general pattern is visible in many software projects of all scales. Development congestion doesn't have to apply to the whole codebase. Sometimes it's limited to a part of the code, perhaps a shared library or a particular subsystem, that attracts many different teams. The consequence is that the schemas we developers need to build up get invalidated on a regular basis. In such situations true expertise in a system cannot be maintained. Not only is it expensive and frustrating—there are significant quality costs, too. Let's explore them.

Quality Suffers with Parallel Development

Practices like peer reviews and coding standards help you mitigate the problems with parallel development by catching misunderstandings and enforcing a degree of consistency. However, even when done right there are still code-quality issues. We'll investigate the organizational side of technical debt in more detail in Part II of this book, but I want to provide an overall understanding of the main issues now and keep them in the back of our minds as we move on.

Organizational factors are some of the best predictors of defects:

- The structure of the development organization is a stronger predictor of defects than any code metrics. (See *The Influence of Organizational Structure on Software Quality [NMB08]* for the empirical data.)

- The risk that a specific commit introduces a defect increases with the number of developers who have previously worked on the modified code. (See *An Empirical Study on Developer Related Factors Characterizing Fix-Inducing Commits [TBPD15]*.)

- These factors affect us even within a strong quality culture of peer reviews. For example, a research study on Linux found that the modules with the most parallel work showed an increase in security-related bugs (*Secure open source collaboration: an empirical study of Linus' law [MW09]*). This indicates that the open source collaboration model isn't immune to social factors such as parallel development.

Software by its very nature is complex, and with parallel development we add yet another layer of challenges. The more parallel development, the more process, coordination, and communication we need. And when we humans have to communicate around deep technical details like code, things often go wrong. No wonder bugs thrive in congested areas.

Make Knowledge Distribution a Strategic Investment

There's a fine balance between minimizing parallel development and attaining knowledge distribution in an organization. Most organizations want several developers to be familiar with the code in order to avoid depending on specific individuals. Encouraging collaboration, having early design discussions, and investing in an efficient code-review process takes you far. To a certain degree it also works to rotate responsibilities or even let responsibilities overlap. The key is to make code collaboration a deliberate strategic decision rather than something that happens ad hoc due to an organization that's misaligned with the system it builds.

Mine Your Organization's Collective Intelligence

Now that we've seen how multifaceted technical debt is, it's time to discuss what we can do about it. Given this interaction of technical and organizational forces, how do we uncover the areas in need of improvement? Ideally, we'd need the following information:

- *Where's the code with the highest interest rate?* In case we have some subpar code—and which large system doesn't?—we need to know to what degree that code affects our ability to evolve the system so that we can prioritize improvements.

- *Does our architecture support the way our system evolves?* We need to know if our architecture helps us with the modifications we make to the system or if we have to work against our own architecture.

- *Are there any productivity bottlenecks for interteam coordination?* For example, are there any parts of the code where five different teams constantly have to coordinate their work?

The interesting thing is that none of this information is available in the code itself. That means we can't prioritize technical debt based on the code alone since we lack some critical information, most prominently a time dimension and social information. How can we get that information? Where's our crystal ball? It turns out we already have one—it's our version-control system.

Our *version-control data* is an informational gold mine. But it's a gold mine that we rarely dig into, except occasionally as a complicated backup system. Let's change that by having a look at the wealth of information that's stored in our version-control system.

There's More to Code than Code

Each time we make a change to our codebase, our version-control system records that change, as the following figure illustrates.

```
Commit: b557ca5
Date: 2016-02-12
Author: Kevin Flynn

     Fix behavior of StartsWithPrefix

    9    27    src/Mvc.Abstractions/ModelBinding/ModelStateDictionary.cs
                src/Mvc.Core/ControllerBase.cs
                src/Mvc.Core/Internal/ElementalValueProvider.cs
    1    39    src/Mvc.Core/Internal/PrefixContainer.cs

Commit: fd6d28d
Date 2016-02-10
Author: Professor Falken

   Make AddController not overwrite existing IControllerTypeProvider

    8    1    src/Core/Internal/ControllersAsServices.cs
   48    0    test/Core.Test/Internal/ControllerAsServicesTest.cs
   13    0    test/Mvc.FunctionalTests/ControllerFromServicesTests.cs

Commit: 910f013
Date :2016-02-05
Author Lisbeth Salander

   Fixes #4050: Throw an exception when media types are empty.

   20    1    src/Mvc.Core/Formatters/InputFormatter.cs
```

Social Information

A Time Dimension

The figure represents a small chunk from a Git log. Not only does Git know *when* a particular change took place; it also knows *who* made that change. This means we get both our time dimension and social data.

Remember our earlier discussion on large projects? We said that given the complexity, in terms of people and size, no single individual has a holistic overview. Rather, that knowledge is distributed and each contributor has a piece of the system puzzle. This is about to change because your version-control data has the potential to deliver that overview. If we switch perspective, we see that each commit in our version-control system contains important information on how we—as developers—have interacted with the code. Therefore, version-control data is more of a behavioral log than a pure technical solution to manage code. By mining and aggregating that data we're able to piece together the collective intelligence of all contributing authors. The resulting information guides future decisions about our system.

We'll get to the organizational aspects of software development in Part II, but let me give you a brief example of how version-control data helps us with the social aspects of technical debt. Git knows exactly which programmer changed which lines of code. This makes it possible to calculate the main contributor to each file simply by summing up the contributions of each developer. Based on that information you're able to generate a *knowledge map*, as the following figure illustrates.

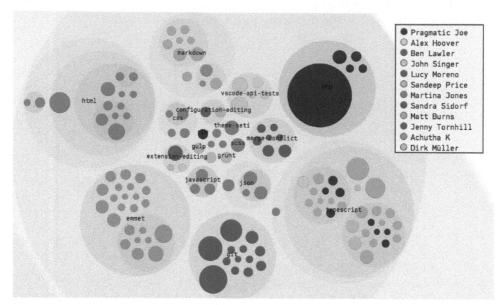

The preceding figure displays a knowledge map for Visual Studio Code, but with pseudonyms replacing the real author names for inclusion in this book.[4] Each source-code file is represented as a colored circle. The larger the circle, the more lines of code in the file it represents, and the color of the circle shows you the main developer behind that module. This is information that you use to simplify communication and to support on- and offboarding.

To evaluate an organization, you aggregate the individual contributions into their respective teams. This lets you detect parts of the code that become team-productivity bottlenecks by identifying modules that are constantly changed by members of different teams, as shown in the parallel development map on page 13.

Just as with the knowledge map, each colored circle in this figure represents a file. However, the color signals a different aspect here. The more red a circle is, the more coordination there is between different teams. In Chapter 7, *Beyond Conway's Law*, on page 117, you'll learn the algorithms behind these social maps, as well as how to act on the information they present. For now you just get a hint of what's possible when we embrace social data.

The time dimension fills a similar role by giving us insights into how our code evolves. More specifically, when you view version-control data as the collective

4. https://github.com/Microsoft/vscode

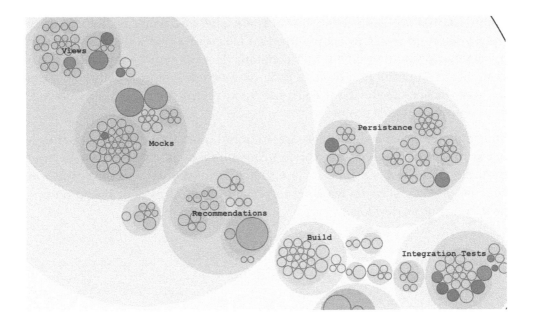

intelligence of the organization, you consider each change to a file as a vote for the relative importance of that code. The resulting data provides the basis for determining the interest rates on technical debt, a topic we'll explore in the next chapter.

Complex Questions Require Context

We often form questions and hypotheses around how well our architecture supports the way our system grows. This information isn't directly available because tools like Git don't know anything about our architectural style; they just store content. To step up to this challenge we need to augment the raw version-control data with an architectural context. Part II of this book shows you how it's done.

Prioritize Improvements Guided by Data

In a large system improvements rarely happen at the required rate, mainly because improvements to complex code are high risk and the payoff is uncertain at best. To improve we need to prioritize based on how we actually work with the code, and we just saw that prioritizing technical debt requires a time dimension in our codebase.

Organizational factors also have a considerable impact on our ability to maintain a codebase. Not only will we fail to identify the disease if we mistake organizational problems for technical issues; we also won't be able to apply the proper remedies. Our coding freedom is severely restricted if we attempt to refactor a module that's under constant development by a crowd of programmers compared to a piece of code that we work on in isolation. Unless we take the social side of our codebase into account we'll fail to identify significant maintenance costs.

This chapter promised to fill those informational holes by introducing a behavioral data source, our version-control systems. We saw some brief examples and now it's time to put that information to use on real-world codebases. Let's start by learning to prioritize technical debt based on our past behavior as developers.

Nature is exceedingly simple.

➤ *Isaac Newton*

CHAPTER 2

Identify Code with High Interest Rates

We've seen that prioritizing technical debt requires a time dimension in our code. Now you'll learn how hotspots provide that dimension by letting you identify code with high interest rates on both the file and function levels.

We'll put hotspots to work on a well-known codebase where we identify a small section of code, just 197 lines, as a specific initial target for improvements. You'll learn how we can be confident that an improvement to those 197 lines will yield real productivity and quality gains. So follow along as we dive into how code evolves and explore a technique that will change how we tackle legacy code.

Measure Interest Rates

Refactoring complex code is a high-risk and expensive activity, so you want to ensure your time is well invested. This is a problem because legacy codebases often contain tons of code of suboptimal quality. You know, that kind of module where we take a deep breath before we dive in to look at it and hope we don't have to touch the code. Ever. Given such vast amounts of code in need of improvement, where do we start? A behavioral code analysis provides an interesting answer to that puzzle. Have a look at the figure on page 16 to see what I mean.

These graphs present an evolutionary view of three distinct codebases. We've sorted the files in each codebase according to their change frequencies—that is, the number of commits done to each file as recorded in the version-control data, with the y-axis showing the number of commits.

This figure shows data from three radically different systems. Systems from different domains, of different size, developed by different organizations, and of different age. Everything about these systems is different. Yet all three

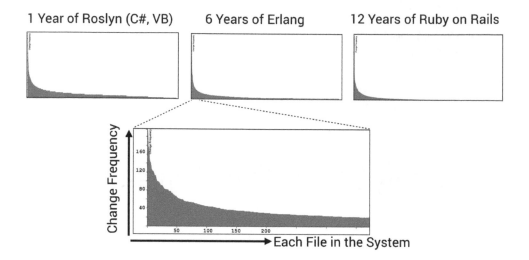

graphs show exactly the same pattern. They show a *power law distribution*. And this is a pattern that I've found in every codebase I've ever analyzed.

The distribution means that the majority of our code is in the long tail. It's code that's rarely, if ever, touched. Oversimplified, this characteristic suggests that most of our code isn't important from a cost or quality perspective. In contrast, you see that most development activity is focused on a relatively small part of the codebase. This gives us a tool to prioritize improvements, as the following figure illustrates.

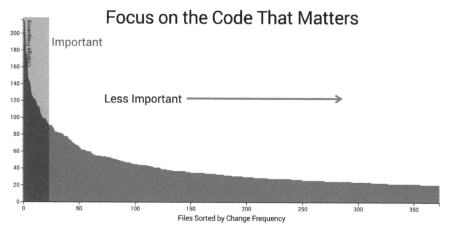

The red area in the preceding figure highlights where we spend most of our development work. These are the files where it's most important that the code be clean and easy to evolve. In practice, more often that not, files with high change frequencies suffer quality problems (we'll have plenty of opportunities to see that for ourselves later on in this book). This means that any improvements we make to the files in the red area have a high likelihood of providing productivity gains. Let's see how you identify such refactoring candidates in your own code.

A Proxy for Interest Rate

Change frequency is a simple algorithm to implement. You just count the number of times each file is referenced in your Git log and sort the results. The book *Git Version Control Cookbook [OV14]* includes a recipe that lets you try the algorithm on your own repository by combining Bash and commands with Git's log option. Just open a Bash shell—or Git Bash if you're on Windows—and go to one of your repositories. Enter the following command:

```
adam$ git log --format=format: --name-only | egrep -v '^$' | sort \
      | uniq -c | sort -r | head -5
1562 actionpack/CHANGELOG
1413 activerecord/CHANGELOG.md
1348 activerecord/CHANGELOG
1183 activerecord/lib/active_record/base.rb
 800 activerecord/lib/active_record/associations.rb
```

The --format=format: option to git log gives us a plain list of all files we've ever changed. The cryptic egrep -v '^$' part cleans our data by removing blank lines from the preceding Git command, and the rest of the shell commands count the change frequencies and deliver the results in sorted order. Finally we limit the number of results with head -5. Just remove this final command from the pipe and redirect the output to a file if you want to inspect the change frequencies of all your code:

```
adam$ git log --format=format: --name-only | egrep -v '^$' | sort \
       | uniq -c | sort -r > all_frequencies.txt
```

The prior code example is from the Ruby on Rails codebase.[1] The first three entries reference the change logs, which are noncode artifacts. But then it gets interesting. The next two files are central classes in the active_record module. We'll talk more about the implications soon, but it's quite typical that the files that attract the most changes are the ones that are central to your system. So have a look at your own list of frequently changed files. Is there a nod of recognition as you inspect the files with the most commits?

The Effectiveness of Change Frequencies

Calculating change frequencies is straightforward, but a practical implementation of the algorithm is trickier since we want to track renamed content.

---

1.   https://github.com/rails/rails

You may also find that your Git log output references files that no longer exist or have been moved to other repositories. In addition, Git only deals with content, so it will happily deliver all kinds of files to you, including those compiled .jar files your former coworker insisted on autocommitting on each build. That's why we need tooling on top of the raw data. We'll meet our tools soon. But let's first look at how well this simple metric performs.

Since code is so complicated to develop and understand, we often like to think that any model of the process has to be elaborate as well. However, like so much else in the world of programming, simplicity tends to win. Change to a module is so important that more elaborate metrics rarely provide any further value when it comes to fault prediction and quality issues. (See, for example, *Does Measuring Code Change Improve Fault Prediction? [BOW11]* and *A Comparative Analysis of the Efficiency of Change Metrics and Static Code Attributes for Defect Prediction [MPS08]* for empiric research on the subject.) So not only do our change frequencies let us identify the code where we do most of the work; they also point us to potential quality problems.

Despite these findings our model still suffers a weakness. Why? Because all code isn't equal. There is a huge difference between increasing a version number in a single-line text file and correcting a bug in a module with 5,000 lines of C++ littered with tricky, nested conditional logic. The first kind of change is low risk and can for all practical purposes be ignored. The second type of change needs extra attention in terms of test and code inspections. That's why we need to add a second dimension to our model in order to improve its predictive power. We need to add a complexity dimension.

Add a Language-Neutral Complexity Dimension

Software researchers have made several attempts at measuring software complexity. The most well-known approaches use the McCabe cyclomatic complexity and Halstead complexity measures.[2] [3] The major drawback of these metrics is that they are language specific. That is, we need one implementation for each of the programming languages that we use to build our system. This is in conflict with most modern systems, which tend to combine multiple languages. Ideally we'd like to take a language-neutral approach, but without losing precision or information.

Fortunately, there's a much simpler complexity metric that performs well enough: the number of lines of code. Yes, the number of lines of code is a

2. https://en.wikipedia.org/wiki/Cyclomatic_complexity
3. https://en.wikipedia.org/wiki/Halstead_complexity_measures

rough metric, but that metric has just as much predictive power as more elaborate constructs like cyclomatic complexity. (See the research by Herraiz and Hassan in *Making Software [OW10]*, where they compare lines of code to other complexity metrics.) The advantage of using lines of code is its simplicity. Lines of code is both language neutral and easy to interpret. So let's combine our complexity dimension with a measure of change frequency to identify hotspots that represent code with high interest rates.

Calculate Lines of Code With cloc

 The open source command-line tool cloc lets you count the lines of code in virtually any programming language. The tool is fast and simple to use, so give it a try on your codebase. You can get cloc from its GitHub page.[4]

Prioritize Technical Debt with Hotspots

A hotspot is complicated code that you have to work with often. Hotspots are calculated by combining the two metrics we've explored:

1. Calculating the change frequency of each file as a proxy for interest rate

2. Using the lines of code as a simple measure of code complexity

The simplest way is to write a script that iterates through our table of change frequencies and adds the lines-of-code measure to each entry. We can also visualize our data to gain a better overview of where our hotspots are.

Let's look at an example from the online gallery,[5] where you see a visualization like the figure on page 20 of a hotspot analysis on *ASP.NET Core MVC*. This codebase, from Microsoft, implements a model-view-controller (MVC) framework for building dynamic websites.[6]

This type of visualization is called an *enclosure diagram*. (See *Visualizations*, on page 217, for details on how to make your own.) We'll use enclosure diagrams a lot in our visualizations since they scale well with the size of the codebase. Here's how to interpret the visualization:

*   Hierarchical: The visualization follows the folder structure of your codebase. Look at the large blue circles in the figure on page 20. Each one of them represents a folder in your codebase. The nested blue circles inside represent subfolders.

---

4. https://github.com/AlDanial/cloc
5. https://codescene.io/projects/1690/jobs/4245/results/code/hotspots/system-map
6. https://github.com/aspnet/Mvc

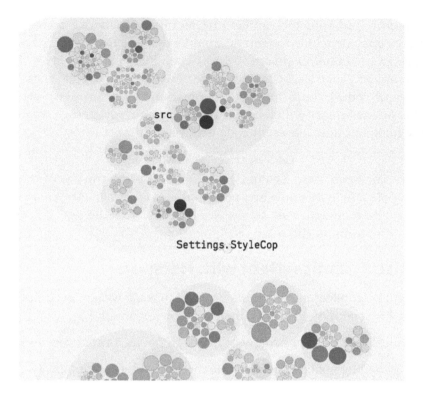

- Interactive: To work with large codebases the visualizations have to be interactive. This means you can zoom in on the code of interest. Click on one of the circles representing folders in the codebase to zoom in on its content.

When you zoom in on a package you'll see that each file is represented as a circle. You'll also note that the circles have different sizes and opacities. That's because those dimensions are used to represent our hotspot criteria, as illustrated in the next figure.

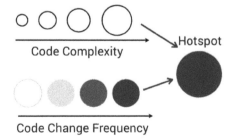

The deeper the red color, the more commits have been spent on that code. And the larger the circle, the more code in the file it represents.

The main benefit of enclosure diagrams is that they let us view the whole codebase at a glance. Even so, there are other options to visualize code. A popular alternative is *tree maps*. Tree maps are a hierarchical visualization that present a more compact view of large codebases. The next figure shows an example from *Your Code as a Crime Scene [Tor15]* where the hotspots are visualized as a tree map.

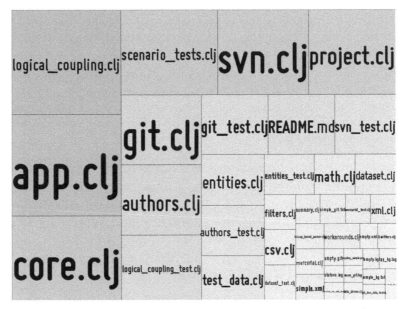

The JavaScript library *D3* provides an easy way to experiment with tree maps.[7] Together with the cloc tool and the git log trick we saw earlier, you have all the data you need to visualize your hotspots.

No matter what visualization style you choose, you're now ready to uncover hotspots with high interest rates.

Locate Your Top Hotspots

A hotspot analysis takes you beyond the current structure of the code by adding a time dimension that is fundamental to understanding large-scale systems. As we saw earlier, development activity is unevenly distributed in your codebase, which implies that not all code is equally important from a maintenance perspective. Consequently, just because some code is badly written or contains excess accidental complexity, that doesn't mean it's a problem. Low-quality code matters only when we need to work with it, perhaps to fix a bug or extend an existing feature—but then, of course, it becomes a true nightmare.

---

7.   https://d3js.org/

\\//   **Joe asks:**
ʒʃ   # Are You Telling Me Code Quality Isn't Important?

No, this is not intended to encourage bad code. The quality of your code *is* important —code is the medium for expressing your thoughts—but context is king. We talk about legacy code. Code is hard to get right; requirements change and situational forces have to be considered. That means every large codebase has its fair share of troubled modules. It's futile to try to address all those quality problems at once because there's only so much time we can spend on improvements, so we want to ensure we improve a part that actually matters.

The reason many well-known speakers and authors in the software industry obsess about keeping all code nice and clean is because we can't know up front which category code will fall into. Will this particular code end up in the long tail that we rarely touch, or will we have to work with this piece of code on a regular basis? Hotspots help us make this distinction.

So let's get specific by analyzing Microsoft's ASP.NET Core MVC. It's a .NET codebase, but the steps you learn apply to code written in any language. You can also follow along online with the interactive analysis results on the URL that we opened earlier.[8]

Prioritize Hotspots in ASP.NET Core MVC

ASP.NET Core MVC is a framework for building dynamic websites. It's a midsize codebase with around 200,000 lines of code, most of it C#. In larger codebases we need a more structured approach, which we'll discuss in Chapter 6, *Spot Your System's Tipping Point*, on page 93, but ASP.NET Core MVC is small enough that we can use a powerful heuristic—our visual system. Let's have another look at our hotspot map, shown in the top figure on page 23.

See the large red circle in the lower part of the figure? That's our top hotspot. It's code that's likely to be complex, since there's a lot if it, and the code changes at a high rate. Zoom in on that hotspot by clicking on it to inspect its details, as shown in the next figure on page 23.

Our main suspect, the unit test ControllerActionInvokerTest.cs, contains around 2,500 lines of code. That's quite a lot for any module, in particular for a unit test. Unit testing is often sold as a way to document behavior. That potential advantage is lost once a unit test climbs to thousands of lines of code. You also see that the developers of ASP.NET Core MVC have made more than 100 commits to that code.

---

8.   https://codescene.io/projects/1690/jobs/4245/results/code/hotspots/system-map

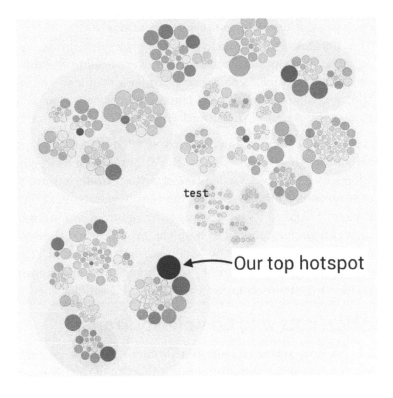

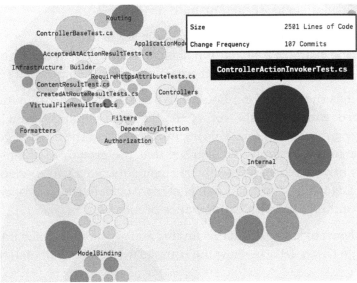

This means that our hotspot, ControllerActionInvokerTest.cs, is a crucial module in terms of maintenance efforts. Based on this information let's peek into that file and determine whether the code is a problem.

Use Hotspots to Improve, Not Judge

The *fundamental attribution error* is a principle from social psychology that describes our tendency to overestimate the influence of personality—such as competence and carefulness—as we explain the behavior of other people. The consequence is that we underestimate the power of the situation.

 It's easy to critique code in retrospect. That's fine as long as we remember that we don't know the original context in which the code was developed. Code is often written under strong pressures of time constraints and changing requirements. And often that pressure exerted its force while the original developers tried to build an understanding of both the problem and the solution domain. As we inspect the code, perhaps months or years later, we should be careful to not judge the original programmers, but rather use the information we gather as a way forward.

Evaluate Hotspots with Complexity Trends

We can find out how severe a potential problem is via a *complexity trend* analysis, which looks at the accumulated complexity of the file over time. The trend is calculated by fetching each historic version of a hotspot and calculating the code complexity of each historic revision.

You will soon learn more about how complexity is calculated, but let's start with a specific example from our top hotspot. As you see in the figure on page 25, ControllerActionInvokerTest.cs has become much more complicated recently.[9]

The trend tells the story of our hotspot. We see that it grew dramatically back in May 2016. Since then the size of the file hasn't changed much, but the complexity continues to grow. This means the code in the hotspot gets harder and harder to understand. We also see that the growth in complexity isn't followed by any increase in descriptive comments. So if you ever struggled to justify a refactoring ... well, it doesn't get more evident than in cases like this. All signs point to a file with maintenance problems.

We'll soon learn to follow up on this finding and get more detailed information. Before we go there, let's see how the complexity trend is calculated and why it works.

---

9. https://codescene.io/projects/1690/jobs/4245/results/code/hotspots/complexity-trend?name=Mvc/test/
Microsoft.AspNetCore.Mvc.Core.Test/Internal/ControllerActionInvokerTest.cs

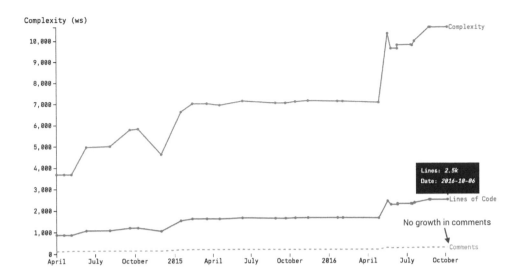

What Is Complexity, Anyway?

While we used lines of code as a proxy for complexity in our hotspot analysis, the same metric won't do the trick here. We'll get more insights if the trend is capable of differentiating between growth in pure size versus growth in complexity. This latter case is typical of code that is patched with nested conditionals; the lines of code probably grow over time, but the complexity of each line grows more rapidly. To make this distinction we need to measure a property of the code, not just count lines.

The *indentation-based complexity* metric provides one such approach. It's a simple metric that has the advantage of being language neutral. The figure on page 26 illustrates the general principle.

With indentation-based complexity we count the leading tabs and whitespaces to convert them into logical indentations. This is in stark contrast to traditional metrics that focus on properties of the code itself, such as conditionals and loops. This works because indentations in code carry meaning. Indentations are used to increase readability by separating code blocks from each other. We never indent code at random (and if we do, we have more fundamental problems than identifying hotspots). Therefore, the indentations of the code we write correlate well with traditional complexity metrics. (See *Reading Beside the Lines: Indentation as a Proxy for Complexity Metrics. Program Comprehension, 2008. ICPC 2008. The 16th IEEE International Conference on [HGH08]* for an evaluation of indentation-based complexity on 278 projects compared to traditional complexity metrics.) I did say it was simple, didn't I?

```
internal void InvokeEvents(object sender, PollEvents events)
{
    if (!m_isClosed)
    {
        m_socketEventArgs.Init(events);

        if (events.HasFlag(PollEvents.PollIn))
        {
            var temp = m_receiveReady;
            if (temp != null)
            {
                temp(sender, m_socketEventArgs);
            }
        }

        if (events.HasF
        {
            var temp =
            if (temp != null)
            {
                temp(sender, m_socketEventArgs);
            }
        }
    }
}
```

We normally consider the code when we discuss complexity...

...but there is a simpler view of code complexity!

Know the Biases in Complexity Trends

In all fairness, the simplicity of our metric comes with some trade-offs. First, the actual complexity number represents the number of logical indentations, so it makes little sense to discuss thresholds or compare complexity values across languages. It's the trend that's important, not the absolute values.

The use of leading whitespace makes the algorithm sensitive to mid-project changes in indentation style. If that happens you'll see a sudden spike or drop in complexity without the code actually being changed. In that case the trend will still be meaningful, but you have to mentally ignore the sudden spike. Just remember that—like all models of complex processes—complexity trends are heuristics, not absolute truths.

Now that we know how complexity trends are calculated, let's move on and discover detailed refactoring candidates.

Calculate Complexity Trends with Python

The complexity trend algorithm is straightforward to implement. CodeScene adds a bit of filtering on top of it, but if you just want the raw data you can script it in no time. I've also open-sourced an implementation in Python as an example and inspiration for your own scripts.[10]

---

10. https://github.com/adamtornhill/maat-scripts/blob/master/miner/git_complexity_trend.py

Use X-Rays to Get Deep Insights into Code

Our analysis let us significantly reduce the amount of code we need to consider. We started with an entire codebase and narrowed it down to a single file where improvements matter. For smaller files that's enough information to start improving the code, but we need to do even better if we come across large hotspots.

Our main suspect in this case is a file with 2,500 lines of code. It's a lot, for sure, but as we'll see later in this book, hotspots with more than 10,000 lines of code are fairly common out in the wild. How useful would it be to know that a file with thousands of lines of code is a hotspot? Where do we look? How do we act on that information? The most common answer is that we don't. We need much more detailed information.

Remember when we saw that not all code is equal? That's true at the function/method level too. A large file is like a system in itself. During maintenance you'll spend more time on some methods than on others. You can capitalize on this aspect by running a hotspot analysis on the method level to identify the segments of code that contribute the most to the file being a hotspot. We'll refer to this analysis as an *X-Ray* to distinguish it from file-level analyses. It's exactly the same algorithm we used earlier, only the scope differs, as the following figure illustrates.

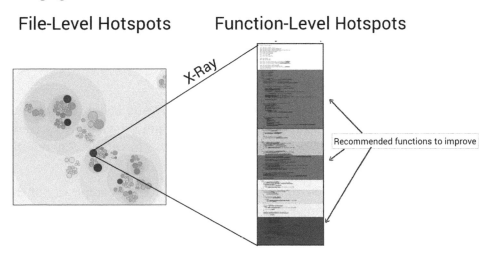

An X-Ray gives you a prioritized list of the methods to inspect and, possibly, refactor. Let's try it on our main suspect. Click on the ControllerActionInvokerTest.cs hotspot in the visualization to bring up the context menu, and select the X-Ray option.

An X-Ray analysis involves the following steps:

1. Fetch the source code for each historic revision of our hotspot from Git.

2. Run a git diff on every subsequent revision of the code. The diff output shows us where—in the historic file—the developers made modifications.

3. Match the diff results to the functions/methods that existed in that particular revision. This means we need to parse the source code to know which functions were affected in a particular commit.

4. Perform a hotspot calculation on the resulting set of changed functions over all revisions of the hotspot. The algorithm is identical to what we used to detect file-level hotspots, but the scope differs. The change frequency represents the number of times we modified a function, and the length of the function gives us the complexity dimension.

With the basic algorithm covered, let's see what the X-Ray analysis reveals inside ControllerActionInvokerTest.cs.[11] As you see in the following figure, the top hotspot on a method level is CreateInvoker.

⇕ Function	⌄ Change Frequency	⇕ Lines of Code
CreateInvoker	68	197
Invoke_UsesDefaultValuesIfNotBound	52	59
InvokeAction_InvokesAsyncExceptionFilter_WhenActionThrows	10	45
InvokeAction_InvokesAsyncAuthorizationFilter_ShortCircuit	10	43
InvokeAction_InvokesExceptionFilter_ResultIsExecuted_WithoutResultFilters	10	27

Like the hotspot analysis, a complexity trend analysis is also orthogonal to the level it operates on. That means you can calculate the complexity trend of the CreateInvoker method. Just click the trend button in your X-Ray results and inspect the trend.[12]

As you see in the trend picture on page 29, the exploding complexity of the CreateInvoker method is responsible for the degenerating trend of the ControllerActionInvokerTest.cs class. The X-Ray table shows that CreateInvoker consists of 197

---

11. https://codescene.io/projects/1690/jobs/4245/results/files/hotspots?file-name=Mvc%2Ftest%2FMicrosoft.AspNet-Core.Mvc.Core.Test%2FInternal%2FControllerActionInvokerTest.cs

12. https://codescene.io/projects/1690/jobs/4245/results/files/functions/complexity-trend?file-name=Mvc%2Ftest%2FMicrosoft.AspNetCore.Mvc.Core.Test%2FInternal%2FControllerActionInvokerTest.cs&func-tion-name=CreateInvoker

lines of code, which is way too much for a single method. But it's much less than 2,500 lines, which is the size of the total file, and it's definitely less than 200,000 lines, which is the size of the total codebase. This means we're now at a level where we can act on the information.

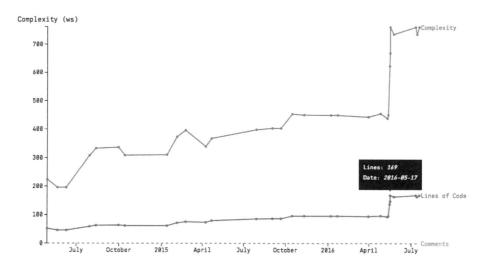

Inspect the Code

The big win with a hotspot analysis is that it lets us minimize our manual efforts while ensuring a high probability that we focus on the right parts of the code. This is important, because at some point in our hunt for technical debt we want to look at the code.

When we view the file ControllerActionInvokerTest.cs, we see that CreateInvoker is actually three overloaded methods, as shown in the next figure.

```
private TestControllerActionInvoker CreateInvoker(
    IFilterMetadata filter,
    bool actionThrows = false,
    int maxAllowedErrorsInModelState = 200,
    List<IValueProviderFactory> valueProviderFactories = null)
{
    return CreateInvoker(new[] { filter }, actionThrows);
}

private TestControllerActionInvoker CreateInvoker(
    IFilterMetadata[] filters,
    bool actionThrows = false,
    int maxAllowedErrorsInModelState = 200,
    List<IValueProviderFactory> valueProviderF
{
    ...
}

private TestControllerActionInvoker CreateInvoker(
    IFilterMetadata[] filters,
    string methodName,
    IDictionary<string, object> arguments,
    int maxAllowedErrorsInModelState = 200)
{
    ...
```

Overloaded methods with the same name are calculated as one logical unit.

Our X-Ray analysis combines all the methods into a single hotspot. This is an implementation detail for sure, and you may choose to keep overloaded methods separate. However, grouping them together lets you consider all overloaded methods as one logical unit when you refactor.

But let's not get lost in the details—investigating a hotspot takes time and requires domain expertise. Besides, you may not be that interested in C#. So let's keep our investigation high level and see if we can spot some common code smells. Have a look at the first few lines of code shown in the following figure.

```csharp
private TestControllerActionInvoker CreateInvoker(
    IFilterMetadata[] filters,
    bool actionThrows = false,
    int maxAllowedErrorsInModelState = 200,
    List<IValueProviderFactory> valueProviderFactories = null)
{
    var actionDescriptor = new ControllerActionDescriptor()
    {
        FilterDescriptors = new List<FilterDescriptor>(),      Control coupling that
        Parameters = new List<ParameterDescriptor>(),          leads to both conditional
    };                                                         complexity and DRY violations

    if (actionThrows)
    {
        actionDescriptor.MethodInfo = typeof(ControllerActionInvokerTest).GetMethod(
            nameof(ControllerActionInvokerTest.ThrowingActionMethod));
    }
    else
    {
        actionDescriptor.MethodInfo = typeof(ControllerActionInvokerTest).GetMethod(
            nameof(ControllerActionInvokerTest.ActionMethod));
    }
```

As you see in the previous annotated code, there's a classic case of control coupling through the Boolean actionThrows parameter. Such flags are a problem since they introduce conditional logic and lower cohesion by enforcing additional state. Such control coupling also leads to subtle duplication of code. These design choices don't play well with maintenance.

Refactor Control Coupling

 Control coupling is common in legacy code. Fortunately, it's simple to refactor locally. You do that by encapsulating the concept that varies between different callers of the method and parameterizing with the behavior, expressed as an object or lambda function, instead of using a flag. As a bonus, your calling code will communicate its intent better, too.

Now let's look at one more maintenance aspect to emphasize that hotspots often point to real problems. If you scroll through the implementation of CreateInvoker you see that the complicated setup of mock objects in the code is worrisome, as the figure on page 31 illustrates.[13]

---

13. https://en.wikipedia.org/wiki/Mock_object

```
formatter
    .Setup(f => f.WriteAsync(It.IsAny<OutputFormatterWriteContext>()))
    .Returns<OutputFormatterWriteContext>(async c =>
    {
        await c.HttpContext.Response.WriteAsync(c.Object.ToString());
    });

var options = new MvcOptions();
options.OutputFormatters.Add(formatter.Object);

var optionsAccessor = new Mock<IOptions<MvcOptions>>();
optionsAccessor
    .SetupGet(o => o.Value)
    .Returns(options);

httpContext
    .Setup(o => o.RequestServices.GetService(typeof(IOptions<MvcOptions>)))
    .Returns(optionsAccessor.Object);
httpContext.SetupGet(c => c.Items)
        .Returns(new Dictionary<object, object>());

httpContext
    .Setup(o => o.RequestServices.GetService(typeof(ObjectResultExecutor)))
    .Returns(new ObjectResultExecutor(
        optionsAccessor.Object,
        new TestHttpResponseStreamWriterFactory(),
        NullLoggerFactory.Instance));

if (routeData == null)
{
    routeData = new RouteData();
}
```

Excess mocking breaks encapsulation and tests a mechanism rather than a behavior.

A null check shouldn't be needed in code whose callers you control.

Mocks have their place, but excess mocking breaks encapsulation and tests a mechanism rather than a behavior. (See *To Mock or Not To Mock? An Empirical Study on Mocking Practices [SABB17]* for research on the uses and misuses of mocks, and see *Growing Object-Oriented Software, Guided by Tests [FP09]* for the cure.) Each time the implementation in the code under test changes, CreateInvoker has to be updated, too. Not only is this error prone and expensive, but you also lose the advantage of unit tests as a true regression suite. In addition, a complicated unit test may well be the messenger telling us to rethink the code under test.

We could go on like this and dissect the rest of code, but that would distract us from the more general use of hotspots. So let's look at some additional use cases for hotspots before we move on to other analyses.

Use the Setup Heuristic

The length of a test's setup method is often inversely related to the readability of the code under test. So start from the unit tests when reviewing code; they indicate the design issues you need to look out for in the application code.

Escape the Technical-Debt Trap

A hotspot analysis is an efficient strategy to prioritize technical debt. Hotspots gives you a prioritized list of the parts of your codebase where you're likely to spend most of your time. This means you can take an iterative approach as you drive improvements based on data from how you have worked with the code so far.

Back in Chapter 1, *Why Technical Debt Isn't Technical*, on page 3, we talked about a system that had accumulated 4,000 years of technical debt. It's a high number, but all too common in legacy codebases. Now we've seen that not all technical debt is important. Using hotspots, you can ignore most of those 4,000 years of technical debt and focus on the parts that really matter to your ability to maintain the system. With behavioral code analysis we have that code narrowed down in just a few minutes.

A hotspot analysis also serves multiple audiences. While developers use hotspots to identify maintenance problems and focus code reviews, testers use the same information to select a starting point for exploratory tests. A hotspot analysis is an excellent way for a skilled tester to identify parts of the codebase that seem unstable due to lots of development activity.

Work with Untouchable Code

Sometimes I come across organizations that have decided to avoid touching their worst code. Thus, a hotspot analysis on the recent development activity would fail to highlight the most serious source of technical debt.

This situation is no different from a codebase built around any third-party framework or library—the only distinction is that the third-party code originated from within the same organization. If you're in a similar situation, you use the hotspot analysis to supervise all the code that does get worked on to ensure it won't end up sharing a similar fate and become the untouchable code to your next generation of developers.

As we'll see in Part II, behavioral code analysis is also useful for exploring unknown code. Version-control data lets us travel in time and uncover the patterns of the original developers, which helps us understand the structure of seemingly impenetrable code. It may be hard, but if people managed to decipher the hieroglyphs and sequence the human genome, it should be possible to cast light on a legacy codebase, too. With hotspots as a guide, that work becomes more pleasant.

There's More to Hotspots

There are several reasons why code grows into hotspots. The most common reason is *low cohesion*, which means that the hotspot contains several unrelated parts and lacks modularity.[14] Such hotspots attract many commits because they have too many responsibilities and those responsibilities tend to be central to your domain, which is why they change. This is a problem that gets worse with the scale of the organization. In Chapter 7, *Beyond Conway's Law*, on page 117, you'll see that there's a social cost to hotspots, too.

Another fascinating aspect of hotspots is that they tend to stay where they are and remain problematic for years. As an example, I've used ControllerAction-InvokerTest.cs as a case study in my workshops on hotspot detection for a year now. In that time the code has accumulated even more complexity. Often, that's because refactoring hotspots is hard and high risk, and we discuss patterns that help us refactor such hotspots in Chapter 4, *Pay Off Your Technical Debt*, on page 51. But before that our next chapter explores how we can detect maintenance issues across whole clusters of files.

Exercises

The following exercises let you uncover technical debt in popular open source projects. You also learn how the combination of hotspots and complexity trends lets you follow up on the improvements you make in the code. That is, instead of focusing on problems, you get to use the analysis techniques to identify code that has been refactored.

Remember the document linked in *How Should You Read This Book?*, on page xiii, which specifies a single page with all the exercise URLs. It'll save you from having to type out all URLs in case you're reading the print version.

Find Refactoring Candidates in Docker

- Repository: https://github.com/moby/moby

- Language: Go

- Domain: Docker automates the deployment of applications inside containers that hold everything needed to run the system.

- Analysis snapshot: https://codescene.io/projects/169/jobs/3964/results/code/hotspots/system-map

The top hotspot in our case study of ASP.NET Core MVC was a unit test. This is a common finding; we developers tend to make a mental divide between application code (which we know is important to keep clean and easy to maintain) and test code (which often receives considerably less love at code

---

14. https://en.wikipedia.org/wIki/Cohesion_(computer_science)

reviews). This is a dangerous fallacy since from a maintenance perspective the test code is *at least* as important as the application code.

Inspect the hotspots in Docker from the perspective of test automation. Are there any maintenance problems? In what direction does the code evolve? Where would you suggest that we focus improvements?

Follow Up on Improvements to Rails

- Repository: https://github.com/rails/rails

- Language: Ruby

- Domain: Rails is a server-side web application framework built on the model-view-controller pattern.

- Analysis snapshot: https://codescene.io/projects/1699/jobs/4265/results/code/hotspots/system-map

We've seen how complexity trends gives us more information on how a hotspot evolves. The trends are also great as a follow-up to subsequent improvements. After a large refactoring, perhaps to simplify conditional logic or to extract cohesive modules from the hotspot, we want to ensure that our complexity trend goes down and stays there.

Explore the two frequently changed files, activerecord/lib/active_record/base.rb and activerecord/lib/active_record/associations.rb, that we identified in code on page 17. Investigate their trends for signs of successful refactorings. Do either of the files give us a false positive with respect to the hotspot criteria? You get bonus points if you can think of a way to filter out refactored code that is no longer a problem from the hotspot results. (In Chapter 5, *The Principles of Code Age*, on page 73, we discuss information that helps us with the task.)

The backbone of surprise is fusing speed with secrecy.

➢ *Carl von Clausewitz*

CHAPTER 3

Coupling in Time: A Heuristic for the Concept of Surprise

In this chapter we explore a concept called *change coupling*. You'll see how change coupling helps us design better software as we uncover expensive change patterns in our code. You'll also learn to uncover subtle relationships across clusters of files by analyzing change patterns between functions located in different files. This gives us a powerful strategy for iteratively improving our design based on feedback from how we work with the code.

As always, we'll study the techniques on a real-world codebase to identify real problems. We'll continue to explore ASP.NET Core MVC. We'll also see that change coupling is a language-neutral concept by peeking at systems written in C, Erlang, and Python. Come along and learn how software evolution helps us improve code based on our past behavior as developers.

Uncover Expensive Change Patterns

Quick—how do we know if a software design is any good? Most answers concern facets of programming such as the importance of naming, testability, and cohesion. We'll go beyond that and assert that none of those qualities matter unless our software design supports the kind of changes we need to make to the code.

This insight isn't revolutionary in itself. What's surprising is that we, as an industry, haven't attempted to measure this aspect of code quality before. The main reason for our negligence is that time is invisible in code. As a consequence, we don't have any detailed mental models of how our codebase evolves. Sure, we may remember the implementation of some large feature that transformed parts of the system architecture. But in a large project the details of how our codebase grows are distributed in the minds of hundreds of different programmers. Additionally, code under active development is a moving target, and details get lost over time due to the frailties of human memory and changes in staff.

Fortunately, our version-control system remembers our past. Once we embrace that data source, we're able to factor in aspects of software development that we haven't been able to measure before. One such aspect is *change coupling.*

What Is Change Coupling?

Change coupling is different from how we programmers typically talk about coupling. First, change coupling is invisible in the code itself—we mine it from our code's history and evolution. Second, change coupling means that two (or more) files change together over time, as shown in the next figure.

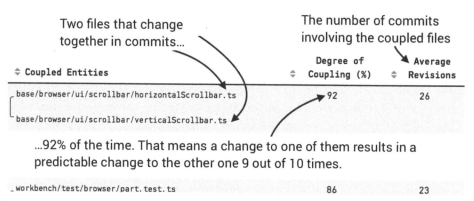

There are several criteria for change coupling. The first coupling criterion is when files are changed within the same commit. This is the simplest case and we'll stick to it in this chapter. In Chapter 9, *Systems of Systems: Analyzing Multiple Repositories and Microservices*, on page 165, you'll learn more advanced strategies to identify change patterns that ripple across Git repository boundaries. Now let's look at an example of cochanging files.

The figure on page 37 shows a simple system with just three modules. We note that the FuelInjector and Diagnostics modules change together in both the first and the third commit. If this trend continues, there has to be some kind of relationship between the two modules that explains their intertwined evolution.

Of course, a cochange between two modules could be accidental, so we need some kind of threshold that helps us avoid false positives. The algorithm we use in this chapter considers two or more files to be coupled in time if 1) they change together in at least 20 commits and 2) the files are changed together in at least 50 percent of the total commits done to either file. That is, if I do

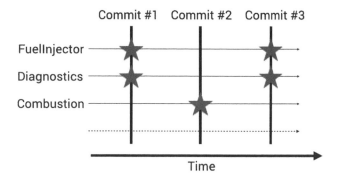

30 commits to file A and file B also gets changed in at least 20 of those commits, then we have change coupling.

Change Coupling Both Is and Isn't Temporal Coupling

In my previous writings—and occasionally in the tooling—you may come across the term *temporal coupling* instead of *change coupling*. This is unfortunate since it overloads the term. The fault is all mine; I chose the temporal coupling name—unaware that it had a previous use—to emphasize the notation of cochange in time.

In its original use, *temporal coupling* refers to dependencies in call order between different functions. For example, *always invoke function Init before calling the AccelerateToHyperspeed method or bad things will happen.* This kind of temporal coupling is a code smell and is discussed in *The Pragmatic Programmer: From Journeyman to Master [HT00]*.

With that covered, let's put change coupling to work by uncovering hidden dependencies in Microsoft's ASP.NET Core MVC codebase.[1] Since we used the same codebase back in Chapter 2, *Identify Code with High Interest Rates*, on page 15, you've already explored parts of it. Just note that the code in the official repository is likely to have changed since this book was written, so point your browser to our forked snapshot to inspect the source code exactly as it looked at the time of this case study.[2]

Detect Cochanging Files

The thresholds serve to limit the amount of change coupling we need to inspect. Even with those thresholds we may find a lot of change coupling in

---

1.   https://github.com/aspnet/Mvc
2.   https://github.com/SoftwareDesignXRays/Mvc

a system. That means we need a way to filter the results and focus on the parts that are most likely to illustrate flawed designs and true technical debt.

My favorite heuristic is the concept of surprise. That is, you want to look for surprising patterns when investigating change coupling. There are two reasons for using surprise as a starting point:

1. *Surprise is one of the most expensive things you can put into a software architecture.* In particular, the poor maintenance programmer coming after us is likely to suffer the consequences of any surprising change pattern we've left in the design. Software bugs thrive on surprises.

2. *Change coupling itself is neither good nor bad; it all depends on context.* A unit test that changes together with the code under test is expected. In fact, we should be worried if that dependency weren't there since it would indicate that our tests aren't kept up to date. On the other hand, if two seemingly independent classes change together over time we might have discovered an erroneous abstraction, copy-pasted code, or—as is often the case—both.

Let's look at the change-coupling results from ASP.NET Core MVC. As usual you can follow along online and interact with the visualizations.[3] As you see in the figure on page 39, the analysis identifies a cluster of unit tests that tend to change together.

This visualization style is a *hierarchical edge bundle,* which is straightforward to implement using the JavaScript library D3.js.[4] In a hierarchical edge bundle visualization, each file is represented as a node and the change dependencies are shown as links between them. The files have also been sorted based on their containing folder, so files within the same folder are next to each other.

If you follow along interactively, you can hover over a file to highlight its change couplings. You see an example in the figure on page 39, where a unit test, FormTagHelperTest.cs, has temporal dependencies on five other files.

When evaluating a change coupling analysis you also want to consider the degree of coupling, as we covered earlier in this chapter. In this case, that cluster of files has a high degree of coupling, ranging from 53 to 90 percent. That means that in more than half the changes you make to any of those files, there's a predictable change to the other files in the cluster. Not only is

---

3. https://codescene.io/projects/1690/jobs/4245/results/code/temporal-coupling/by-commits
4. https://d3js.org/

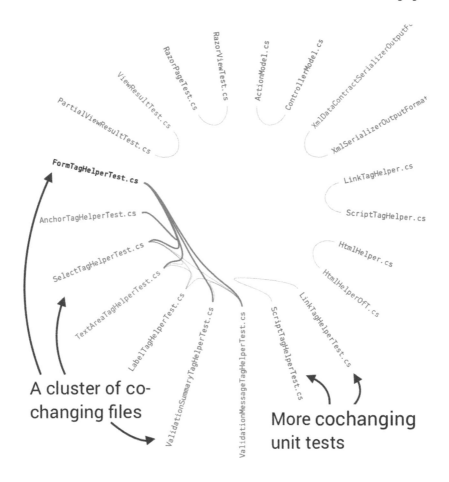

A cluster of co-changing files

More cochanging unit tests

it expensive to maintain code like this, but it also puts us at risk of forgetting to update one of the files, with potentially severe consequences.

So why would seemingly unrelated unit tests change together? ASP.NET Core MVC is a framework for building dynamic web applications. If we look at our change coupling visualization in the preceding figure, it's not entirely clear why a FormTagHelperTest.cs should be modified together with an AnchorTagHelperTest.cs. These files model different aspects of the problem domain and we'd expect them to evolve independently.

If we inspect the code, we see that there's no direct dependency between any of the files in the change-coupling cluster. That is, there's nothing on the code level that suggests why these unit tests evolve together. This is in contrast to the case where, say, an interface and the classes implementing that interface change together. We've found our first surprise! Let's see why seemingly unrelated code changes together.

Minimize Your Investigative Efforts

A change coupling analysis gives us information on how our code grows, which lets us detect implicit dependencies that point to code that's hard to maintain. Information is useful only if we act upon it, and a surprising change coupling relationship may be extremely time-consuming to investigate in more depth. Change coupling is something that happens over time, so we have to inspect the changes between different revisions of the involved files. That is, we need to inspect multiple historic revisions and try to spot some pattern. This is impractical and tedious, which means it's unlikely to ever happen.

Our case study of ASP.NET Core MVC shows why that's the case. The unit tests we need to inspect are fairly large files with about 1,000 lines of code each. In addition we have around 50 revisions to inspect. That boils down to a large amount of code distributed over time. So while a change coupling analysis is a great starting point to detect expensive change patterns in a codebase, it may be hard to act on that information.

However, the harder the problem the greater the reward. We covered X-Ray analysis back in Chapter 2, *Identify Code with High Interest Rates*, on page 15, as we identified refactoring targets inside a hotspot. Now we'll use the same algorithm to identify the methods inside our cluster that are responsible for the change coupling. Just as we ran a hotspot analysis on a function/method level, we'll now run a change coupling analysis on the methods in the different files in our cluster. This step will bring us to a level where we can act on the analysis information.

Calculate Change Coupling from the Command Line

 The open source tool code-maat lets you calculate change coupling from the command line. While code-maat doesn't support the X-Ray level of analysis, it does give you enough information to launch your own investigation into unexpected change patterns. Check out Appendix 2, *Code Maat: An Open Source Analysis Engine*, on page 215 for more details.

If you follow along interactively, you can launch an X-Ray analysis by clicking on one of the files in the change coupling cluster, as shown in the figure on page 41.

An X-Ray analysis has to parse the methods in each file, map them to the hunks that differ in each commit, and finally run a change coupling calculation on the resulting dataset. Note that the change coupling algorithm is identical to the one we used between files—only the level of detail is different. Let's

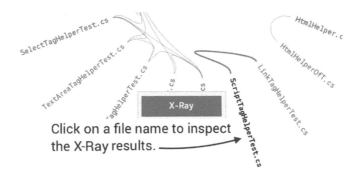

Click on a file name to inspect
the X-Ray results.

start with the dependency between LinkTagHelperTest.cs and ScriptTagHelperTest.cs since these two files have the strongest change coupling, with 90 percent. The following figure visualizes the cochanging methods in those files as a dependency wheel.

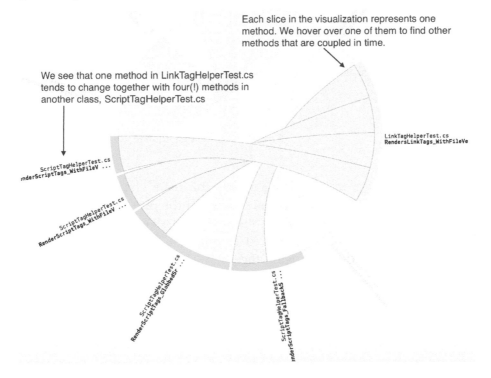

Each slice in the dependency wheel represents a method in a specific file. Since it's an interactive visualization you can hover over any of the methods to highlight its dependents. In this case we see that the method RendersLink-Tags_WithFileVersion in LinkTagHelperTest.cs changes together with four (!) methods in another unit test, ScriptTagHelperTest.cs. This looks expensive to maintain, so we should investigate this finding.

Every time we have a cluster of unit tests that evolve together we also need to inspect the code being tested. Our coupled unit tests may just be the messenger—not the problem itself—trying to tell us about a design issue in the application code. So have one more look at your change coupling between files, replicated in the following figure. Can you spot any change dependency from our cluster of unit tests to the application code?

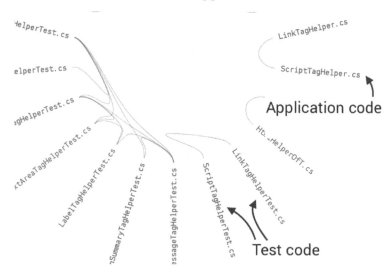

Interestingly enough, in this case the two unit tests change together more frequently (90 percent of all commits) than what the unit tests and their corresponding application code do (just 49 percent of all commits). At the same time we see that two classes related to our test suite, LinkTagHelper.cs and ScriptTagHelper.cs, also keep changing together. This is another surprise, and we'll return to it in the exercises at the end of this chapter. For now, we just note that individual commits don't tell the whole story. Sometimes you come across the pattern where a developer updates the unit tests in one commit and the related application code in another commit. Since we just look for change coupling inside the same commit, our algorithm misses such cases. In Part II of this book you'll learn about a powerful extension to the change coupling analysis that lets us uncover change coupling that's invisible in the code as well as in Git's commit log.

But for now we want to inspect any potential quality problems with the unit-test code. Our starting point is to look for the usual suspects: missing abstractions or duplications in the test data. For example, the coupled methods may share the same input data or, more commonly, contain repeated and duplicated assertion statements. Let's look at an example from ScriptTagHelperTest.cs:

```
Assert.Equal("script", output.TagName);
Assert.False(output.IsContentModified);
Assert.Empty(output.Attributes);
Assert.True(output.PostElement.GetContent().Length == 0);
```

If you scroll through the file you see that this group of assertions is a pattern that's repeated, with small variations, in different methods across the files in our cluster. It's a duplication of knowledge since it repeats the postconditions of each test, with the consequence that we introduce undesirable change coupling. This, in turn, leads to expensive change patterns as minor modifications to the application code set off waves of changes that ripple across the methods in the unit tests.

If we look closer at the specific assertions in the code above we note two missing abstractions:

- *Test Data*: We need to model the domain of our tests and express the concept of test data. In the example code above we could introduce an ExpectedScriptTagOutput class to capture the repeated pattern, and each test could then instantiate an object of that class and parameterize it with the few context-specific values.

- *Assertions*: We need a specialized assertion statement that encapsulates our test criteria. We won't bother with the implementation details, but after a refactoring according to these recommendations, the previous group of assertions is replaced by a single statement: AssertContent(expected, output).

By encapsulating both the test data and the assertion statements you introduce a model that's much more likely to stand the test of time, which means you no longer have to do shotgun surgery as you update a unit-test criterion.

There Is No Such Thing as Just Test Code

The design problem we just discussed is way too common. As a consequence, some of the worst hotspots and design issues tend to be in automated tests. My hypothesis is that we developers make a mental divide. On one hand we have the application code, and we know that it's vital to keep it clean and easy to evolve. On the other hand we have the test code, which we know isn't part of our production environment. The consequence is that the test code often receives considerably less love.

This is a dangerous fallacy because from a maintenance perspective there's really no difference between the two. If our tests lack quality, they will hold us back. That's why you should focus your analysis efforts on test code, too. Another important point is to make sure your test code passes through the same quality gates (for example, code reviews and static analysis) as your application code. With this in mind, let's discuss our findings in more detail so we're prepared to deal with the issue when it occurs in our own code.

Behavioral code analysis helped us narrow down the problem in the case study to just five methods that we had to inspect. This, in turn, let us focus our refactoring efforts on the code that needs it the most. Now we'll take it a step further as we dive into the dirty secret of copy-paste and how it relates to unit tests.

The Dirty Secret of Copy-Paste

While visualizations are important to get the overall picture, the numbers from an X-Ray analysis often provide more details that help uncover design issues. The next figure shows the detailed results from the X-Rays of Link-TagHelperTest.cs and ScriptTagHelperTest.cs.

| Copy-paste detection | Coupling | | Similarity |
⇕ Coupled Functions	⇕ (%)	⇕ Commits	⌄ (%)
┌ LinkTagHelperTest.cs/RunsWhenRequiredAttributesArePresent └ ScriptTagHelperTest.cs/RunsWhenRequiredAttributesArePresent	44	41	98
┌ LinkTagHelperTest.cs/MakeTagHelperOutput └ ScriptTagHelperTest.cs/MakeTagHelperOutput	32	41	87
┌ LinkTagHelperTest.cs/DoesNotRunWhenARequiredAttributeIsMissing └ ScriptTagHelperTest.cs/DoesNotRunWhenARequiredAttributeIsMissing	32	41	87
	--	..	--

The table in the preceding figure presents an interesting finding. We see that several methods have a high degree of *code similarity*. That is, the implementation of several methods is very similar, which is an indication of copied-and-pasted code. For example, the highlighted row shows that there's a code similarity of 98 percent between two methods in different files. The figure on page 45 shows part of the code, and you see that there's a shared test abstraction wanting to get out.

Since these methods are changed together in almost half the commits that touch those files, this is copy-paste that actually matters for your productivity. Let me clarify by revealing a dirty secret about copy-paste.

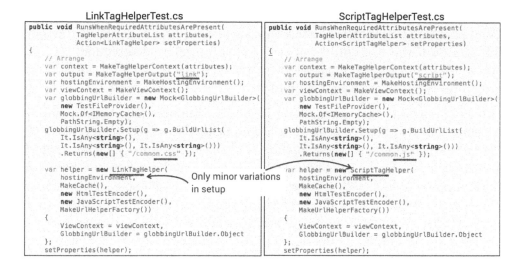

In the previous chapter we saw that low-quality code isn't necessarily a problem. Now we'll challenge another wide-spread belief by asserting that copy-paste code isn't always bad.

---

5. https://en.wikipedia.org/wiki/Abstract_syntax_tree
6. http://clonedigger.sourceforge.net/
7. http://www.harukizaemon.com/simian/

Like everything else, the relative merits of a coding strategy depend on context. Copy-paste isn't a problem in itself; copying and pasting may well be the right thing to do if the two chunks of code evolve in different directions. If they don't—that is, if we keep making the same changes to different parts of the program—that's when we get a problem.

This is important since research on the topic estimates that in your typical codebase, 5–20 percent of all code is duplicated to some degree. (See *On Finding Duplication and Near-Duplication in Large Software Systems [Bak95]* and *Experiment on the Automatic Detection of Function Clones in a Software System Using Metrics [MLM96]* for studies of commercial software systems.) That's a lot of code. We can't inspect and improve all of it, nor should we. Just as with hotspots, we need to prioritize the software clones we want to get rid of. The change coupling analysis combined with a code-similarity metric is a simple and reliable way to identify the software clones that really matter for your productivity and code quality. Again, note that this is information you cannot get from the code alone; we need a temporal perspective to prioritize the severity of software clones.

Once we've identified the software clones that matter, we want to refactor them. We typically approach that refactoring by extracting the repeated pattern into a new method and parameterizing it with the concept that varies. This makes the code a little bit cheaper to maintain as our temporal dependency disappears. We also get less code, and that's good because all code carries a cost. It's a *liability.*[8] The more code we can remove while still getting the job done, the better. Killing software clones is a good starting point here.

The Power of Language-Neutral Analyses

So far we've been torturing ASP.NET Core MVC—a .NET codebase. However, these techniques aren't limited to a particular technology. The analyses are language neutral, which means we can analyze any kind of code and use the same measures to reason about it.

The power of language-neutral analyses is that we can spot relationships between files implemented in different languages. This is important because today's systems are often polyglot codebases. We have an example in the implementation of the programming language Erlang, as shown in the figure on page 47.[9]

---

8. https://blogs.msdn.microsoft.com/elee/2009/03/11/source-code-is-a-liability-not-an-asset/
9. https://codescene.io/projects/1707/jobs/4287/results/code/temporal-coupling/by-commits

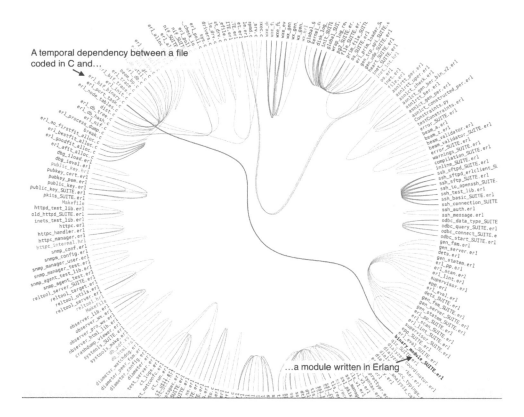

A temporal dependency between a file coded in C and…

…a module written in Erlang

That figure shows a change coupling between erl_bit_binary.c, written in C, and binary_module_SUITE.erl, written in Erlang. We could X-Ray those two files to find out why, but for now we've gotten a hint of the power of language-neutral software analyses.

Being language neutral means we're able to uncover change patterns that ripple across our technology stack—for example, front-end code that changes together with server-side logic and database scripts. This is information that we use to understand a codebase by uncovering how different pieces of code fit together. (The pioneering research in this area is documented in *Mining Version Histories to Guide Software Changes [ZWDZ04]* and shows the value of this much underused technique.)

We return to this topic in the exercises and we'll explore it in much more depth in the second part of this book. I promise.

Learn More About Change Coupling

Change coupling helps us determine if our design fits the way we work with the code. We saw how a change coupling analysis helped us identify missing abstractions in unit tests and possible design issues in the corresponding application code. We still had to analyze the problematic code and come up with remedies ourselves. The big win is that we can now focus our expertise to where it's likely to pay off, and ensure our refactorings have a real impact on our ability to maintain the system.

There's much more to say about change coupling. Just as we can drill deeper from files to change coupling between methods, we can also travel in the opposite direction and analyze change coupling between components and subsystems, which we'll study in depth in the second part of this book.

By combining hotspots with change coupling we're able to detect maintenance issues in individual files and across clusters of related files. Now we need to react to that information. The next chapter addresses the challenges of improving code that's under active development by multiple programmers and teams.

Exercises

Once you start to apply change coupling analyses to your own code, you'll discover that the information is useful beyond uncovering technical debt. The following exercises let you explore different use cases for the analysis information. You also get to fill in the missing piece in our ASP.NET Core MVC case study as you uncover software clones in application code.

Learn from the Change Patterns in a Codebase

- Repository: Roslyn[10]

- Language: Visual Basic and C#

- Domain: Roslyn implements the C# and Visual Basic compilers, including an API for code analysis.

- Analysis snapshot: https://codescene.io/projects/1715/jobs/4299/results/code/temporal-coupling/by-commits

Surprisingly, most of our work as developers doesn't involve writing code. Rather, most of our time is spent understanding existing code. Change coupling provides a learning vehicle that lets us uncover how different pieces of code fit together. Therefore, a change coupling analysis is a good way to explore a new codebase and identify change patterns that would otherwise surprise us. This is particularly useful in polyglot codebases.

---

10. https://github.com/dotnet/roslyn

Go to the change coupling analysis for Roslyn and look for files with a strong degree of change coupling, like 90 percent. Investigate the change patterns and determine if they are expected or surprising.

Detect Omissions with Internal Change Coupling

- Repository: TensorFlow[11]
- Language: Python
- Domain: TensorFlow is a machine-learning library originating at Google.
- Analysis snapshot: https://codescene.io/projects/1714/jobs/4295/results/files/internal-temporal-coupling?file-name=tensorflow/tensorflow/contrib/layers/python/layers/layers.py

Change coupling is capable of providing design insights on a single file, too. We'll explore that in more detail in the next chapter, but the basic principle is that you look for functions in a single file that tend to change together. In particular, you want to look for functions with a high degree of similarity since those often point to a missing abstraction and an opportunity to refactor the code.

In this exercise we'll look at two such functions. Run an X-Ray of tensorflow/contrib/layers/python/layers/layers.py. Inspect the *internal change coupling* results and compare the two functions convolution2d_transpose and fully_connected. Look at the chunks of code that differ between the two files. Are there any possible omissions that show the presence of potential bugs? Any style issues to be aware of?

Hint: Investigate and compare the conditional logic between the two functions.

Kill the Clones

- Repository: ASP.NET Core MVC[12]

- Language: C#

- Domain: This codebase implements a model-view-controller framework for building dynamic websites.

- Analysis snapshot: https://codescene.io/projects/1690/jobs/4245/results/code/temporal-coupling/by-commits

In this chapter we saw that unit tests coupled in time often hint at a deeper design problem with the code under test. That means we should explore the

---

11. https://github.com/tensorflow/tensorflow
12. https://github.com/aspnet/Mvc

code under test, too, once we find a surprising change pattern between seemingly unrelated unit tests.

Go to the change coupling analysis of ASP.NET Core MVC and explore the change coupling between LinkTagHelper.cs and ScriptTagHelper.cs. Run an X-Ray analysis on these two classes and see if you can detect any quality issues. In particular, look at the code-similarity metrics and see if you can suggest a refactoring that breaks the change coupling.

Mathematicians are like managers–they want improvement without change.

➣ Edsger Dijkstra

CHAPTER 4

Pay Off Your Technical Debt

Now that we've uncovered hotspots and surprising temporal coupling in our codebase, we need to put that information to use. This is often easier said than done. Even armed with the existing catalogs of refactoring techniques, we need to consider the people side of code, too. Refactoring code that's under heavy development, perhaps even shared between multiple teams, adds another dimension to the problem.

This chapter introduces refactoring strategies that let you improve code iteratively to limit the disturbance to the rest of the business. The strategies build on the evolutionary analyses you mastered in the earlier chapters, which lets you drive refactoring by using data about how your team works with the code.

This chapter is also the most technical one in the book, so feel free to skip ahead to the next chapter if you're more interested in the strategic importance of the analysis information. If you're still here, let's get ready for proximity—a much underused design principle.

Follow the Principle of Proximity

The principle of proximity focuses on how well organized your code is with respect to readability and change. Proximity implies that functions that are changed together are moved closer together. Proximity is both a design principle and a heuristic for refactoring hotspots toward code that's easier to understand.

Let's pretend you run an X-Ray analysis on a large hotspot and as you look at its internal change coupling, you identify several cases of obvious code duplication.

You see an example of such code duplication in the figure on page 52, and the gut reaction is to extract the commonalities into a shared abstraction. In

⇕ Coupled Functions	Degree of Coupling ⤵ (%)	Average ⇕ Revisions	Similarity ⇕ (%)
OfType_Select OfType_Select_OfType_Select	100	41	93
String_EndsWith_MethodCall String_StartsWith_MethodCall	100	33	85
String_Contains_MethodCall String_EndsWith_MethodCall	100	33	56
String_Contains_MethodCall	100	33	51

many cases that's the correct approach, but sometimes a shared abstraction actually makes the code *less* maintainable. Follow along as we explore an example and come up with a better alternative.

The preceding change coupling results are from an X-Ray of the hotspot test/EFCore.SqlServer.FunctionalTests/QuerySqlServerTest.cs in the codebase for Entity Framework Core, which is an object-relational mapper for .NET.[1] You can view the whole file on GitHub,[2] in the state it was at the time of writing, or follow along in the online analysis results.[3]

These analysis results show that the methods String_EndsWith_MethodCall and String_StartsWith_MethodCall change together in 100 percent of commits and have done that in 33 shared commits. This is a strong temporal dependency and the similarities in method names indicate that the responsibilities are closely related. Let's look at the code, shown in the figure on page 53, to see how we can refactor it.

As you see in the figure on page 53, there's a fair chunk of duplication between these two implementations. Take a minute and think about how you'd refactor away from that duplication before you read on. I'll do some thinking on my side, too, and wait for you here.

---

1. https://github.com/aspnet/EntityFrameworkCore
2. https://github.com/SoftwareDesignXRays/EntityFrameworkCore/blob/dev/test/EFCore.SqlServer.FunctionalTests/QuerySqlServerTest.cs
3. https://codescene.io/projects/1716/jobs/4314/results/files/internal-temporal-coupling?file-name=EntityFrameworkCore/test/EFCore.SqlServer.FunctionalTests/QuerySqlServerTest.cs

```
public override void String_StartsWith_MethodCall()
{
    base.String_StartsWith_MethodCall();

    AssertSql(
        @"@__LocalMethod1_0: M (Size = 4000)

SELECT [c].[CustomerID], [c].[Address], [c].[City], [c].[CompanyName], [c].[ContactName],
    [c].[ContactTitle], [c].[Country],
    [c].[Fax], [c].[Phone], [c].[PostalCode], [c].[Region]
FROM [Customers] AS [c]
WHERE (([c].[ContactName] LIKE @__LocalMethod1_0 + N'%' AND (LEFT([c].[ContactName],
    LEN(@__LocalMethod1_0)) = @__LocalMethod1_0)) OR (@__LocalMethod1_0 = N'')");
}

...<snip>...

public override void String_EndsWith_MethodCall()
{
    base.String_EndsWith_MethodCall();

    AssertSql(
        @"@__LocalMethod2_0: m (Size = 4000)

    SELECT [c].[CustomerID], [c].[Address], [c].[City], [c].[CompanyName], [c].[ContactName],
        [c].[ContactTitle], [c].[Country],
        [c].[Fax], [c].[Phone], [c].[PostalCode], [c].[Region]
    FROM [Customers] AS [c]
    WHERE (RIGHT([c].[ContactName], LEN(@__LocalMethod2_0)) = @__LocalMethod2_0) OR
        (@__LocalMethod2_0 = N'')");
}
```

A fundamental principle of software design is to encapsulate the concept that varies. Applied to our case we could

1. introduce a common test method that encapsulates the bulk of our SQL query;

2. parameterize our new, shared method with the differences in the respective WHERE clauses; and

3. make the test data-driven, which removes all traces of any duplication.

While those steps would get rid of the duplication, the new abstractions would leave the code in a *worse* state. To abstract means to take away. As we raise the abstraction level through a shared method, the two test cases lose their communicative value. Unit tests serve as an excellent starting point for newcomers in a codebase. When we take abstractions too far we lose that advantage by obscuring the behavior we want to communicate through the tests.

As programmers we are conditioned to despise copy-paste code, but there's always a trade-off as we refactor two methods into a shared abstraction. Even when the original code is nearly identical, the two methods may well model different aspects of the problem domain. When we refactor such code into a shared representation we give that new method different reasons to change, and when that happens our shared abstraction breaks down in a heavy rain of control flags and Boolean parameters, which is a worse problem than the original duplication.

The amount of duplicated knowledge is simply too small in this case to motivate a shared abstraction. This is a hard balance because we do want to simplify future maintenance and at least warn future developers of the deliberate code duplication. Let's see how the principle of proximity helps us achieve these goals.

Use Your Perception

A century ago the movement of *Gestalt psychology* formed theories on how we make sense of all chaotic input from our sensory systems.[4] The *proximity principle* is a Gestalt theory that specifies that objects or shapes that are close to each other appear to form groups. This is why our brains sometimes perceive multiple, distinct parts as a whole, as the following figure illustrates.

The proximity principle lets you perceive
objects close to each other as more related.

If we translate the proximity principle to software, it means we should favor a structure that guides our code-reading brain toward interpreting related parts of the source file as a group. Let's look at a specific example by considering the information carried by the changes we make to our code, shown in the figure on page 55.

In the this figure, both case A and B show three hypothetical changes that form a single commit. However, there's a different effort behind them although the same amount of code gets changed. Remember that as developers we spend most of our time trying to understand existing code. With the proximity principle in mind, case A exhibits a change pattern that suggests a group of related functionality. This is in contrast to case B, where the parts that make up a concept are distributed, which means we initially—and falsely—perceive these as unrelated functions.

---

4. https://en.wikipedia.org/wiki/Gestalt_psychology

"belong together"   "separate"

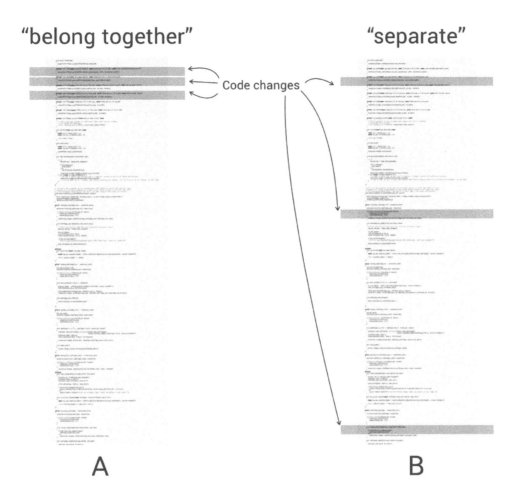

Code changes

A   B

Now, let's return to the code duplication we identified in Entity Framework Core, where we found the methods String_EndsWith_MethodCall and String_StartsWith_MethodCall change together. If you look at the whole file you see that there are 50 lines of code between these two methods. More important, there are three other methods modeling different behavior interspersed between them. We improve this code, as the figure on page 56 illustrates, by moving methods that belong together close to each other.

The proximity principle is a much-underused refactoring technique that uses feedback from how our code evolves. By ordering our functions and methods according to our change patterns we communicate information that isn't expressible in programming-language syntax. That information serves as a powerful guide to both the programmer and, more important, the code reader on which parts belong together and how we expect the code to grow.

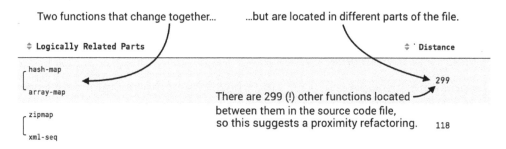

```
public override void String_StartsWith_MethodCall()
{
    base.String_StartsWith_MethodCall();

    AssertSql(
        @"@__LocalMethod1_0: M (Size = 4000)

SELECT [c].[CustomerID], [c].[Address], [c].[City], [c].[CompanyName], [c].[ContactNam
FROM [Customers] AS [c]
WHERE [[c].[ContactName] LIKE @__LocalMethod1_0 + N'%' AND (LEFT([c].[ContactName], LE
```

```
public override void String_EndsWith_Literal()
{
    base.String_EndsWith_Literal();

    AssertSql(
        @"SELECT [c].[CustomerID], [c].[Address], [c].[City], [c].[CompanyName
FROM [Customers] AS [c]
WHERE RIGHT([c].[ContactName], LEN(N'b')) = N'b'");
}
```

Proximity refactoring: move related code together

```
public override void String_EndsW
{
    base.String_EndsWith_Identity(

    AssertSql(
        @"SELECT [c].[CustomerID], [c].[Address], [c].[City], [c].[CompanyName
FROM [Customers] AS [c]
WHERE (RIGHT([c].[ContactName], LEN([c].[ContactName])) = [c].[ContactName]) OR ([c].[
}
```

```
public override void String_EndsWith_Column()
{
    base.String_EndsWith_Column();

    AssertSql(
        @"SELECT [c].[CustomerID], [c].[Address], [c].[City], [c].[CompanyName
FROM [Customers] AS [c]
WHERE (RIGHT([c].[ContactName], LEN([c].[ContactName])) = [c].[ContactName]) OR ([c].[
}
```

```
public override void String_EndsWith_MethodCall()
{
    base.String_EndsWith_MethodCall();

    AssertSql(
        @"@__LocalMethod2_0: m (Size = 4000)

SELECT [c].[CustomerID], [c].[Address], [c].[City], [c].[CompanyName], [c].[ContactNam
FROM [Customers] AS [c]
WHERE (RIGHT([c].[ContactName], LEN(@__LocalMethod2_0)) = @__LocalMethod2_0) OR (@__Lo
```

Automate Proximity Recommendations

Software evolution lets you take the concept a step further and get automated
recommendations on proximity refactorings. Let's look at the following figure,
which shows an example from the implementation of the programming language *Clojure*.[5]

Two functions that change together...   ...but are located in different parts of the file.

```
⇕ Logically Related Parts                                    ⇕ Distance
─────────────────────────────────────────────────────────────────────
  hash-map
[                                                                   299
  array-map

                        There are 299 (!) other functions located
                        between them in the source code file,
  zipmap                so this suggests a proximity refactoring.    118
[
  xml-seq
```

5.   https://github.com/clojure/clojure

The recommendations in the figure are built on change coupling, where you identify pairs of functions that evolve together. Once you've found your pairs of cochanging functions, it's straightforward to calculate the distance between them. This example uses the number of intervening functions as a distance metric (the Distance column in the preceding table). An alternative would be to count the number of lines of code separating the functions, which captures declarations too.

The main advantage of a proximity refactoring is that it carries low risk. If you detect copy-paste code the day before a critical deadline, it may just not be the right time to abstract away the duplication. A proximity refactoring presents a viable alternative that serves as a mental note that the two functions belong together, which reduces the risk that the next programmer will forget to update one of the clones. It's that simple.

You also use the principle of proximity as you write new code. Each module has methods on different levels of abstraction. The major distinction is between the *external protocol* of your module (the public API) and the private methods used to implement it (the *internal protocol*). In well-designed code you want to express the concepts of your internal protocol on a granular level, which means you tend to get several small functions that together represent a specific concept. To maintain a brain-friendly structure you need to keep those related functions close to each other in your source code.

 Joe asks:

What If I Have a Cluster of Methods That Coevolve?

That happens, and it's usually an indication that there's a missing abstraction looking to get out. In that case, check if it makes sense to extract those methods into their own module. Often, you can also introduce a method representing the higher-level concept and let that method compose calls to the lower-level methods. Organize the affected methods in reading order.

Refactor Congested Code with the Splinter Pattern

The *splinter pattern* provides a structured way to break up hotspots into manageable pieces that can be divided among several developers to work on, rather than having a group of developers work on one large piece of code. You use the splinter pattern to improve code that's gone too far over the edge of complexity.

The main reason a piece of code grows into a hotspot is because it has accumulated several central responsibilities. As a consequence, the hotspot has many reasons to change. This leads to a downward spiral where every interesting new feature has to touch the hotspot code, which reinforces its change rate by adding yet another responsibility. Unless we catch that downward spiral early—for example, by supervising our complexity trends—we end up with code that's both hard and risky to refactor. Let's look at an example in the following figure.

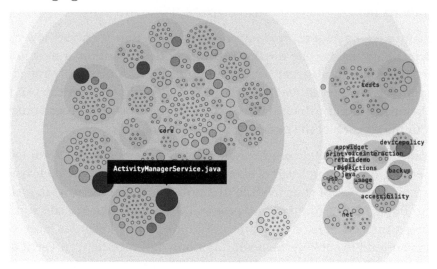

This figure shows the main hotspots in a part of the *Android* system.[6] The top hotspot, ActivityManagerService.java, is a file with almost 20,000 lines of code. Its complexity trend, shown in the figure on page 59, reveals that the file has grown by 7,000 lines over the past four years. That's a lot of new behavior.

A hotspot like ActivityManagerService.java is likely to continue to grow and each additional line of code will come at a high cost in terms of future maintenance. If we find similar hotspots in our own code we have to react and start to invest in improvements. That is, we need to refactor.

There a several good books that help you refactor existing code. *Refactoring: Improving the Design of Existing Code [FBBO99]* and *Working Effectively with Legacy Code [Fea04]* are both classics that offer practical and proven techniques. *Refactoring for Software Design Smells: Managing Technical Debt [SSS14]* is a new addition that is particularly valuable if you work with object-oriented techniques. However, in a case like the preceding Android hotspot we need preparatory steps before we can apply those refactoring techniques. Let's investigate why that's the case.

6.　https://github.com/android/platform_frameworks_base

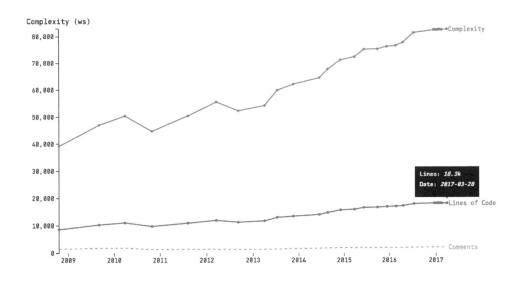

Parallel Development Is at Conflict with Refactoring

Refactoring a hotspot like ActivityManagerService.java takes months, and during that time you want to minimize any feature development and bug fixes in your refactoring target. However, there will likely be lots of parallel work in the hotspots as they represent critical parts of the codebase. This leads to high-risk merges as multiple development teams constantly modify the same code you're trying to refactor. As a result, our refactoring goal conflicts with the short-term evolution of the overall system, and most organizations just cannot afford to pause ongoing work so that we can refactor in a safe, development-free vacuum.

The splinter pattern resolves this dilemma by recognizing that refactoring a hotspot is an iterative process that stretches over multiple incarnations of the code. In a splinter refactoring you won't even improve the code quality as such, but rather transform the code to a structure where multiple people can work together in parallel toward the overall refactoring goal.

Split a Hotspot File Along Its Responsibilities

The intent of the *splinter* pattern is to break a hotspot into smaller parts along its responsibilities while maintaining the original API for a transient period. Just like real-world splinters are small, sharp objects, you probably find that the resulting set of modules aren't optimal. They have their edges and rough corners, but

remember—we're not after perfection here. We just want to take the first, albeit hardest, step toward a more maintenance-friendly design.

The following figure shows a hypothetical refactoring of ActivityManagerService.java from the Android codebase. As you see, we've identified four behaviors that we extract into new and more cohesive classes. You also see that we keep the original method signatures and replace the method bodies with a simple delegation to the extracted modules. This is to protect the rest of the system from changes related to our refactoring. Remember, you use splinter refactoring in code that's under heavy parallel development. If we broaden our scope too early we expose the rest of the organization to conflicting changes, which is why we take this extra step and limit the ripple effects across other modules.

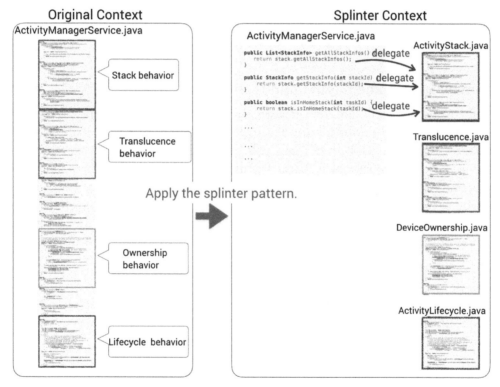

Here are the steps behind an iterative splinter refactoring:

1. *Ensure your tests cover the splinter candidate.* If you don't have an adequate test suite—few hotspots do—you need to create one, as discussed in *Build Temporary Tests as a Safety Net*, on page 64.

2. *Identify the behaviors inside your hotspot.* This step is a code-reading exercise where you look at the names of the methods inside the hotspot and identify code that forms groups of behaviors.

3. *Refactor for proximity.* You now form groups of functions with related behavior inside the larger file, based on the behaviors you identified earlier. This proximity refactoring makes your next step much easier.

4. *Extract a new module for the behavior with the most development activity.* Use an X-Ray analysis to decide where to start, then copy-paste your group of methods into a new class while leaving the original untouched. Remember to put a descriptive name on your new module to capture its intent.

5. *Delegate to the new module.* Replace the body of the original methods with delegations to your new module. This allows you to move forward at a fast pace, which limits the risk for conflicting changes by other developers.

6. *Perform the necessary regression tests to ensure you haven't altered the behavior of the system.* Commit your changes once those tests pass.

7. *Select the next behavior to refactor and start over at step 4.* Repeat the splinter steps until you've extracted all the critical hotspot methods you identified with your X-Ray analysis.

The key to a successful splinter refactoring is to prioritize your next move with evolutionary data, because there's no way we can refactor a major hotspot in one sweep. The X-Ray analysis you learned in *Use X-Rays to Get Deep Insights into Code*, on page 27, lets you identify the code with the highest interest rate inside your hotspot. Therefore, an X-Ray analysis serves well to prioritize splinters.

Use Static Analysis to Guide Code Explorations

 Static analysis tools such as PMD, NDepend, and SonarQube complement evolutionary analyses and provide additional insights —for example, by detecting dependency cycles between methods.[7]

Separate Code with Mixed Content

Files that contain more than one language add another challenge to the splinter pattern. This is often the case in legacy technologies that encourage a mixture of application logic and presentation elements in the same file. PHP is the most notorious example, but you find the same pattern in other languages too. For example, a Java Server Pages (JSP) file could well mix JavaScript, HTML, SQL, and CSS into its Java code.

---

7. https://pmd.github.io/, http://www.ndepend.com/, https://www.sonarqube.org/

Before you apply a splinter refactoring you need to extract the different implementation languages into separate files. That is, you start from a technical perspective and split your hotspot based on technical content. The following figure shows an example.

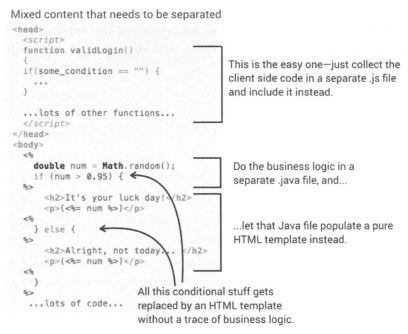

Once you've done that separation it will be much easier to identify the behaviors hiding in the original technology soup. An added advantage is that you can now start to use tools like *Lint* that help you catch common mistakes in the client-side code.

Signal Incompleteness with Names

During a splinter refactoring you may find that a particular cluster of behavior shares code with other seemingly unrelated methods in the original hotspots. Such dependencies hinder the refactoring, so let's discuss the viable strategies.

The figure on page 63 shows a common case where a piece of code is shared between two potential splinter candidates.

In such cases you have two choices:

1. Duplicate the shared method in your splinters, or

2. maintain a shared abstraction in a new module that both splinters depend upon.

```
                              public List<StackInfo> getStackInfo() {
         Depends on a            ...lots of code...
                                } finally {
         shared method            restoreIdentity(originalIdentity, true);
                                }

                              }

                                ...

                              public void respondTo(ExternalCaller caller) {
                                ...lots of code...          Depends on the same
                                                            shared method
                                restoreIdentity(clientIdentity, false);
                              }

                                ...

                              private restoreIdentity(Identity id, boolean isOriginal) {
                                ...lots of code...
                              }
```

As you refactor to a splinter you may find that duplicating previously shared code isn't that bad since you're often able to simplify it by removing branches and arguments. That's possible because shared code inside a hotspot tends to become "reused" to support additional scenarios. (You see an example with the Boolean argument in the preceding figure.) In your new splinter, special cases lose relevance since the context is narrower, which means you're free to remove the corresponding conditional logic.

If you chose the second alternative you have the opportunity to signal a potentially low cohesion of the code by introducing a name that communicates incompleteness. That is, avoid generic names like misc, util, or common and choose a provocative name like Dumpster.java. That name makes it clear the shared module needs future work and discourages subsequent growth of the module. After all, who wants to put their carefully crafted code in a dumpster?

Know the Consequences of Splinters

A splinter refactoring creates a new context where you address a larger problem by breaking it into smaller parts. The hotspot now acts as a facade that maintains the original API, which in turn shields the clients of the hotspot from impact. Without this first step your changes ripple across modular boundaries, which increases the risk of the refactoring because you're no longer dealing with a local change.

Once you've extracted all splinters you're ready to apply traditional refactorings. For example, the next step after creating a splinter is to remove the middle man (a refactoring described in *Refactoring: Improving the Design of Existing Code [FBBO99]*) and let the clients of the original hotspot access the splinters directly without any delegation.

You may also find that several splinter modules won't need refactorings. The power law curve of development activity that we discussed back in Chapter 2, *Identify Code with High Interest Rates*, on page 15, holds true for splinter modules too. The implication is that some new modules are likely to be stable in terms of future work and you identify those modules with a hotspot analysis at a later date. However, in that analysis you only include the development activity that took place *after* your splinter refactoring:

- To only get commits that are more recent than your refactoring, you provide a --after=<date> flag to git. This makes it easy to calculate interest rates like we did in the code on page 17.

- If you use CodeScene you just go to your analysis project and specify the desired start date.

Used this way a hotspot analysis takes on the role of a guide that lets you prioritize future refactorings based on recent development patterns.

Even with splinters, refactoring a hotspot is high risk and it may be tempting to do it on a separate branch. Don't go there, as the key driver behind a splinter refactoring is short lead times. You need to deliver new splinters fast—like in one or two hours tops—to minimize the disturbance to the rest of your team, and branches are at odds with that goal.

I experienced this myself as, years ago, I and a coworker launched an ambitious effort to modularize a hotspot with more than 10,000 lines of C++ that plagued the codebase. We made the mistake of branching out, and a branch gives a false sense of safety, which led us to take too-large steps. Even though we rebased our branch multiple times a day, we lost lots of time as we had to understand and merge work from the master branch to code that we had extracted and moved. Short splinter lead times let you avoid that catch-up game.

Build Temporary Tests as a Safety Net

Before you apply a splinter refactoring you have to ensure that you won't break the behavior of the code. Unfortunately, most hotspots lack adequate test coverage and writing unit tests for a hotspot is often impossible until we've refactored the code. Let's look at an example from the Android codebase that we discussed earlier.

As you see in the figure on page 65, there's a big difference in the amount of application code in Android's core package versus the amount of test code in the test package.

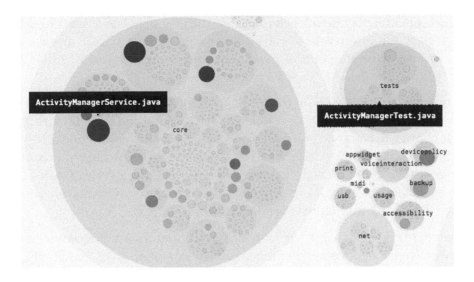

That figure should put fear into any programmer planning a refactoring, because the unit test for the main hotspot, ActivityManagerService.java, with 20,000 lines of code, is a meager 33 (!) lines of test code. It's clear that this test won't help us refactor the code.

In situations like this you need to build a safety net based on *end-to-end tests*. End-to-end tests focus on capturing user scenarios and are performed on the system level. That is, you run with a real database, network connections, UI, and all other components of your system. End-to-end tests give you a fairly high test coverage that serves as a regression suite, and that test suite is the enabler that lets you perform the initial refactoring without breaking any fundamental behavior.

The type of end-to-end tests you need depends upon the API of your hotspot. If your hotspot exposes a REST API—or any other network-based interface—it's straightforward to cover it with tests because such APIs decouple your test code from the application. A UI, like a web page or a native desktop GUI, presents more challenges as it makes end-to-end tests much harder to auto-mate. Our cure in that situation comes with inconvenient side effects but, just like any medicine, if you need it you really need it. So let's look at a way to get inherently untestable code under test.

Introduce Provisional End-to-End Tests

The trick is to treat the code as a black box and just focus on its visible behavior. For web applications, tools like Selenium let you record existing interactions and play them back to ensure the end-user behavior is unaffected.[8] This gives you a way to record the main scenarios that involve your hotspot from a user's point of view. Tools like Sikuli let you use the same strategy to cover desktop UI applications with tests.[9]

The test strategy is based on tools that capture screen shots and use image recognition to interact with UI components. The resulting tests are brittle—a minor change to the style or layout of the UI breaks the regression suite—and expensive to maintain. That's why it's important to remember the context: your goal is to build a safety net that lets you refactor a central part of the system. Refactoring, by its very nature, preserves existing behavior since it makes for a safer and more controlled process.

Thus, we need to consider our UI-based safety net as a temporary creation that we dispose of once we've reached our intermediate goal. You emphasize that by giving the temporary test suite a provocative name, as we discussed in *Signal Incompleteness with Names*, on page 62.

Finally, measure the *code coverage* of your test suite and look for uncovered execution paths with high complexity.[10] You use that coverage information as feedback on the completeness of your tests and record additional tests to cover missing execution paths. You could also make a mental note to extract that behavior into its own splinter module.

Maintainable Tests Don't Depend on Details

 Maintainable end-to-end tests don't depend on the details of the rendered UI. Instead they query the DOM based on known element identities or, in the case of desktop applications, the identity of a specific component.

Reduce Debt by Deleting Cost Sinks

It's a depressingly common case to find hotspots with inadequate test coverage. That doesn't mean there aren't any tests at all, just that there aren't any tests where we would need them to be. Surprisingly often, organizations have unit-test suites that don't grow together with the application code, yet add to the maintenance costs. Let's look at the warning signs in the figure on page 67.

As you see in the figure, the ratio between the amount of source code versus test code is unbalanced. The second warning sign is that the complexity trends

---

8.   http://www.seleniumhq.org/

9.   http://www.sikuli.org/

10.   https://en.wikipedia.org/wiki/Code_coverage

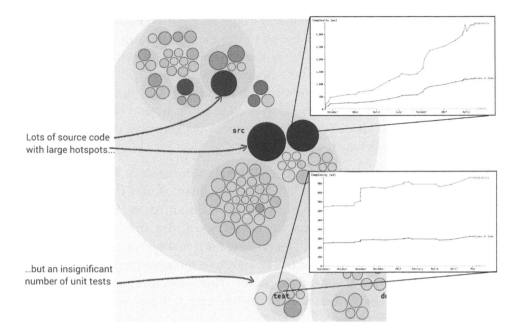

Lots of source code with large hotspots...

...but an insignificant number of unit tests

show different patterns for the hotspot and its corresponding unit test. This is a sign that the test code isn't doing its job by growing together with the application code, and a quick code inspection is likely to confirm those suspicions.

This situation happens when a dedicated developer attempts to introduce unit tests but fails to get the rest of the organization to embrace the technique. Soon you have a test suite that isn't updated beyond the initial tests, yet needs to be tweaked in order to compile so that the automated build passes.

You won't get any value out of such unit tests, but you still have to spend time just to make them build. A simple cost-saving measure is to delete such unit tests, as they do more harm than good.

Turn Hotspot Methods into Brain-Friendly Chunks

The advantage of a refactoring like the splinter pattern is that it puts a name on a specific concept. Naming our programming constructs is a powerful yet simple technique that ties in to the most limiting factor we have in programming—our *working memory*.

Working memory is a cognitive construct that serves as the mental workbench of your brain. It lets you integrate and manipulate information in your head. Working memory is also a strictly limited resource and programming tasks stretch it to the maximum.

We saw back in *Your Mental Models of Code*, on page 7, that optimizing code for programmer understanding is one of the most important choices we can make. This implies that when we're writing code our working memory is a dimensioning factor that's just as important as any technical requirements. Since we, at the time of this writing, unfortunately can neither patch nor upgrade human working memory, we need to work around that mental bottleneck rather than tackle it with brute force. Let's get some inspiration from chess masters to see how it's done.

Chess masters are capable of playing chess simultaneously with tens of different people and, without even looking at the board, know the precise positions in every single game. This sure seems like an amazing feat of memory. However, if you were to rearrange the chess pieces into an order that cannot occur naturally during a game, like putting both bishops on the same color, suddenly the chess master wouldn't be able to remember the positions of the pieces any better than a non–chess player. This is because a chess master's memory isn't necessarily better than anyone else's; it just works differently in that domain of expertise.

Chess masters don't really recall individual pieces. Instead they remember patterns, which represent whole groups of pieces, as illustrated in this figure. Cognitive psychologists call these groups *chunks*, and chunks hold the key to readable code, too. Let's translate the principle of chunks to programming through an example from Craft.Net, a .NET library used to interact with Minecraft.[11]

The Sicilian Opening = A Chunk

If an analysis is run on the Craft.Net repository, the file Craft.Net/source/Craft.Net.Server/MinecraftServer.cs turns up as the main hotspot. A subsequent X-Ray analysis reveals that the method NetworkWorker represents code with high interest rates inside that file. Let's look at the code, shown in the figure on page 69.

This code reveals accidental complexity that makes the code tricky to understand; we have thread-synchronization primitives, nested conditionals, and

---

11. https://github.com/SirCmpwn/Craft.Net

```
private void NetworkWorker()
{
    while (true)
    {
        UpdateScheduledEvents();
        lock (NetworkLock)
        {
            for (int i = 0; i < Clients.Count; i++)
            {
                var client = Clients[i];                     Periodic IO for clients
                PeriodicIoFor(client);
            }
        }
        if (LastTimeUpdate != DateTime.MinValue)
        {
            if ((DateTime.Now - LastTimeUpdate).TotalMilliseconds >= 50)
            {
                Level.Time += (long)((DateTime.Now -             Track playtime on current level
                            LastTimeUpdate).TotalMilliseconds / 50);
                LastTimeUpdate = DateTime.Now;
            }
        }
        if (NextChunkUpdate < DateTime.Now)
            NextChunkUpdate = DateTime.Now.AddSeconds(1);       Track time to refresh
        Thread.Sleep(10);                                       Release the CPU (flawed)
    }
}
```

loops. That means we should introduce chunks to uncover the different
behaviors of the NetworkWorker and to improve our understanding of the algorithm. As you see in the preceding figure, we have already taken the first
steps by identifying the individual steps of the algorithm. When we put a
name on each of those steps we transform the original code by raising its
abstraction level to a point where the big picture emerges, as the following
code listing shows.

```
private void NetworkWorker()
{
    while (true)
    {
        UpdateScheduledEvents();

        PeriodicIoFor(Clients);
        TrackPlaytimeOnCurrentLevel();
        TrackTimeToRefresh();

        FlawedThreadDeactivation();
    }
}
```

When you introduce chunks, you want to express the different steps in the
method on roughly the same level of abstraction as recommended in
Implementation Patterns [Bec07]. In the preceding example we used whitespace
to separate groups of related steps. Such whitespace separation leaves additional clues to readers of our code, and suggests future refactoring directions
by identifying potential abstractions on an even higher level. There's power
in negative space.

Unfortunately, most hotspot methods are more complicated than the preceding
example—and the NetworkWorker is no exception. In fact, the annotated code

you saw earlier has already been simplified; only a small chunk of it would fit into this book. The PeriodicIoFor() method encapsulates a chunk with 50 lines of code that were originally part of the NetworkWorker method.[12] (You can view the full code sample on its GitHub page.)

When you split a hotspot method into a group of chunks, consider leaving the code as is and follow up with an X-Ray analysis on your refactored code a month later. Chances are that most of your chunks have remained stable, which means you can ignore them and instead focus your refactoring efforts on the few parts that continue to evolve.

Introducing brain-friendly chunks is a simple refactoring that does wonders for our ability to evolve code. It's also a quick procedure since most refactoring plugins automate the mechanics (see the refactoring *Extract Method*[13]), which means short lead times that minimize the exposure to conflicting changes from other developers on your team.

On a related note, data types are chunks too. In a statically typed language you want to replace primitive types such as integers, floats, and strings with types whose names carry a meaning in your domain. String arguments in particular are so common that they deserve special mention. If there were such a thing as a legacy code scale, we could bet that it would include the number of string arguments as its main metric. Instead of a string, introduce a descriptive domain type that communicates information to a human reader and lets the compiler ensure correct semantics in the process.

The Curse of a Successful System

Ironically, much code decay isn't due to incompetence but rather is owed to the success of an evolving product. As we discussed earlier, code grows into hotspots because we change it a lot, and those changes are driven by user needs—both real and perceived. Writing code always involves exploring and understanding both the problem and the solution domain. Thus it's inevitable that we turn down the wrong road every now and then, and the pressure of completing a feature makes it hard to stop and backtrack. The codebase of a successful system is an ugly place to visit.

It doesn't have to be that way if we actively attend to the health of our codebase and take countermeasures when needed. In this chapter you learned how refactoring support is another area where behavioral code analysis techniques

---

12. https://github.com/SirCmpwn/Craft.Net/blob/bc20a3d3f6c60957ecd04cc7388e225387158eb1/source/
    Craft.Net.Server/MinecraftServer.cs#L341
13. https://refactoring.com/catalog/extractMethod.html

shine. Guided by data, you're more likely to identify the true maintenance bottlenecks in your codebase and get information that advises you on a specific refactoring. You also learned the importance of considering the social side of refactoring code that's under development by your peers, and we discussed a number of refactoring patterns that help you limit risks and code conflicts.

The next step is to consider higher-level building blocks. You'll see how behavioral code analysis helps us refactor package structures, too. Follow along as we discuss the age of code and the insights it gives us.

It is not well to make great changes in old age.

➤ *Charles Spurgeon*

CHAPTER 5

The Principles of Code Age

In this chapter we explore package-level refactorings as we see how to organize code by its age. We measure the age of code as the time since the last modification, so that we can separate code we recently worked on from old and stable parts. Code age is a much-underused driver of software design that strengthens our understanding of the systems we build. Code age also helps us identify better modular boundaries, suggests new libraries to extract, and highlights stable aspects of the solution domain.

You use code age analysis to evolve systems toward increased development stability, where the resulting structure offers lower cognitive overhead. As a bonus, you also learn about the link between code age and defects, so let's dive in and see why it's important to stabilize code from both a quality and a cost perspective.

Stabilize Code by Age

Back in Chapter 2, *Identify Code with High Interest Rates*, on page 15, we saw that some parts of our code change more frequently than others. Architectures–the real, physical kind—face the same challenges since buildings aren't permanent either. Buildings change over time to adapt to new uses, and different parts of a building change at different rates, much like software. This led the writer Stewart Brand to remark that a building tears itself apart "because of the different rates of change of its components." (See *How Buildings Learn: What Happens After They're Built [Bra95].*)

Similarly, different rates of change to software components may tear a system apart, resulting in code that's hard to understand and consequently hard to change. The forces that tear codebases apart are the frailties of human memory and the need to communicate knowledge across time and over corporate boundaries. To counter those forces we need to take a time perspective on our code.

The age of code is a factor that should—but rarely does—drive the evolution of a software architecture. Designing with code age as a guide means that we

1. organize our code by its age;

2. turn stable packages into libraries; and

3. move and refactor code we fail to stabilize.

Following these principles gives us a set of advantages:

- *Promotes long-term memory models of code*: Stable packages serve as chunks that remain valid over time, which means our expectations of a piece of code won't be broken. (See *Turn Hotspot Methods into Brain-Friendly Chunks*, on page 67, for a discussion on how chunks help us understand code.)

- *Lessens cognitive load since there's less active code*: The more code you manage to stabilize, the less knowledge you need to keep in your head. This property translates to a positive onboarding effect. New team members can focus on the smaller amount of code under active development without being misled into exploring code that won't change.

- *Prioritizes test suites to shorten lead times*: Automated tests are wonderful until they kill your build times. Getting back on track takes time, and in the meantime you're at risk for dysfunctional practices that long build times encourage. Code age buys you time for proper remedies since it serves as a decision point (potentially automated) on which parts of the software you can safely skip test runs.

Each of the previous advantages plays a part in our larger quest to optimize code for ease of understanding. We'll soon see how these aspects of code age are important from a quality perspective too, but before we go there we have to learn to calculate code age.

The Business Domain Is Above Age

 In Part II of this book we'll look at the importance of structuring software architectures around features, use cases, and domain concepts. The code age heuristic in this chapter applies in that context and within such boundaries. That is, code should be structured by age *within* its containing business context.

Calculate the Age of Code

Measuring age requires us to agree on a reference, a point in time, that specifies the most recent date for our code. The most straightforward implementation is to use the current date as a point of reference, which works fine for a codebase under active development.

However, consider the case where an organization decides to pause its work on a particular system. If you run a code age analysis a few months later the code will look stable, which is misleading since that stability only reflects lack of development work rather than properties of the system evolution itself. In such a case the date of the most recent commit is a better point of reference.

Choose the strategy that fits your situation. In this chapter we use an absolute measure—that is, the current analysis date—as a reference, but it's easy to switch to the other metric. Before we go there, let's see how you get the raw age data of your source code.

Git's log command is a Swiss army knife for repository mining. We used log back in Chapter 2, *Identify Code with High Interest Rates*, on page 15, to calculate change frequencies. Now we use a variation on the command to fetch the last modification date of the files in a repository. Here's an example from the Ruby on Rails codebase:[1]

```
adam$  git log -1 --format="%ad" --date=short \
                -- activerecord/lib/active_record/base.rb
2016-06-09
adam$  git log -1 --format="%ad" --date=short \
                -- activerecord/lib/active_record/gem_version.rb
2017-03-22
```

The key to smooth data mining with git log is to specify a --format that limits the result to the information of interest. In this case we specify "%ad" as a shortcut for *author date*, which gives us the last modification time of the file. Since we don't need the timestamp we simplify the output further by telling Git to just give us the date using the option --date=short.

A simple output means simpler scripting, and now that we have a way of getting the modification date of individual files, we need to scale our data mining to operate on whole systems. Again, Git provides the basic tools you need, so let's look at the code age algorithm, shown in the figure on page 76.

---

1. https://github.com/rails/rails

Algorithm	Intermediate Result
1. Retrieve a list of your repository content using the command `git ls-files`	List of all files actioncable/actioncable.gemspec actioncable/javascripts/action_cable.coffee.erb actioncable/javascripts/action_cable/connection.coffee
2. Iterate over your list of files and apply the `git log` command we used earlier to fetch the modification date	Last modification date actioncable/actioncable.gemspec 2017-05-10 actioncable/javascripts/action_cable.coffee.erb 2016-01-02 actioncable/javascripts/action_cable/connection.coffee 2016-03-15
3. Calculate an age metric for each file based on the current date as reference. Here we use 2017-06-10 as reference date.	Age in months relative to 2017-06-10 actioncable/actioncable.gemspec 1 actioncable/javascripts/action_cable.coffee.erb 17 actioncablejavascripts/action_cable/connection.coffee 14

As that figure shows, we retrieve a list of all files in the repository, fetch their last modification date, and finally calculate the age of each file. The analysis results in this chapter build on that algorithm, and since it is straightforward to automate the steps in a command line–friendly language like Python or in shell scripts, you may want to give it a try and gain experience with repository mining. You also have another tooling option in Code Maat, which provides a code age analysis. (See Appendix 2, *Code Maat: An Open Source Analysis Engine*, on page 215, to get started.)

With the algorithm covered, let's learn how to interpret the resulting code age data.

Exclude Autogenerated Content

Many Git repositories contain generated content such as project files used by your IDE, package manager configurations, and so on. Generated content shows up as noise in the analyses and you want to exclude it. The Git commands we use support command-line flags like --exclude for that purpose, and in CodeScene your analysis configuration provides the same exclusion support.

The Three Generations of Code

The code age analysis was inspired by the work of Dan North, who introduced the idea of short *software half-life* as a way to simplify code. North claims that we want our code to be either very recent or old, and the kind of code that's hard to understand lies in between these two extremes.[2] North's observation ties in with how human memory works, so let's take a brief detour into the science of forgetting before we return to code age and see how it impacts our ability to understand systems.

---

2.   https://leanpub.com/software-faster

In *Your Mental Models of Code*, on page 7, we saw how our brain makes sense of code by building cognitive schemas. Unfortunately, those mental models aren't fixed. That's why we may find ourselves cursing a particular design choice only to realize it's code written by our younger selves in a more ignorant time. We humans forget, and at a rapid pace.

Back in 1885 the psychologist Hermann Ebbinghaus published his pioneering work on how human memory functions. (See *Über das Gedächtnis. Untersuchungen zur experimentellen Psychologie. [Ebb85]*.) In this research, Ebbinghaus studied his own memory performance by trying to remember as many made-up nonsense syllables as possible (kind of like learning to code in Perl). Ebbinghaus then retested his memorization after various periods of time, and discovered that we tend to forget at an exponential rate. This is bad news for a software maintainer.

The next figure shows the *Ebbinghaus forgetting curve*, where we quickly forget information learned at day one. To retain the information we need to repeat it, and with each repetition we're able to improve our performance by remembering more.

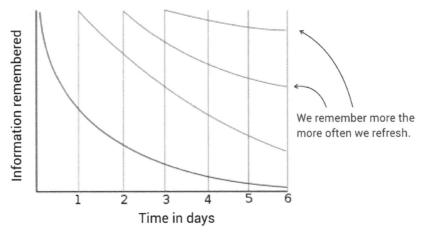

Now, think back to North's claim that code should be either recent or old. This works as a design principle because it aligns with the nature of the Ebbinghaus forgetting curve. Recent code is what we extend and modify right now, which means we have a fresh mental model of the code and we know how it achieves its magic. In contrast, old code is by definition stable, which means we don't have to modify it, nor do we have to maintain any detailed information about its inner workings. It's a black box.

The Ebbinghaus forgetting curve also explains why code that's neither old nor recent is troublesome; such code is where we've forgotten much detail, yet we need to revisit the code at times. Each time we revisit mid-aged code we need to relearn its inner workings, which comes at a cost of both time and effort.

There's also a social side to the age of code in the sense that the older the code, the more likely the original programmer has left the organization. This is particularly troublesome for the code in between—the code we fail to stabilize—because it means that we, as an organization, have to modify code we no longer know. David Parnas labeled such modifications "ignorant surgery" as a reference to changing code whose original design concept we fail to understand. (See *Software Aging [Par94]*.)

The first ignorant surgery is an invitation for others to follow. Over time the code gets harder and harder to understand, which leaves us with a technical debt that's largely due to the organizational factor of failing to maintain mastery of the system. Such code also becomes brittle, which means it's important to stabilize code from a quality perspective too.

Your Best Bug Fix Is Time

Back in my days as a consultant I was hired to do a code review of a database framework. The code, which had been around for years, was a monument to accidental complexity and the basis of many war stories among the senior staff. The code review soon confirmed that the design was seriously flawed. However, as we followed up with a code age analysis, we noted that the code had barely been touched over the past year. So what was all the fuss about? Why spend time reviewing that code?

Well, this organization faced lots of technical debt—both reckless and strategic—and now was the time to pay it off. The database framework was the starting point since that's what everyone complained the most about and had the urge to rewrite. However, those complaints were rooted in folklore rather than data. Sure, the code was messy to work with, so the few people brave enough to dive into it did raise valid complaints, but it had cooled down significantly and was no longer a hotspot. And to our surprise the code wasn't defect-dense either.

Software bugs always occur in a context, which means that a coding error doesn't necessarily lead to a failure. Historically, that database framework had its fair share of critical defects, but it had since been patched into correctness by layers of workarounds delivered by generations of programmers. Now it just did its job and it did it fairly well.

The risk of a new bug decreases with every day that passes. That's due to the interesting fact that the risk of software faults declines with the age of the code. A team of researchers noted that a module that is a year older than a similar module has roughly one-third fewer faults. (See *Predicting fault incidence using software change history [GKMS00]*.) The passage of time is like a quality verdict, as it exposes modules to an increasing number of use cases and variations. Defective modules have to be corrected. And since bug fixes themselves, ironically, pose a major risk of introducing new defects, the code has to be patched again and again. Thus, bugs breed bugs and it all gets reflected as code that refuses to stabilize and age.

Test Cases Don't Age Well

 While old code is likely to be good code in the sense that it has low maintenance costs and low defect risk, the same reasoning doesn't apply to test cases. Test cases tend to grow old in the sense that they become less likely to identify failures. (See *Do System Test Cases Grow Old? [Fel14]*.) Tests are designed in a context and, as the system changes, the tests have to evolve together with it to stay relevant.

Even when a module is old and stable, bad code may be a time bomb and we might defuse it by isolating that code in its own library. The higher-level interface of a library serves as a barrier to fend off ignorant surgeries. Let's see how we get there by embarking on our first code age analysis.

Refactor Toward Code of Similar Age

We've already learned to calculate code age, so let's import the raw numbers into a spreadsheet application and generate a histogram like the one in the next figure.

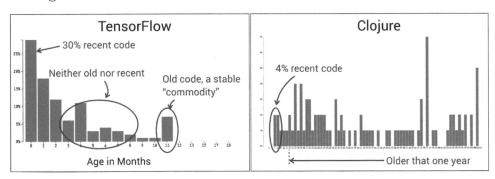

The preceding figure shows the code age distribution of two codebases in radically different states of development: Google's machine-learning service TensorFlow and the programming language Clojure.[3][4]

---

3. https://github.com/tensorflow/tensorflow
4. https://github.com/clojure/clojure

At this time of writing, TensorFlow is under heavy development and that's reflected in its age profile; much of the code shows up as recent. This is in contrast to the age profile of the Clojure code, where most of it hasn't been touched in years. The age distribution of Clojure shows a stable codebase that has found its form.

Code age, like many of the techniques in this book, is a heuristic. That means the analysis results won't make any decisions for us, but rather will guide us by helping us ask the right questions. One such question is if we can identify any high-level refactoring opportunities that allow us to turn a collection of files into a stable package—that is, a mental chunk.

The preceding age distribution of TensorFlow showed that most code was recent, but we also identified a fair share of old, stable code. If we can get that stable code to serve as a chunk, we'll reap the benefits of an age-oriented code organization that we discussed earlier. So let's project TensorFlow's age information onto the static structure of our code.

The next figure shows CodeScene's *age map* zoomed in on TensorFlow's core/lib package. As usual, you can follow along interactively in the pregenerated analysis results.[5]

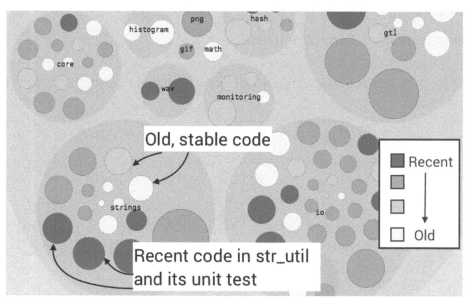

You may recognize the visualization style as an enclosure diagram, just like the one we used in *Prioritize Technical Debt with Hotspots*, on page 19. The difference here is that the color signals the age of the files rather than change frequencies—everything else is the same. The dark blue circles represent recent code and the lighter blue shades indicate code of increasing age.

We start our investigation at the strings package in the lower-right corner. The reason we start there is because the visualization indicates that the package contains code of mixed age. There are no precise rules, so we rely on this visual heuristic instead. If you inspect the actual age of each file, you find that most code is between eight and eleven months old. That's close to ancient, given the rapid development of TensorFlow. However, we also note that the module str_util.cc and its corresponding unit test are recent and thus prevent us from stabilizing the whole package.

Domain Knowledge Drives Refactorings

 The strings package refactoring in this TensorFlow example is chosen as a simple example because we don't want to get sidetracked by domain details; strings are a universal programming construct. A code age analysis on your own code may point you toward more complex refactorings. Should the refactoring turn out to be too hard, take a step back—which is easy with version control—and restart it using the splinter pattern. (See *Refactor Congested Code with the Splinter Pattern*, on page 57.)

Back in *Signal Incompleteness with Names*, on page 62, we saw that generic module names like str_util.cc signal low cohesion. Given the power of names—they guide usage and influence our thought processes—such modules are quite likely to become a dumping ground for a mixture of unrelated functions. This is a problem even when most of the existing functions in such utility-style files are stable, as the module acts like a magnet that attracts more code. This means we won't be able to stabilize the strings package unless we introduce new modular boundaries.

A quick code inspection of str_util.cc confirms our suspicions as we notice functions with several unrelated responsibilities:[6] some escape control characters, others strip whitespace or convert to uppercase, and much more. To stabilize the code we extract those functions into separate modules based on the different responsibilities. We also take the opportunity to clarify the intent of some functions by renaming them, as the figure on page 82 illustrates.

---

6. https://github.com/tensorflow/tensorflow/blob/2ca7c2bdc269b73803d6fa7c199667b987ebeb66/tensorflow/core/lib/strings/str_util.cc

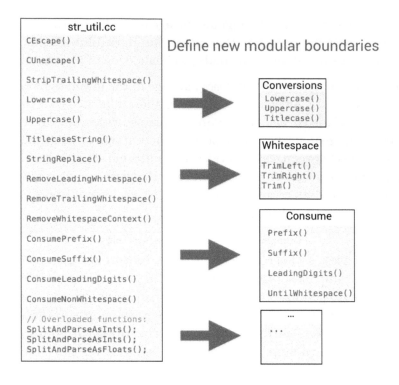

If this were our own code we would continue to split the corresponding unit test str_util_test.cc too. But let's leave that for now and reflect on where our refactoring would take us:

- Each new module is more cohesive, with a clear responsibility.
- The name of each module suggests a usage related to the solution domain.
- As string objects represent a largely fixed problem space, it's likely that several of our new modules won't be touched again. Stable code!

This single refactoring won't be enough to turn the whole strings package into a stable chunk that we can extract into a library. However, we've taken the first step. From here we identify the next young file inside strings, explore why it fails to stabilize, and refactor when needed. Such refactorings have to be an iterative process that stretches over time, and as we move along we can expect to stabilize larger and larger chunks of our code.

Refactor Your Package Structure

Our previous example was a file-level refactoring, but a code age analysis lets us use the same principle to align package structures with how the code evolves. To illustrate the idea we turn to a codebase with a rich history: the

Python programming language.[7] We use the same basic age data as we saw earlier in this chapter, so either clone the Python repository and generate the code age data or follow along in the prepared analysis results.[8]

The Python repository has a history that goes 25 years back, which makes this wonderful language about as old as some of humanity's other great achievements, namely the Hubble space telescope and MTV's *Unplugged* broadcasts. You won't need that much data to detect trends in your own codebase—a few months is usually enough—but the history of Python makes a good case study as it amplifies long-term trends in code age.

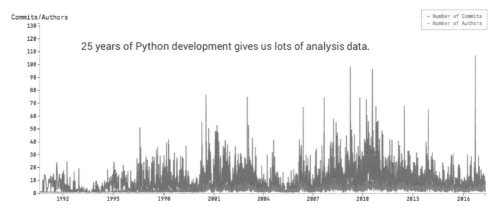

We start our analysis by following the same visual heuristic we used for TensorFlow, where we look for packages with code of different age. There are several candidates, so let's pick one and start with the Modules package, illustrated in the top figure on page 84.

The Modules package is the part of Python's standard library that's implemented in the C programming language.[9] As such, the package is more a collection of building blocks than the realization of a specific domain concept. As the previous figure reveals, one of those building blocks—the cjkcodecs package—matches our heuristic. Let's zoom in and inspect the details of cjkcodecs, as shown in the next figure on page 84.

The analysis reveals a large discrepancy in age between the different files, as some haven't been touched in a decade while multibytecodec.c has been modified recently. Code that changes at different rates within the same package is a warning sign that means either of the following:

---

7. https://github.com/python/cpython

8. https://codescene.io/projects/1693/jobs/4253/results/scope/system-trends/by-date

9. https://docs.python.org/devguide/

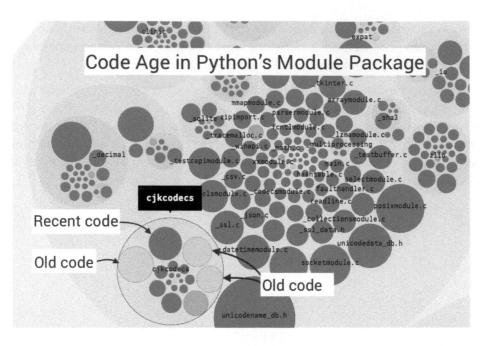

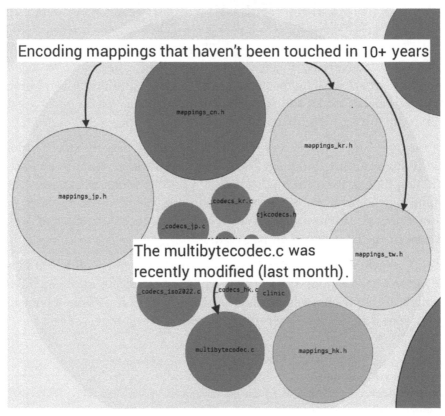

- Some of the code may have quality issues and we need to patch it frequently (hence its younger age).

- Individual files stabilize at different ages because they model different aspects of the problem domain.

Often these two facets come together to explain the differentiation in age. That's why we follow up with an X-Ray analysis (see *Use X-Rays to Get Deep Insights into Code*, on page 27) to get a quick assessment of potential quality issues in the part of the package we fail to stabilize—the file multibytecodec.c, as shown in the following figure.[10]

Some functions would benefit from refactoring.

⇕ Function	⇕ Change Frequency	⇕ Lines of Code ⇕	Cyclomatic Complexity
multibytecodec_encerror	38	154	48
mbstreamreader_iread	38	104	33
_multibytecodec_MultibyteStreamWriter _reset_impl	32	34	6
multibytecodec_decerror	30	103	41
multibytecodec_encode	30	86	28

This figure shows that the hotspots on the function level are way too large, with 100–150 lines of code. The X-Ray results also include a cyclomatic complexity measure that we haven't discussed before. Cyclomatic complexity is a measure of the number of branches (for example, conditional logic and loops) and is used to complement our hotspot criteria as a rough estimate of how tricky the code is. We won't put a lot of weight on the complexity number—the lines of code tell much the same story—but suffice to say that 48 branches in a single function puts a massive tax on our working memory.

While the multibytecodec.c would benefit from targeted refactorings, code complexity doesn't tell the whole story. If you look at the previous age map, you see that the stable parts are encoding pages that specify how text is represented for different natural languages. Encodings tend to be a stable domain since the writing systems of natural languages rarely change.

This is in contrast to the multibytecodec.c file that provides the actual mechanism of encoding and, as such, solves a more general problem. That is, the multibytecodec.c isn't specific to the language mappings and could be reused in other

---

10. https://codescene.io/projects/1693/jobs/4253/results/files/hotspots?file-name=cpython/Modules/cjkcodecs/multibytecodec.c

applications. We can express that in our design by separating the content of cjkcodecs into separate packages, as shown in the following figure.

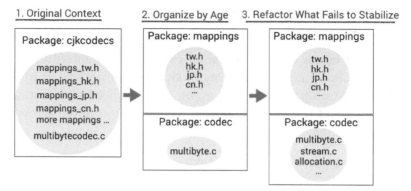

The next step, if this were our codebase, would be to refactor multibytecodec.c using the patterns from Chapter 4, *Pay Off Your Technical Debt*, on page 51, as illustrated in the previous figure. Over time we'd be able to stabilize more and more of the codec implementation, and eventually we could extract the whole package into its own Git repository and make it available to other applications.

This package-level refactoring increases the cohesion of the system by being better aligned with the domain; when different modules in the same package change at different rates, there's a good chance that they represent separate concepts that we've mistaken as the same previously. Our case study illustrates that. The age-driven separation of the codec mechanism from the language mappings also follows the *common closure principle*, which states that classes/files that change together should be packaged together. (See *Clean Architecture: A Craftsman's Guide to Software Structure and Design [Mar17]*.)

We arrived at our suggested improvements by learning from how our code evolves; software design is much more opportunistic and less formal than we'd like to think, which is why we won't be able to get everything right with the initial design. The strength of software evolutionary analyses is that they give us feedback that help us address the gap between the current state of the code and where we'd like it to be.

Dead Code Is Stable Code

In large codebases with a rich history you're likely to find whole packages that are old. Make sure that code is still in use before you extract it into a library. I've seen several commercial codebases where the only reason a package stabilizes is that the code is dead. In this case it's a quick win since you can just delete the code. Remember, deleted code is the best code.

Scale from Files to Systems

A code age analysis complements hotspots by helping you evolve your codebase in a direction where the system gets easier to maintain as you stabilize increasingly large parts of it. A failure to stabilize means that you need to maintain a working knowledge of those parts for the lifetime of the system.

Code age also guides code reorganizations toward the common closure principle, which is basically a specialization of the more general concept of cohesion applied on the package level. As a nice side effect, new programmers who join your organization experience less cognitive load, as they can now focus their learning efforts to specific parts of the solution domain with a minimum of distracting code.

The code age measure we used is shallow—that is, making a tiny change to a file is enough for it to be considered modified and recent. Used this way, our measure errs on the side of the extreme, which means we may miss some refactoring opportunities. However, the advantage is that we can rest assured that if we identify old code we know it's been untouched. This is important from a quality perspective because, as we saw, the risk of bugs decreases with code age.

Finally, we saw that code age is a heuristic, and that no tool will ever be able to do the thinking for us. Instead we use the analysis results to complement our domain expertise and focus our attention to where it's likely to be needed the most.

As we've now reached the end of Part I in this book, we have the fundamental tools to uncover the technical debt with the highest interest rate and react to our findings. However, large systems with millions of lines of code present their own set of challenges. That's why Part II scales the analyses to an architectural level that gives you insights on the system as a whole.

Exercises

As we saw in this chapter, a common reason that we fail to stabilize a piece of code is that it's low on cohesion and, hence, has several reasons to change. In these exercises you get the opportunity to investigate a package, uncover parts with low cohesion, and suggest new modular boundaries. You also get to pick up a loose end and come up with a deeper measure of code age that addresses the shortcomings we noted.

Cores All the Way Down

- Repository: TensorFlow[11]

- Language: C++ and Python

- Domain: TensorFlow is a machine-learning library from Google used to build neural networks.

- Analysis snapshot: https://codescene.io/projects/1714/jobs/4295/results/code/hotspots/system-map

Earlier in this chapter we suggested a hypothetical refactoring of TensorFlow's strings package. That package is located under TensorFlow's core/lib structure. In the TensorFlow analysis you will see that there is another core package nested inside the core structure. We note that a generic name like core hints at low package cohesion and, since we have two levels of generic names—a core package inside a core package—we suspect there are refactoring opportunities here.

The following figure shows an age map of TensorFlow's core/lib/core package. Your task is to suggest a new modular structure of that package to suggest usage of the groups of files and stabilize larger chunks of the code. To get you started, the following figure highlights a threadpool module that you can use as a starting point for code to extract.

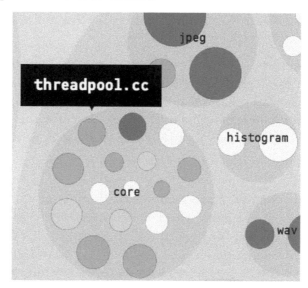

---

11. https://github.com/tensorflow/tensorflow

Deep Mining: The Median Age of Code

So far in the book we've used variations on the git log command for our data mining. That strategy works surprisingly well in providing us with the bulk of information we need. But for more specific analyses we need to dig deeper.

One such analysis is a possible extension to the age analysis in this chapter, where we used a shallow measure for code age. Ideally, we'd like to complement our age metric with a second one that goes deeper. One promising possibility is to calculate the median age of the lines of code inside a file. A median code age value would be much less sensitive to small changes and likely to provide a more accurate picture. How would you calculate the median age of code?

Hint: The key to successful data mining is to have someone else do the job for us. Thus, look to outsource the bulk of the job to some of Git's command-line tools that operate on individual files. There are multiple solutions.

Part II

Work with Large Codebases
and Organizations

Part I provided the basic tools to prioritize technical debt. Now we scale those concepts to work at an architectural level to gain insights into the system as a whole. You'll see how the same techniques help us build new code as we use the information proactively to counter potential problems before they become maintenance issues.

There are no rules of architecture for a castle in the clouds.

> ➤ *Gilbert K. Chesterton*

CHAPTER 6

Spot Your System's Tipping Point

Changes and new features often become increasingly difficult to implement over time, and many systems eventually reach a tipping point beyond which the codebase gets expensive to maintain. Since code decay is a gradual process, that tipping point is often hard to spot when you're in the middle of the work on a large and growing codebase.

In this chapter we use social code analysis to make sense of large-scale systems by breaking them down into subsystems. The strategies you learn let you distill millions of lines of code, authored by hundreds of developers, into a set of specific and focused refactoring tasks. To pull this off we generalize the concepts of hotspots and complexity trend analyses to an architectural level.

We use the Linux kernel as a practical case study and you get the chance to detect maintenance issues in one of the most prominent open source projects of our time. The techniques you learn apply to any larger software system, so let's get going.

Is Software Too Hard?

I spent six years of my career studying psychology at the university. During those years I also worked as a software consultant, and the single most common question I got from the people I worked with was why it's so hard to write good code. This is arguably the wrong question because the more I learned about cognitive psychology, the more surprised I got that we're able to code at all. Given all the cognitive bottlenecks and biases of the brain—such as our imperfect memory, restricted attention span, and limited multitasking abilities —coding should be too hard for us. The human brain didn't evolve to program.

Of course, even if programming should be too hard for us, we do it anyway. We pull this off because we humans are great at workarounds, and a lot of the practices we use to structure code are tailor-made for this purpose. Abstraction, cohesion, and good naming help us stretch the amount of information we can hold in our working memory and serve as mental cues to help us counter the Ebbinghaus forgetting curve. We use similar mechanisms to structure our code at a system level. Functions are grouped in modules, and modules are aggregated into subsystems that in turn are composed into a system. When we succeed with our architecture, each high-level building block serves as a mental chunk that we can reason about and yet ignore its inner details. That's powerful.

Even when we manage to follow all these principles and practices, large codebases still present their own set of challenges. The first challenge has to do with the amount of information we can keep up with, as few people in the world can fit some million lines of code in their head and reason efficiently about it. A system under active development is also a moving target, which means that even if you knew how something worked last week, that code might have been changed twice since then by developers on three separate teams located in different parts of the world. Detailed knowledge in the solution domain gets outdated fast.

Large systems become even more complex once we add the social dimension of software development. As a project grows beyond 12 or 15 developers, coordination, motivation and communication issues tend to cause a significant cost overhead. We've known that since Fred Brooks stressed the costs of communication efforts on tasks with complex interrelationships—the majority of software tasks—in *The Mythical Man-Month: Essays on Software Engineering [Bro95]* back in the 1970s. Yet we, as an industry, are still not up to the challenge. For example, we have tons of tools that let us measure *technical aspects* like coupling, cohesion, and code complexity. While these are all important facets of a codebase, it's often even more important to know if a specific part of the code is a coordination bottleneck. And in this area, supporting tools have been sadly absent.

Societies within a Software System

The social dimension of software impacts any system that grows beyond a handful of contributors. We'll investigate codebases of different scales later in the book, but let's start with an extreme example—Linux. Take a look at the figure on page 95.

The high-profile Linux kernel attracts lots of contributors, and the figure shows a slight exaggeration of the number of Linux contributors. In reality, the number of contributors isn't infinite—which would be a management

dream—but a number so large that GitHub doesn't display it.[1] If we calculate it ourselves, which is straightforward through the shell command git shortlog -s | wc -l, we note that there are 16,241 contributors to Linux.

Given we just learned how communication is a major issue in software development, this number of contributors prompts the question of what the coordination costs are on projects of that scale. To answer it we need to dig deeper; without more context the number of contributors is really just that—a number.

Raise the Abstraction Level

The scale of a codebase has to be reflected in both the organization of people and the architecture of the system. (In a small codebase you have to work hard to fail no matter how you organize.) Linux, for example, has taken the route of a modular system so that people can work independently on isolated parts with a minimum of disturbance.[2] High modularity doesn't mean coordination comes for free—just that it's possible in practice.

This means our true measure of effective collaboration is how well our modular boundaries hold up. That is, instead of focusing on individual files we need to move our analyses to the level of modules and subsystems. Analyses on a subsystem level are also a better fit for large organizations because improvements to different areas can—and should—proceed in parallel. With higher-level analyses, each team gets its own prioritized hotspots to work on—the technical debt that matters the most in their context.

When we raise the abstraction level of the social code analyses, we also provide better means of communication with nontechnical stakeholders. Communicating technical debt via file names is of limited value since people who don't code are unlikely to be familiar with specific files. File names also change as a product evolves, so we want our shared vocabulary to focus on the more enduring names of subsystems and components.

---

1. https://github.com/torvalds/linux
2. http://users.ece.utexas.edu/~perry/education/382v-s08/papers/moon.pdf

Our exploration of large systems starts from a technical perspective. These results are useful in themselves, but they also lay the foundation for the social measurements of interteam coordination that we meet in the next chapter. It all starts with a divide-and-conquer approach, so let's explore what that means.

Divide and Conquer with Architectural Hotspots

A divide-and-conquer strategy helps you split the code investigation into smaller tasks that are easier to reason about than the system as a whole. Let's look at the general strategy before we dive into the practicalities of each step.

1. *Identify your architectural boundaries.* Sometimes those boundaries are documented and, if you're lucky, the documentation may even be correct. If not, you need to reverse-engineer those boundaries, and a good starting point is to base them on the folder structure of the codebase.

2. *Run a hotspot analysis on an architectural level.* This lets you identify the subsystems with the most development effort and, as we'll see later, visualize the complexity trend of a whole architectural component.

3. *Analyze the files in each architectural hotspot.* In this step we're back to individual files, but our analysis scope is smaller since we focus on one subsystem at a time.

The main reason we go through these steps and split the codebase into multiple analysis projects is because each subsystem has a different audience. Our goal is to partition the analysis information on a level where each analysis result is tailored to the people working on that part. We discuss that analysis in detail later in this section, but the general idea is to aggregate the statistics of individual files into logical components, as illustrated in the figure on page 97.

Finally, note that when we speak of the complexity of large systems, the main driver comes from organizational size rather than lines of code. Surprisingly, there's no strong correlation between the two; a system of two million lines of code may be maintained by anywhere from 30 to 300 developers. In the former case, an analysis of the whole system is likely to be good enough to prioritize improvements, whereas the latter requires individual analyses that mirror the areas of responsibility for the different teams.

With the overall analysis process covered, let's apply it to divide and conquer the Linux kernel.

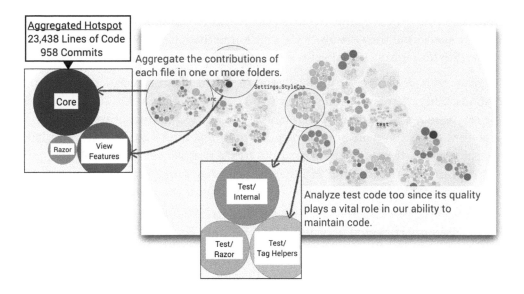

A Language for Specifying Architectural Boundaries

Architectural analyses are based on the same basic data as we used back in Chapter 2, *Identify Code with High Interest Rates*, on page 15. That is, we start from the change frequencies of each file in the codebase, as illustrated by the following command run in the Linux Git repository:[3]

```
adam$ git log --format=format: --name-only --after=2016-01-01 \
    | sort | uniq -c | sort -r | head -10
 621 MAINTAINERS
 542 drivers/gpu/drm/i915/intel_display.c
 503 drivers/gpu/drm/i915/i915_drv.h
 343 drivers/gpu/drm/i915/i915_gem.c
 245 drivers/staging/wilc1000/host_interface.c
 240 drivers/gpu/drm/i915/intel_drv.h
 235 drivers/gpu/drm/i915/intel_pm.c
 228 drivers/gpu/drm/amd/amdgpu/amdgpu.h
 221 drivers/gpu/drm/i915/intel_ringbuffer.c
 207 drivers/net/wireless/realtek/rtl8xxxu/rtl8xxxu.c
```

To script your own hotspot analysis you pipe this data to a file, as shown in the following command:

```
adam$ git log --format=format: --name-only --after=2016-01-01 \
    | sort | uniq -c | sort -r > all_frequencies.txt
```

---

3. https://github.com/torvalds/linux

Note that this time we limit the analysis period to the evolution over the past year by specifying the --after=2016-01-01 option to the Git log. We do this to avoid having historic data that obscures more recent trends.

In your own codebase you also want to focus on the areas within your responsibility. After all, that's where you're most likely to be able to act on the analysis results. Unless you're one of the 16,000 Linux contributors, you probably won't have an area of responsibility, so let's analyze the complete codebase. This gives us the opportunity to see how we can pick up 15 million lines of unfamiliar code and, within a few minutes, suggest a specific refactoring based on how the developers have worked with the code so far. If we pull that off, the scariness factor of most legacy systems goes down because we have techniques that make us more comfortable working with those systems.

Our first step is to identify our architectural boundaries. In a modular architecture like Linux, the folder names in the codebase reflect domain concepts, which simplifies our task because we map each folder to an architectural boundary as the following figure illustrates.

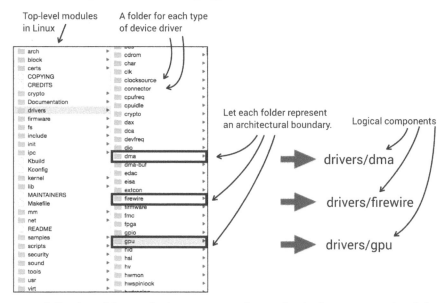

These architectural boundaries represent our *logical components*. A logical component is a construct that aggregates multiple files into an analysis unit that carries meaning on an architectural level. We can go to any level of detail we want here, but it's best to start with a rough model and, if needed, provide more detailed boundaries based on feedback from the analysis results.

In this case we provided a one-to-one mapping of the top-level source code folders to logical components. However, as the preceding figure shows, Linux's drivers package is huge, so let's split it into several components, as well. For drivers, we map each of its subfolders to a unique component name. As you see in the following figure, the transformation to logical components is a straightforward text transformation.

Transform file names from the Git log
to names of logical components.

```
3040 drivers/gpu/drm/i915/intel_display.c        3040 drivers/gpu
2055 drivers/gpu/drm/i915/i915_drv.h             2055 drivers/gpu
1496 sound/pci/hda/patch_realtek.c               1496 sound
1193 arch/x86/kvm/x86.c                          1193 arch
1179 net/core/dev.c                              1179 net
...                                              ...
```

There are two obvious mechanisms to perform this transformation:

- *Glob patterns* let you specify paths and file names by use of wildcards.[4] For example, the glob pattern drivers/gpu/** would match all files and subfolders under the drivers/gpu folder.

- *Regular expressions* are supported by all major scripting languages, including the shell. That makes them an attractive candidate. The disadvantage is that all file names from Git are given in the UNIX-style path format, with forward slashes as separators between directories, and the forward slash is a reserved character in regular expressions. This means we need to escape it, which makes our patterns more cluttered because the equivalent to the simple glob pattern drivers/gpu/** would be ^drivers\/gpu\/.+

Since both approaches work, choose the one you're most comfortable with for your own scripting. If you rely on existing tooling, check out Code Maat (see *Run Architectural Analyses*, on page 216); it uses regular expressions for this purpose, whereas CodeScene lets you specify glob patterns.

Summarize Change Frequencies by Component

Once our Git log is transformed to represent the change frequencies of logical components, we could combine the data with complexity metrics to get more insights. In that case we'd use the lines of code as we saw in *Add a Language-Neutral Complexity Dimension*, on page 18. Since line-counting tools like cloc deliver textual output (see *A Brief Introduction to cloc*, on page 223, for specific commands), you just transform the results using the same patterns as for the Git log.[5]

---

4. https://en.wikipedia.org/wiki/Glob_(programming)
5. https://github.com/AlDanial/cloc

From here we summarize the data for each logical component, and the following figure shows the results from the Linux kernel visualized in an enclosure diagram that you can inspect in the online gallery, too.[6]

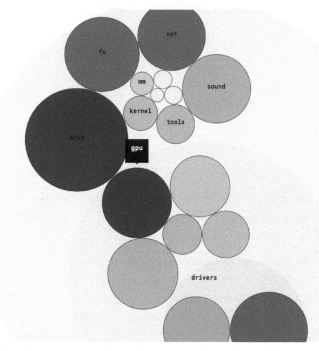

The visualization shows that the top architectural hotspot in Linux is the drivers/gpu module. That means the Linux authors have spent most development effort during 2016 on code inside that package. If we look at the aggregated data from the Git log, we see that a total of 6,481 commits have been done to that code and that it now consists of 685,260 lines of application code.

That's a respectable amount of code, and we could use this information to specify more narrow logical components and divide drivers/gpu even more. However, based on experience we should be on a level of scale where we can act, so let's focus a file-level analysis on the content of the drivers/gpu module.

Analyze Subsystems

To dive into a subsystem we exclude all code contributions except the ones that touch the drivers/gpu module. This is straightforward, as git log already implements the functionality we need. We just need to specify an optional path, as shown in the following shell command:

---

6. https://codescene.io/projects/1737/jobs/4353/results/architecture/hotspots

```
adam$ git log --format=format: --name-only --after=2016-01-01 \
    -- drivers/gpu/ | sort | uniq -c | sort -r | head -5
 542 drivers/gpu/drm/i915/intel_display.c
 503 drivers/gpu/drm/i915/i915_drv.h
 343 drivers/gpu/drm/i915/i915_gem.c
 240 drivers/gpu/drm/i915/intel_drv.h
 235 drivers/gpu/drm/i915/intel_pm.c
```

The argument -- drivers/gpu/ instructs git log to show only commits relating to the content in our folder of interest. Based on this data we perform a file-level hotspot analysis on the content of this subsystem, which reveals that the Intel graphics driver, intel_display.c, is our top hotspot during 2016,[7] as shown in the following figure.

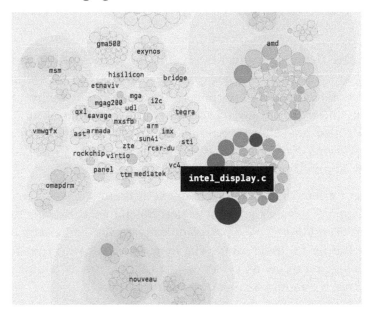

However, remember that just because some code is a hotspot, that doesn't necessarily mean it's a problem. Rather, a hotspot means we've identified a part of the code that requires our attention since it attracts many changes. And the more often something is changed, the more important it is that the corresponding code is of high quality so all those changes are simple and low risk. Thus, our next step is to gather more data to find out how intel_display.c evolves.

In *Evaluate Hotspots with Complexity Trends*, on page 24, we saw how to calculate complexity trends, so let's apply it to intel_display.c. This time we run the analysis on the complete history of the file to detect long-term trends, as shown in the figure on page 102.

---

7. https://codescene.io/projects/1738/jobs/4354/results/code/hotspots/system-map

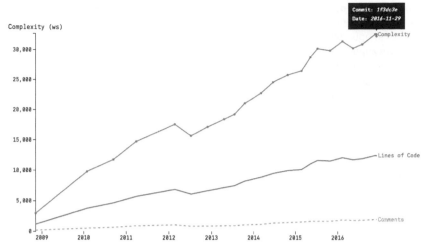

The complexity trend shows two interesting properties of intel_display.c. First, the file has doubled its lines of code over the past four years and it now contains approximately 12,000 lines of code. Size alone may be problematic, as large files are likely to contain many different responsibilities and be hard to navigate. We also note that the complexity of the code has grown steadily, with only two signs of refactorings (the dips in complexity in 2012 and 2015), and it's now at an all-time high.

At this point we have all the information we need to suggest a refactoring of our main suspect. It's a large unit, we need to change the code often, and as we do we keep adding even more complexity to the code, which makes it harder and harder to understand. The longer we wait with that refactoring, the worse it's going to be, as evidenced by the increasing complexity trend. Let's see where we should focus our improvements.

Prioritize Function Hotspots and Code Clones

A file like intel_display.c with 12,000 lines of C code becomes like a system in itself, where parts of the code are likely to remain stable for years while others keep changing. We want to focus on the latter. The X-Ray analysis we covered in *Use X-Rays to Get Deep Insights into Code*, on page 27, helps us with the task by calculating change frequencies on the function level, as shown in the figure on page 103.

The figure shows the X-Ray results of intel_display.c.[8] In most cases, this information serves as a prioritized list of refactoring candidates. Sure, there may

---

8. https://codescene.io/projects/1738/jobs/4354/results/files/hotspots?file-name=linux/drivers/gpu/drm/i915/
    intel_display.c

⇕ Function	⇕ Change Frequency	⇕ Lines of Code	⇕ Cyclomatic Complexity
intel_crtc_page_flip	82	238	52
intel_dump_pipe_config	64	98	10
intel_atomic_commit_tail	58	167	19
i9xx_update_primary_plane	56	66	7
intel_framebuffer_init	53	173	63

be severe structural problems within a hotspot, but in a large file with thousands of lines of code you need to start somewhere. In this case our top refactoring candidate is the function intel_crtc_page_flip, whose code you can view on GitHub.[9] The analysis results reveal that this function consists of 238 lines of code and has been changed 82 times over the past year.

You can get more insights through the complexity trend of the code in the intel_crtc_page_flip function, as the following figure illustrates.

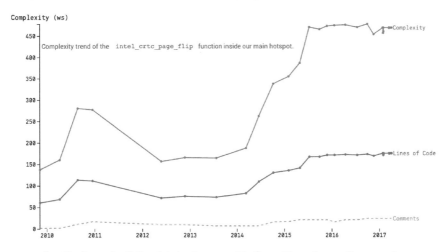

The complexity trend of the intel_crtc_page_flip function doesn't reveal any recent dramatic changes to the code. Instead we see that there was a steep increase in complexity back in 2014 and the code has since continued to evolve at a high but stable complexity level. This indicates that most recent commits are relatively small fixes. However, given the size of the function, it's likely that

9.   https://github.com/torvalds/linux/blob/e93b1cc8a8965da137ffea0b88e5f62fa1d2a9e6/drivers/gpu/drm/i915/intel_display.c#L12120

those more recent commits are expensive in terms of understanding the existing code. If we could simplify future changes we would lower both effort and risks, as the code is likely to continue to evolve.

We also note that intel_crtc_page_flip has a high cyclomatic complexity of 52 branches, which indicates that the code contains lots of conditional logic. Based on this data we should focus our initial refactorings on reducing the overall complexity and size, as we saw in *Turn Hotspot Methods into Brain-Friendly Chunks*, on page 67.

X-Ray Hotspots with the Git Log

A bulletproof X-Ray has to be language aware in the sense your tooling needs to parse the code and understand its syntax. However, there's a simple shortcut based on Git's log option that serves as a useful heuristic to count change frequencies and complexity trends of individual functions: Use the -L option to instruct Git to fetch each historic revision based on the range of lines of code that make up a function. You can even specify the name of the function and have Git resolve the line numbers for you. Here's an example on our Linux hotspot: git log -L:intel_crtc_page_flip:drivers/gpu/drm/i915/intel_display.c.

Look for Quick Wins

Refactoring a complex, evolving piece of code like intel_crtc_page_flip is hard and must be an iterative process. It has to be done, but if we need a quick win first to boost morale we look to identify code clones like we did in *The Dirty Secret of Copy-Paste*, on page 44.

Our tool in this case is a change coupling analysis to detect modification patterns between functions inside intel_display.c, as shown in the next figure.[10]

⇕ Coupled Functions ▼	Degree of Coupling (%) ⇕	Average Revisions ▼	Similarity (%)
intel_finish_page_flip_cs intel_finish_page_flip_mmio	100	11	99
i9xx_find_best_dpll pnv_find_best_dpll	100	21	95
intel_gen4_queue_flip intel_gen6_queue_flip	100	20	83

---

10. https://codescene.io/projects/1738/jobs/4354/results/files/internal-temporal-coupling?file-name=linux/drivers/gpu/drm/i915/intel_display.c

The change coupling results reveal that the functions intel_finish_page_flip_cs and intel_finish_page_flip_mmio are modified together in every commit that touches any of them. The clone-detection algorithm presented in the Similarity column in the preceding table presents a code similarity of 99 percent between the functions. Let's compare the code, as shown in the following figure.

Function Comparison

```
void intel_finish_page_flip_cs(              void intel_finish_page_flip_mmio(
    struct drm_i915_private *dev_priv,           struct drm_i915_private *dev_priv,
    int pipe)                                    int pipe)
{                                            {
    struct drm_device *dev = &dev_priv->drm;     struct drm_device *dev = &dev_priv->drm;
    struct intel_crtc *crtc =                    struct intel_crtc *crtc =
      intel_get_crtc_for_pipe(dev_priv, pipe);     intel_get_crtc_for_pipe(dev_priv, pipe);
    struct intel_flip_work *work;                struct intel_flip_work *work;
    unsigned long flags;                         unsigned long flags;

    /* Ignore early vblank irqs */               /* Ignore early vblank irqs */
    if (!crtc)                                   if (!crtc)
        return;                                      return;

    /*                                           /*
     * This is called both by irq handlers and the reset   * This is called both by irq handlers and the reset
     * code (to complete lost pageflips) so needs the       * code (to complete lost pageflips) so needs the
     * full irqsave spinlocks.                              * full irqsave spinlocks.
     */                                          */
    spin_lock_irqsave(&dev->event_lock, flags);  spin_lock_irqsave(&dev->event_lock, flags);
    work = crtc->flip_work;                      work = crtc->flip_work;

    if (work != NULL &&                          if (work != NULL &&
        !is_mmio_work(work) &&                       is_mmio_work(work) &&
        pageflip_finished(crtc, work))              pageflip_finished(crtc, work))
        page_flip_completed(crtc);                  page_flip_completed(crtc);

    spin_unlock_irqrestore(&dev->event_lock, flags);   spin_unlock_irqrestore(&dev->event_lock, flags);
}                                            }
```

You need to look carefully at the preceding code since there's only a single character difference between the two functions: a negation (!) character. That leaves us with a clear case of code duplication, and we also know that the duplication matters since the change coupling tells us that these two clones evolve together. Software clones like these are good in the sense that they represent low-hanging fruit where we can factor out the commonalities to get an immediate drop in the amount of hotspot code.

Ask the Right Questions

In an internal change coupling analysis we look for functions with high degrees of similarity since those often point to missing abstractions. However, once you start to investigate the code, you may detect possible omissions instead that you need to follow up on.

If you look back at the preceding coupling analysis of intel_display.c, you note that the second row shows two functions, i9xx_find_best_dpll and pnv_find_best_dpll, with 95 percent code similarity. Let's explore the differences this time in the figure on page 106.

Our first pair of software clones revealed classic code duplication, but the functions in the figure paint a more worrisome picture. You don't have to be a C coder to notice that the function to the left, i9xx_find_best_dpll, contains a conditional statement that isn't present in the clone to the right. Without

Function Comparison

```
static bool                                              static bool
i9xx_find_best_dpll(const struct intel_limit *limit,     pnv_find_best_dpll(const struct intel_limit *limit,
             struct intel_crtc_state *crtc_state,                 struct intel_crtc_state *crtc_state,
             int target, int refclk, struct dpll *match_clock,    int target, int refclk, struct dpll *match_clock,
             struct dpll *best_clock)                             struct dpll *best_clock)
{                                                        {
    struct drm_device *dev = crtc_state->base.crtc->dev;    struct drm_device *dev = crtc_state->base.crtc->dev;
    struct dpll clock;                                      struct dpll clock;
    int err = target;                                      int err = target;

    memset(best_clock, 0, sizeof(*best_clock));            memset(best_clock, 0, sizeof(*best_clock));

    clock.p2 = i9xx_select_p2_div(limit, crtc_state, target);   clock.p2 = i9xx_select_p2_div(limit, crtc_state, target);

    for (clock.m1 = limit->m1.min; clock.m1 <= limit->m1.max;   for (clock.m1 = limit->m1.min; clock.m1 <= limit->m1.max;
         clock.m1++) {                                          clock.m1++) {
        for (clock.m2 = limit->m2.min;                           for (clock.m2 = limit->m2.min;
             clock.m2 <= limit->m2.max; clock.m2++) {               clock.m2 <= limit->m2.max; clock.m2++) {
            if (clock.m2 >= clock.m1)                               for (clock.n = limit->n.min;
                break;                                                  clock.n <= limit->n.max; clock.n++) {
            for (clock.n = limit->n.min;
                 clock.n <= limit->n.max; clock.n++) {       ..<snip>..
                for (clock.p1 = limit->p1.min;
                                                            return (err != target);
    ..<snip>...                                            }

    return (err != target);
}
```

more context we can't tell if this is a conditional that's only needed in a particular calling context, or if the comparison reveals a latent bug where a developer forgot to update one of the clones.

This is a common case often found in real-world codebases, so it pays off to investigate the root cause of the differences when you find the same pattern in your own code. If it's a bug, your analysis may have saved the organization from a future failure. You investigate it deeper by running the git blame command on the file, which reveals the author of the lines, and then talk to the developer who made the particular change.[11] Should you find that the code is correct, make sure to explain the differing behavior in the code, either by encapsulating the difference in a well-named function or by making a comment.

Rinse and Repeat

Our case study started from architectural-level hotspots, and used the data to initiate an analysis of the gpu subsystem in more depth. Based on the behavioral patterns of the contributors, we identified a main hotspot where we came up with specific refactoring recommendations.

The main advantage of running separate analyses for different subsystems is that inspecting a hotspot is so much easier if you're familiar with the domain and the code. Through the divide-and-conquer strategy we align the scope of the analysis with the expertise of the team that acts upon the results.

If this were your codebase, you'd repeat the process with the other main suspects in the hotspot analysis. There are no hard rules, but with a heuristic you want to inspect the top 10 hotspots in your subsystem. The reason is

---

11. https://git-scm.com/docs/git-blame

that in a large system you can—and should—let different developers work on improving different parts of the code in parallel. By involving more developers in refactorings, you make people aware of the shortcomings of existing code and let them see the effect of improvements. We humans build expertise in complex domains by doing, and refactoring code is an excellent opportunity to sharpen the skills of your team.

Fight the Normalization of Deviance

If you've worked long enough in the software industry, you've probably heard the claim that coding should be more like real engineering. Behind such statements lies a wish for a more rational approach with clear rules and certainty in the outcome. The software field can definitely do better, but as long as we have people in the loop, failures will happen because we people are far from rational and predictable.

A dramatic example took place in 1986 when the space shuttle *Challenger* disintegrated shortly after launch. If you look at the figure on page 108 you see a puff of gray smoke on one of *Challenger*'s solid rocket boosters. That gray smoke shows that hot rocket gases have escaped and are now burning and compromising the structure of the space shuttle.

The sociologist Diane Vaughan used the *Challenger* disaster as a case study on the theory of *normalization of deviance*. (See *The Challenger Launch Decision: Risky Technology, Culture, and Deviance at NASA [Vau97]*.) The technical reason for the *Challenger* disaster was a failure of its solid rocket booster joints, yet the root cause wasn't technical—it was a social issue.

The early testing of the solid rocket boosters a decade previous revealed that the actual performance of their joints deviated from the predicted performance. To make a long story short, a committee was formed, the problem was discussed, and it was passed off as an acceptable risk. Years later the first in-flight tests again showed that the actual performance of the joints deviated from the predicted performance. Again the problem was discussed and passed off as an acceptable risk. Finally, on the eve of the *Challenger* launch a group of engineers raised concerns about the joints due to the cold temperatures in Florida at that time. The problem was discussed and passed off as an acceptable risk, resulting in a tragic—and possibly avoidable—disaster.

Diane Vaughan explains the decision process as an example of the normalization of deviance: each time you accept a risk, the deviations become the new normal. This is of interest to us because normalization of deviance isn't about

spaceships—it's about people, and we've plenty of normalization of deviance in software development.

Let's say you inherit a file with 15,000 lines of code. At first you're probably shocked by the amount of code and the lack of higher-level organization. But if you work with that code long enough, those 15,000 lines become the new normal. Besides, what difference does a few more lines of code make? Soon you have 16,000, then 17,000 lines of code, and so on.

Get a Whistleblower

The normalization of deviance is one reason why whistleblowers in an organization are important. In software, complexity trends serve as excellent whistleblowers by giving us an unbiased frame of reference that helps us detect when we accept a quality ditch too much. Just as we calculate hotspots on the level of logical components, we can do the same for complexity trends. Here are the general steps:

1. Decide upon a sample interval—for example, once per month.

2. Calculate a complexity trend for each file in the logical component with sample points on the dates given by the interval decided in the previous step.

3. Aggregate the individual trends into a single trend.

In our Linux case study, the gpu module is an architectural hotspot. If you look at the next figure, you see that inside the gpu module there's a cluster of hotspots—including our main suspect intel_display.c—within the i915 submodule.

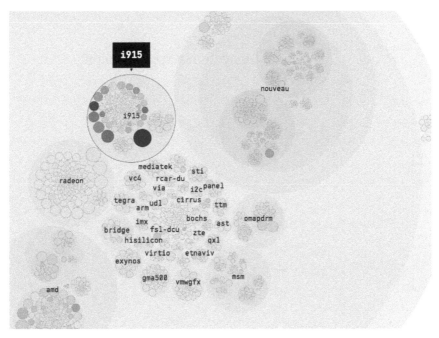

All these files serve to implement the drivers for Intel's graphic card, so let's aggregate their complexity trends as shown in the top figure on page 110.

The aggregated trend of all content in the i915 package doesn't show any dramatic complexity growth. Instead, we see an almost linear trend, which indicates that the module grows in terms of pure size. A much more problematic example is shown in the next figure on page 110, taken from a commercial system.

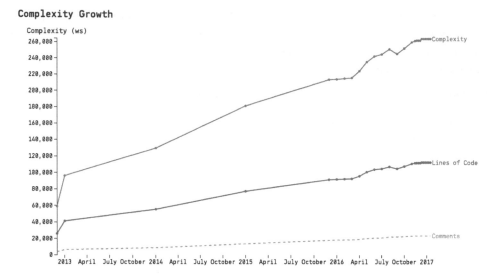

The preceding figure shows a subsystem whose complexity escalates at a rapid rate. This is a sign that the development organization has to take a step back and start investing in improvements. Trends like these may also serve as a warning sign; adding more people to a system whose complexity grows rapidly would be disastrous, so use the trends as a basis for organizational decisions too.

Used this way, complexity trends helps us detect, and possibly predict, when our system reaches its tipping point—beyond which it becomes a maintenance nightmare. Another use of aggregated trends is that they let us track the effects of refactorings that split a single file into multiple files (for example, the splinter pattern, discussed in *Refactor Congested Code with the Splinter Pattern*, on page 57). Over time we would expect a successful refactoring to reduce the overall complexity of the whole package, and aggregated trends let us measure it.

React to Hotspots Today

Linux may be a unique snowflake in terms of scale and development activity, but it still evolves like most other codebases: hotspots tend to stay where they are and they also keep accumulating complexity over several years. As developers, we're often aware of problematic modules, but without visual trends we're destined to miss how serious those hotspots are and how much time we waste maintaining code that's more complex than it should be.

Once we run a complexity trend analysis it becomes obvious that we—as an organization—should have invested in code improvements years ago. We can save our future selves from the same painful insights by reacting today.

Communicate with Nontechnical Managers

Depending on your company culture, you may need management buy-in for large redesigns. I've used the techniques in this chapter to communicate the costs and risks of hotspots.

If you're in that situation, start by calculating the percentage of commits that involve your top hotspots—10 to 15 percent is common—to show your managers how important that code is for your ability to support new features and innovations. Follow up with the corresponding complexity trends to explain that the code gets worse over time, which will slow you down. Add the people side to your presentation to highlight that the hotspots are coordination bottlenecks too.

Later you can visualize the effects of a refactoring with a steep downward trend of your prioritized hotspot. This is most effective when applied on the level of logical components, which tend to carry meaning to nontechnical managers too. As an example, the figure on page 112 shows the effect of a splinter refactoring. Trends like these provide an important part of the feedback loop.

Managers do listen; it's just that we need to give them a chance to understand the pain points of something as technical as code so that they can balance that information with other trade-offs. Data buys trust.

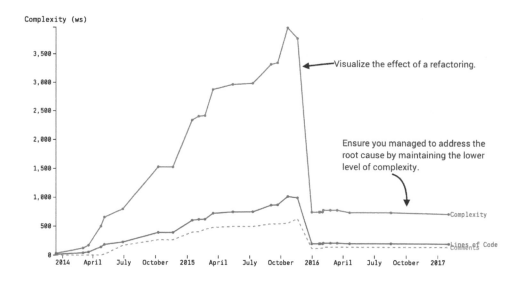

Toward Team-Oriented Measures

In this chapter we climbed the abstraction ladder and analyzed the evolution of complete subsystems. Since the principles for hotspots and complexity trends are orthogonal to the data they operate on, we get to use the same concepts on all levels of detail, be it architectural components, files, or functions. This means you now have the techniques to make sense of a codebase, no matter the scale and size of it.

The way you slice and dice your architectural boundaries varies depending on your architectural style. For example, in a technically oriented architecture like MVC you want to represent each layer as a boundary, whereas you'd specify each microservice as its own logical component. (We'll discuss both cases—with examples—in Chapter 9, *Systems of Systems: Analyzing Multiple Repositories and Microservices*, on page 165.)

It's also important to note that your mapping doesn't have to be one-to-one between folders and logical components, and in practice you often find that a logical component is represented by multiple folders. One typical example is a physical separation of application code and test code into different parallel folder structures, as illustrated in the figure on page 113.

High-level analyses on logical components fill an important role from a communication point of view, too, as nontechnical stakeholders won't gain much information from learning that the code in gtt.c is hard to maintain. By raising the information to the level of components and instead showing a complexity

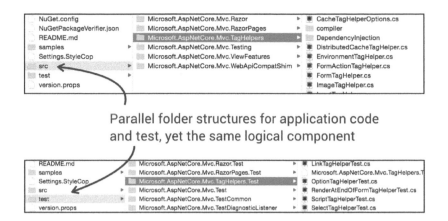

Parallel folder structures for application code
and test, yet the same logical component

trend of the containing component—for example, Intel graphics driver—you tap
into the vocabulary shared between developers and nontechnical people.

We react to architectural hotspots by drilling deeper and uncovering the most
critical file- and function-level hotspots, which serve as prioritized refactoring
targets. Refactoring large hotspots is an iterative process that takes time.
Thus, it's crucial that improvements to different areas can proceed in parallel.

To work in practice, the collaborative model of your organization has to align
with the system's architectural boundaries. Since that's a dimension of software that isn't visible in the code itself, we dedicate the whole next chapter
to it. Come along as we explore how to optimize organizations based on feedback from the coding.

Exercises

The following exercises are designed to let you explore architectural hotspots
on your own. By working through the exercises you also get the opportunity
to explore an additional usage of complexity trends to supervise unit test
practices.

Prioritize Hotspots in CPU Architectures

- Repository: Linux[12]
- Language: C
- Domain: The Linux kernel is an operating system kernel.
- Analysis snapshot: https://codescene.io/projects/1740/jobs/4358/results/code/hotspots/
  system-map

---

12. https://github.com/torvalds/linux

In this chapter we focused our case study on the gpu package since it was the top hotspot. Once we're done with that analysis it's time to move on to the next candidate: the arch package. Located in the top folder of Linux, the arch directory contains a module for each supported computer architecture, like *PowerPC*, *ARM*, and *Sparc*.

Run a subsystem analysis of the arch package and identify its top hotspot. Dig deeper with an X-Ray, look at the code, and come up with a prioritized refactoring target.

Get a Quick Win

- Repository: Erlang[13]

- Language: C

- Domain: Erlang is a functional programming language designed for concurrency, distribution, and fault tolerance.

- Analysis snapshot: https://codescene.io/projects/1707/jobs/4289/results/files/internal-temporal-coupling?file-name=otp/erts/emulator/beam/erl_process.c

Erlang is a wonderful platform for building soft real-time systems. The language provides an interesting model of state and interactions, with the main abstraction being *Erlang processes*. Erlang's processes are lightweight and cheap to create, which is quite different from the processes we know in operating systems.

The code for the process abstraction is located in the file /erts/emulator/beam/erl_process.c. It's a central piece of code with a rich history, which probably explains why the code now exceeds 10,000 lines. Perform an X-Ray on the file and look for internal change coupling that we could eliminate by introducing shared abstractions for similar code. If you succeed, you get a quick win since you manage to reduce the overall complexity of the file.

Supervise Your Unit Test Practices

- Repository: PhpSpreadsheet[14]

- Language: PHP

- Domain: PhpSpreadsheet is a PHP library used to read and write spreadsheet files such as Excel.

---

13. https://github.com/erlang/otp
14. https://github.com/PHPOffice/PhpSpreadsheet

- Analysis snapshot: https://codescene.io/projects/1579/jobs/4888/results/scope/system-trends/by-component

Complexity trends on logical components let us fight the normalization of deviance. Such aggregated trends solve a second problem, too—namely, catching components that abandon unit tests. Instead of considering application code and test code part of the same logical component, calculate separate complexity trends for them and see if they evolve together. All too often, organizations embark on a unit-test strategy only to ignore the tests as soon as the first deadline hits the fan. Aggregated complexity trends help you detect build-ups of technical debt early.

Explore the complexity trends of the logical components in PhpSpreadsheet. Look at the coevolution of application code and test code. Do the trends indicate that unit tests are actively maintained, or are there signs of worry? Think about what the warning signs would look like in terms of trends. (You can always peek at the solutions in *Solutions: Spot Your System's Tipping Point*, on page 229.)

All men's miseries derive from not being able to sit in a quiet room alone.

> ➤ *Blaise Pascal*

CHAPTER 7

Beyond Conway's Law

In Part I we saw that a software project often mistakes organizational problems for technical issues, and treats the symptoms instead of the root cause. This misdirection happens because the organization that builds the system is invisible in our code. We can't tell from the code alone if a piece of code is a productivity bottleneck for five different teams. In this chapter we close this knowledge gap as we use version-control data to measure team efficiency and detect parts of the code with excess coordination needs.

This means we'll be able to measure aspects of software development that we haven't been able to measure before. We'll use this information to see how well our current system aligns with *Conway's law*, which states that "a design effort should be organized according to the need for communication." (See *How do committees invent? [Con68]*.) We'll look at this principle in more detail and make sure to point out the missing pieces in Conway's law by tapping into research from social psychology, which teaches us that there are many other important organizational issues that affect the quality of our work. We'll also draw a distinction between your team's operational boundaries and knowledge boundaries to explain why it's necessary to keep the former more narrow.

The way developers collaborate is crucial to the maintainability of any system, so let's dive in and see how we can guide our organization toward better code.

Software Architecture Is About Making Choices

Software architecture is as much about boxes and arrows as archeology is about shovels. While sketching boxes may be useful as part of a discussion, the real software architecture manifests itself as a set of principles and guidelines rather than a static structure captured in PowerPoint. Such architectural principles work as constraints that limit our design choices to ensure consistency and ease of reasoning in the resulting solution.

A software architecture also goes beyond purely technical concerns, as it needs to address the collaborative model of the people building the system. The general idea is to minimize the coordination and synchronization needs between different teams to achieve short lead times so that an idea can be realized in code with minimal overhead. When we succeed, each architectural boundary serves as a high-level mental chunk that we can reason about even though the modules are developed by our peers on different teams. The extent to which you can implement new features without calling a grand staff meeting is the ultimate test of an architecture's success.

Conway's Law and Its Impact on Modularity

Modularity alone doesn't guarantee a successful architecture that facilitates parallel work. Rather, your modular boundaries need to align with the responsibilities of the teams in your organization. That principle is the core of Conway's law.

To pull this off, your modular boundaries should be based on concepts from the problem domain rather than the solution domain. This is because an architecture oriented around the problem domain provides natural team boundaries, as each team can take on an end-to-end responsibility for a feature, which gives every team a clear purpose that is reflected in its responsibilities and areas of work.

This is in contrast to a technically oriented architecture based on ideas from the solution domain, where concepts like data access, controllers, views, and clients are your main building blocks. This may work fine for a small team, but the architectural style doesn't scale well. Technical building blocks become interconnected and every interesting change to the codebase requires modifications that cut across modular boundaries.

A technically oriented architecture implies that you either get all of your teams working in the same parts of the code all the time—a coordination nightmare—or that each team "owns" a component and consequently becomes a coordination bottleneck to all teams requiring changes to that component. Either way, it's expensive.

In the next chapter we'll analyze these patterns in more detail, but for now we just note that such architectures come with inherent coordination costs for both component- and feature-based organizations. The figure on page 119 illustrates the bottlenecks.

Interteam communication is an inevitable aspect of building large systems, and thus ease of communication should be a key nonfunctional requirement

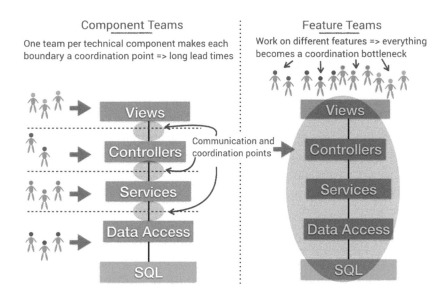

of any architecture. These claims are supported by empirical research, which reports gaps in the required coordination between developers and the actual coordination results in an increase in software defects. The same research also shows development productivity increases with better socio-technical *congruence*. (See *Coordination Breakdowns and Their Impact on Development Productivity and Software Failures [CH13]* for the research findings.)

Congruence means that the actual coordination needs are matched with appropriate coordinating actions, which is a strong case for aligning your architecture and organization since coordination costs increase with organizational distance. Such coordination costs also increase with the number of developers, so let's look into that topic.

Measure Coordination Needs

There's a difference between code developed by a single individual versus code that's more of a shared effort by multiple programmers and, thus, in need of coordination. Excess coordination needs correlate directly to increased lead times. What's more surprising is that there may be a long-term cost, too, as our organizational patterns impact code quality in terms of defects.

In a groundbreaking study, researchers at Microsoft used organizational metrics such as the number of authors, the number of ex-authors, and organizational ownership to measure how well these factors predict the failure proneness of the resulting code. The research shows that organizational factors are better predictors of defects than any property of the code itself, be it code complexity or code coverage. (See *The Influence of Organizational Structure on Software Quality [NMB08]* for the research.) Let's use these insights to uncover the contribution patterns of individual authors with an example from the Linux kernel.

Parallel Development in Linux

In the previous chapter we identified the Intel graphics driver as an architectural hotspot, and now we want to investigate if it also represents a coordination bottleneck in terms of how many authors need to work on it. Social aspects are a bit more complex to measure, so hold tight as we build up our data step by step.

Out-of-the-Box Social Analyses

 All the algorithms in this chapter have open source implementations in Code Maat, as introduced in Appendix 2, *Code Maat: An Open Source Analysis Engine*, on page 215.

Our starting point is to count the number of developers that contribute code to each logical component. As we saw in the previous chapter, the folder structure of the Linux kernel reflects concepts from the problem domain. This simplifies our analysis, as we can count the number of authors of each component by specifying the path to its folder as an argument to Git's shortlog command, which serves to summarize data from git log. Here's what it looks like:

```
adam$ git shortlog -s
  8     D. Cooper
  7     Bob
  2     N. Cross
 37     B. Horn
  ...
```

By providing the -s option to git shortlog we get a list with each author's total commit count. Since each author is represented by one line in the output, we can just count the lines. In a UNIX/Linux shell we pipe the output to the wc -l utility, and on Windows we'd use the find /c /v "" combination or PowerShell. Let's see it in action on Linux:

```
adam$ git shortlog -s --after=2016-09-19 -- drivers/gpu/drm/i915/ | wc -l
    55
adam$ git shortlog -s --after=2016-09-19 -- drivers/gpu/drm/amd/ | wc -l
    44
adam$ git shortlog -s --after=2016-09-19 -- drivers/gpu/drm/i810/ | wc -l
     1
adam$ git shortlog -s --after=2016-09-19 -- drivers/gpu/drm/nouveau/ | wc -l
    22
```

The preceding output shows example results from some of the driver components in Linux. For instance, we note that the Intel graphics driver in drivers/gpu/drm/i915/ has contributions from 55 authors in a timespan of three months, which is quite a lot considering that a total of 169 authors have committed code to any module under drivers/gpu within that time period. This means one-third of all contributors in that area may have to coordinate work in the Intel graphics driver. We haven't yet discussed why we focused on just three months of development activity; we'll cover that as we discuss how to decide on an analysis interval later in this chapter. (Spoiler: it's a heuristic.) First, let's see how to use the data.

The number of authors behind each component provides a shallow indication of coordination needs, and is just a starting point. The quality risks we've discussed are not so much about how many developers have to work with a particular piece of code. Rather, it's more important to uncover how diffused their contributions are, and once more we turn to research for guidance.

In a fascinating study on the controversial topic of code ownership, a research team noted that the number of minor contributors to a module has a strong positive correlation to defects. That is, the more authors that make small contributions, the higher the risk for bugs. Interestingly, when there's a clear main developer who has written most of the code, the risk for defects is lower, as illustrated by the following figure. (See *Don't Touch My Code! Examining the Effects of Ownership on Software Quality [BNMG11]*.)

Each color represents an author. The area of each box shows how much code each author has contributed.

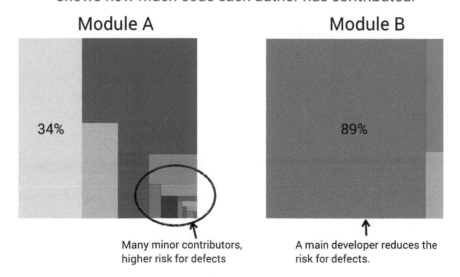

Module A   Module B

34%   89%

Many minor contributors, higher risk for defects

A main developer reduces the risk for defects.

Based on that research alone we can't tell *why* having more minor developers of a module leads to more defects. However, given what we've learned so far, some of the effect is likely due to increased coordination needs combined with an incomplete understanding of the existing design and problem domain. Further, a main developer is likely to mean that the code has a consistent style and idea behind it. As we'll soon see, other psychological factors should influence our code-ownership strategy, but let's not get ahead of ourselves. Let's start by taking the research findings at face value and exploring how we can detect these potential problems.

Rank Code by Diffusion

Our goal is to provide an analysis that ranks all the modules in our codebase based on how diffused the development effort is, and then to use that as a proxy for coordination needs. This is a quantitative metric that we get through a *fractal value* analysis. A fractal value is an algorithm that delivers a normalized value between 0.0 and 1.0 based on how many different authors have contributed and how the work is distributed among them. (See *Fractal Figures: Visualizing Development Effort for CVS Entities [DLG05]* for the research and complete definition.) The next figure shows the fractal value formula, and if you prefer code to math, there's an implementation in Code Maat too.[1]

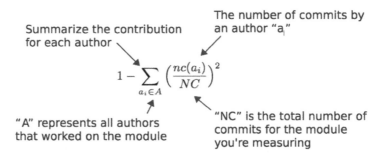

A fractal value of 0.0 means a single author has written all the code, whereas the closer to 1.0 we get, the more contributors there are, as shown in the top figure on page 123.

The git shortlog command we used earlier provides us with all the input data we need for the fractal value computation. Remember that with an -s option, git shortlog includes a summary with the commit count per author. We can then visualize it using enclosure diagrams—just as we did for hotspots—but have the color signal the range of the fractal value instead. The next figure on page 123

---

1. https://github.com/adamtornhill/code-maat/blob/1c867df1e8228c321ddd83bf6679ddb781049116/src/code_maat/analysis/effort.clj#L96

Each box represents a file and each color represents
the relative contribution of an author.

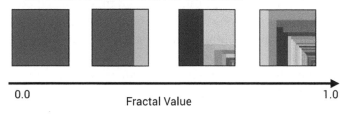

0.0   Fractal Value   1.0

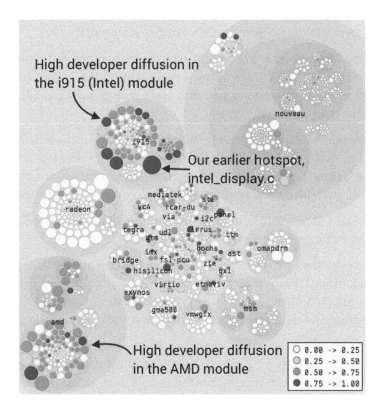

shows the fractal values of the files in the Linux GPU drivers, where the more
intense red color indicates higher fragmentation.[2]

The analysis of the Linux GPU package reveals that the driver modules for
Intel and AMD have the greatest need for coordination. The main hotspot,
intel_display.c, which we identified in the previous chapter, attracted 17 developers over the past three months. Now let's see what this means and how we
would react to similar findings in our own code.

---

2.   https://codescene.io/projects/1738/jobs/4886/results/social/knowledge/individuals

React to Developer Fragmentation

Open source development may be different from many closed source settings, as it encourages contributions to all parts of the code. However, there's evidence to suggest that this collaboration comes with a quality cost. One study on Linux found that code written by many developers is more likely to have security flaws. (See *Secure open source collaboration: an empirical study of Linus' law [MW09]*.) The paper introducing our fractal value metric evaluated it on the Mozilla project, and found a strong correlation between the fractal value of a module and the number of reported bugs. (See *Fractal Figures: Visualizing Development Effort for CVS Entities [DLG05]*.)

Every situation is different. You might have good reasons for multiple developers to work on the same code. However, you can still use the fractal values to reason about risk. Whenever you find code with a high fractal value, use the data to do the following:

- *Prioritize code reviews*. Code reviews done right are a proven defect-removal technique, but they come at a cost. As your organization grows, code-reviewer fatigue becomes a real thing. Given what we know about defects, we should prioritize code reviews of changes done by minor contributors.

- *Focus tests*. Calculate fractal values to identify the areas of the code where you need to focus extra tests.

- *Replan suggested features*. Before you start on a new feature, measure the development fragmentation over the past weeks. If your planned work involves an area of the code with high developer congestion, it could pay off to replan and delay the start on any new feature implementation.

- *Redesign for increased parallelism*. In a large system you need to optimize development for parallel work, so use the fractal values to identify candidates for splinter refactorings allowing people to work more independently.

- *Introduce areas of responsibility*. When you visualize developer patterns you give nontechnical managers insights into development work, providing them a chance to reassess the current ways of working, perhaps by introducing teams that are aligned with the structure of the codebase, an idea we'll explore shortly.

Many fundamental problems in large-scale software development stem from a mindset where programmers are treated as interchangeable cogs—generic resource ready to be moved around and thrown at new problems in different areas. The research we just covered suggests that such a view is seriously flawed. Not all code changes are equal, and the programmer making the change is just as important from a quality perspective as the code itself. With that covered, let's raise these ideas to the level of an organization and start to analyze team work.

Watch Out for Authors with Multiple Aliases

Social metrics such as fractal values identify each developer who contributes code, but unfortunately it's common that developers have multiple Git aliases, which biases the analysis results. You prevent that by providing a .mailmap that resolves the aliases. The Git feature .mailmap is a simple text file that you add to the root of your repository and use to specify a mapping from multiple aliases to a single developer, as shown here.

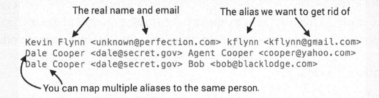

The real name and email   The alias we want to get rid of

```
Kevin Flynn <unknown@perfection.com> kflynn <kflynn@gmail.com>
Dale Cooper <dale@secret.gov> Agent Cooper <cooper@yahoo.com>
Dale Cooper <dale@secret.gov> Bob <bob@blacklodge.com>
```

You can map multiple aliases to the same person.

Code Ownership and Diffusion of Responsibility

So far we've discussed coordination needs mainly in terms of quality: the more developers who touch a piece of code, the higher the risk for defects. But coordination also has a very real direct cost, which is what social psychologists call *process loss*.

Process loss is a concept that social psychologists borrowed from the field of mechanics. The idea is that just as a machine cannot operate at 100 percent efficiency all the time (due to physical factors like friction and heat loss), neither can a team. Part of a team's potential productivity is simply lost. (See *Group Process and Productivity [Ste72]* for the original research.)

The kind of process loss that occurs depends on the task, but in a brain-intensive collaboration like software, most process loss is due to communication and coordination overhead. Process loss may also be driven by motivation losses and other social group factors. These are related to a psychological phenomenon called *diffusion of responsibility*. You notice the most extreme manifestation of diffusion of responsibility if you're unfortunate enough to witness an accident or an emergency; the larger any group of bystanders, the less likely any individual will provide help. Scary.

One of the most important reasons behind diffusion of responsibility is that in larger groups we don't feel a personal sense of responsibility, and we assume someone else should react and help.[3] The consequence is that the group setting makes us act in a way we wouldn't if we were alone.

Diffusion of responsibility usually takes on less dramatic forms in software, but it's still there and the same situational forces have serious implications for code quality and productivity. To counter these effects we must feel that our individual contributions make a difference. Good code has a sense of personal responsibility from everyone involved.

To counter the diffusion of responsibility we need to look for structural solutions. One way of producing personal responsibility is *privatizing*, which is an effective technique for managing shared resources in the real world. (See *The commons dilemma: A simulation testing the effects of resource visibility and territorial division [CE78]* for research on how groups benefit from privatization.) Since code is about knowledge rather than a physical resource, we need to explore the idea of privatizing and its consequences in terms of code ownership.

Immutable Design

Providing a clear ownership model also helps address hotspots. I analyze codebases as part of my day job, and quite often I come across major hotspots with low code quality that still attract 10 to 15 percent of all development efforts.

It's quite clear that this code is a problem, and when we investigate its complexity trends we frequently see that those problems have been around for years, significantly adding to the cost and displeasure of the project. New code gets shoehorned into a seemingly immutable design, which has failed to evolve with the system.

At the same time, such code is often not very hard to refactor, so why hasn't that happened? Why do projects allow their core components to deteriorate in quality, year after year? A look at the diffusion of responsibility provides part of the answer as the developer fragmentation of those hotspots tends to look like the figure on page 127.

This is the software version of a crowd of people looking passively at an accident. Again, the main problem here isn't technical but social, and it's intimately tied to the organization building the code.

Code Ownership Means Responsibility

Code ownership can be a controversial topic as some organizations move to models where every developer is expected to work on all parts of the codebase.

---

3.   https://en.wikipedia.org/wiki/Diffusion_of_responsibility

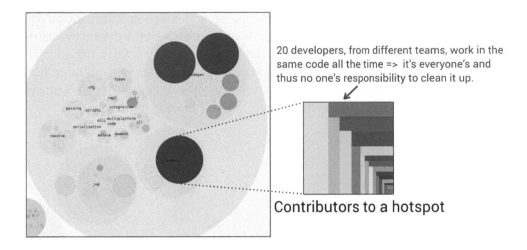

20 developers, from different teams, work in the same code all the time => it's everyone's and thus no one's responsibility to clean it up.

Contributors to a hotspot

The idea of code ownership evokes the idea of *development silos* where knowledge is isolated in the head of a single individual. So let's be clear about this: when we talk ownership, we don't mean ownership in the sense of "This is my code—stay away." Rather, ownership is a mechanism to counter the diffusion of responsibility, and it suggests that someone takes personal responsibility for the quality and future of a piece of code.

That "someone" can be an individual, a pair, or a small team in a larger organization. I've also seen organizations that successfully adopt an open source–inspired ownership model where a single team owns a piece of code, yet anyone can—and is encouraged to—contribute to that code. The owning team, however, still has the final say on whether to accept the contributions. The advantage of this model is that it allows teams to bridge gaps in the alignment between architecture and organization by implementing the functionality they need even when it happens to cross organizational boundaries.

Provide Broad Knowledge Boundaries

The effects we discuss are all supported by data, and whether we like it or not, software development doesn't work well with lots of minor contributors to the same parts of the code. We've seen some prominent studies that support this claim, and there is further research in *Code ownership and software quality: a replication study [GHC15]*, which shows that code ownership correlates with code quality. This research is particularly interesting since it replicates an earlier study, *Don't Touch My Code! Examining the Effects of Ownership on Software Quality [BNMG11]*, which claims that the risk for defects increases with the number of minor developers in a component.

Of course, these findings don't mean you should stop sharing knowledge between people and teams—quite the contrary. It means that we need to distinguish between our *operational boundaries* (the parts where we're responsible and write most of the code) from the *knowledge boundaries* of each team (the parts of the code we understand and are relatively familiar with). We want to keep the latter more broad, as illustrated in the following figure.

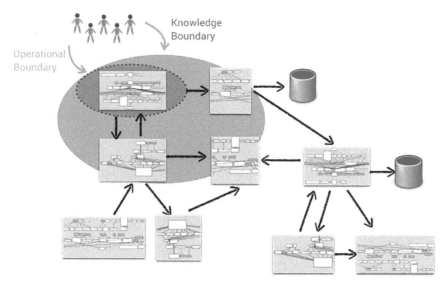

Whereas Conway's law implies that our communication works best with well-defined operational boundaries, broader knowledge boundaries make interteam communication easier since we share parts of each other's context. There's also evidence that broader knowledge boundaries provide our organization with a competitive advantage, enabling us to see opportunities and benefit from innovations outside our area of the code. (See *The Mirroring Hypothesis: Theory, Evidence, and Exceptions [CB16]* for a summary of 142 empirical studies on the topic.)

There are several techniques for broadening your knowledge boundaries, such as inviting people from other teams to code reviews and scheduling recurring sessions where you present walkthroughs of a solution or design. You may also choose to encourage people to rotate teams. When combined, these techniques give your teams a fresh perspective on their work and help foster a culture of shared goals. In addition, few things provide a greater learning opportunity than explaining your code and design to someone else.

The key to finding the right boundaries is to make it a deliberate rather than an accidental designation. We can't measure the precise knowledge boundaries, but we can get an accurate picture of the operational boundaries based on where each developer has contributed code, and use that information to streamline our architecture and organization. We'll cover how to do that in a minute, but as a first step we need to agree on a cutoff date for our analysis.

Specify a Start Date with Organizational Significance

Development organizations aren't static. People move between teams, new teams are formed, and old teams are abandoned. Each organizational change introduces a possible bias into the team-level metrics.

You can avoid these biases by selecting an analysis start date that represents the date of your last organizational change. For example, let's say you changed the team structure in March 2017. In that case you want to limit your version-control data to changes since that date, which you do with the --after option to Git that we discussed earlier. Behavioral data in the shape of version-control commits accumulates quickly, and a few weeks of activity is usually enough to detect the patterns we discuss in this chapter.

Note that the technical analyses, like hotspots and change coupling, are different from social analyses because you want to detect long-term trends. In that case, use a start date that represents a significant event in your product's life cycle, such as a major release or a fairly large redesign. With the analysis time span covered, we're ready to start analyzing team work.

Analyze Operational Team Boundaries

In many situations the coordination unit of interest isn't that of individual developers but rather of teams. This is the case in larger organizations or when using collaborative development techniques like pair programming. Since version-control data doesn't know anything about teams, we need to augment the raw behavioral data with organizational information. This is a matter of scripting a replacement of author names with the names of their teams, as the following figure illustrates.

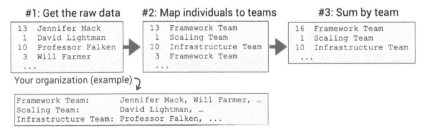

The Git log output in the preceding figure is fetched with the same options, git shortlog -s, that we used in *Parallel Development in Linux*, on page 120. The raw data gives us the number of commits per author and folder, and from here we just replace the author with the name of the team through a simple lookup.

Now we need to iterate through the Git data and summarize the contributions at the team level so that we can calculate a fractal value and detect excess parallel work. This is a mechanical scripting exercise that you could implement yourself, use the open source tooling in Code Maat (see *Measure Conway's Law*, on page 217), or have CodeScene do for you.[4]

Let Git Do the Team Mapping

Git's .mailmap functionality provides a quick way of getting raw data on the team level. Just provide a .mailmap that translates individual authors to the names of their teams, and configure the path to that .mailmap through Git's mailmap.file option. The next time you run a git log command you get team names instead of authors without the need for any extra scripting.

Whatever approach we choose, we want to end up with data that lets us identify components with excess parallel development, as the following figure illustrates.

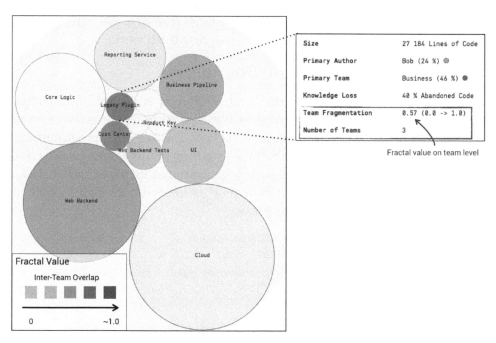

Size	27 184 Lines of Code
Primary Author	Bob (24 %)
Primary Team	Business (46 %)
Knowledge Loss	40 % Abandoned Code
Team Fragmentation	0.57 (0.0 -> 1.0)
Number of Teams	3

Fractal value on team level

Fractal Value
Inter-Team Overlap
0   ~1.0

---

4.   https://codescene.io/docs/guides/architectural/architectural-analyses.html#evaluate-conway-s-law

The preceding figure is from a commercial closed source system that I made anonymous for inclusion as a case study. The most fragmented logical component is the Legacy Plugin, where three teams have made contributions over the past month. In the real application, Legacy Plugin has a more business-oriented name, but legacy it is. It's a subsystem that's been around for years and no one claims to know anything about it except for Bob, its original author, who left in frustration two years ago.

Interestingly, the figure shows that Bob has written only 24 percent of the historic code as measured from version-control data. That means the majority of the code was written by someone else, so how come nobody claims to know anything about the component?

Back in Part I we saw that building and maintaining mental representations of code gets significantly harder in the presence of excess parallel development. In this case there are three teams with between 10 and 15 authors working on the code. However, parallel work is probably only part of the real issue, as the organization faces motivational issues too. The code in the Legacy Plugin was in fairly bad shape, and thus no one took a particular interest in working with it. Instead, most developers made the minimal tweaks their feature required and moved on to greener pastures as fast as possible without retaining much new knowledge about the Legacy Plugin. As a result, the code degrades with each new feature and a complexity trend analysis would reveal that it has reached its tipping point. Let's see how to break out of this downward spiral.

Introduce New Teams to Take on Shared Responsibilities

Code like the Legacy Plugin is both a cost sink and a quality risk, so it's important to get it back on track. The first step is to grant someone ownership over the code and ensure that person gets the necessary time to address the most critical parts. Social code analysis helps us with this task too.

Since we know who has worked where, we can investigate team patterns in more depth. The figure on page 132 shows the distribution of contributions among the teams that work on the Legacy Plugin.

Since all three teams make significant contributions, the organization used this information to assemble a new team with a member from each. A component that attracts teams that are supposed to have distinct responsibilities indicates a lack of symmetry between the organization and the design. By ensuring that people with domain knowledge of the surrounding subsystems are represented, the organization can build on the members' existing communication network and see to it that any design changes fit all clients. In this

Contributions to the Legacy Plugin by Team

case, the new team decided to do a partial rewrite of the Legacy Plugin to separate its responsibilities and better align with the rest of the architecture.

Architectural building blocks tend to get defined early in a product's life cycle, and as the code evolves it's likely that new boundaries are needed, for both components and teams. Unfortunately, this is an aspect that organizations often fail to react to, and the consequences are developer congestion and coordination bottlenecks in the codebase. Such problems sneak up on us, which is why we need to measure and visualize. Let's see how we can get more detailed insights.

So far our team-level analyses have focused on logical components, which is a good starting point since a component represents a semantically interesting unit of work. However, the same analyses can be performed on the file level, too, as the figure on page 133 illustrates.

The advantage of measuring coordination needs at the file level is that it lets you see how diffused the parallel work is. Is it limited to just a few files or is it a general pattern for every entity within the component? The preceding figure shows an example from another commercial system, where most coordination needs are inside the system's integration tests. This is a common pattern since integration tests tend to be collaborative efforts, with each team covering the scenarios for their features.

In this example, you see that the files with integration tests tend to be relatively large compared to the surrounding application code. The actual file sizes for each test ranged between 1,500 and 3,000 lines of code, and a hotspot

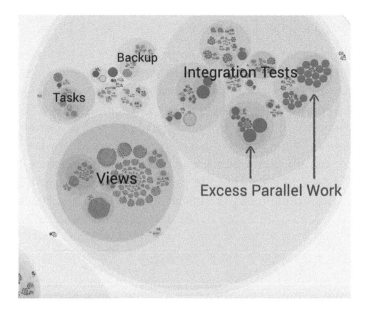

analysis with a subsequent code inspection revealed that the highest technical debt interest rate was in those tests.

These tests were developed by an organization that puts lots of effort into writing maintainable code. The automated integration suite is a key component in that regard, yet it exhibited a noticeably lower quality standard. The test suites contained structural problems, an X-Ray analysis revealed large chunks of copy-pasted code, and the change patterns told a story of strong and surprising coupling between tests that were expected to be independent. Again, the main reasons were social rather than technical, as no one had a holistic overview of the test code, nor did they feel a sense of personal responsibility for it.

The organization reacted to these findings in two ways. First, it took a technical view of the integration-test design. This is important since code attracts many contributors for a reason, which often boils down to low cohesion. By extracting the plumbing—such as initialization code, result reporting, and infrastructure—into a separate library, the test suites could be split more easily to focus on distinct scenarios and thus provide a natural fit for the different feature teams operating on them. Second, the organization introduced a new team to take on the shared responsibility of maintaining the core test functionality. This new team also had the final say on the code that got accepted, which proved useful in establishing and communicating effective integration-test patterns to all teams.

Social Groups: The Flip Side to Conway's Law

So far you've probably gotten the impression that if we just manage to align our operational boundaries with a system's architecture, we're fine. Conway's law is a great observation from the dawn of software development that has received renewed interest over the past few years, mostly as a way to sell the idea of microservices. But from a psychological perspective Conway's law is an oversimplification. Team work is much more multifaceted. The law also involves a trade-off: we minimize communication needs between teams, but that win comes with costs and risks that are rarely discussed in a software setting. Let's look at an example using the knowledge map in the following figure.

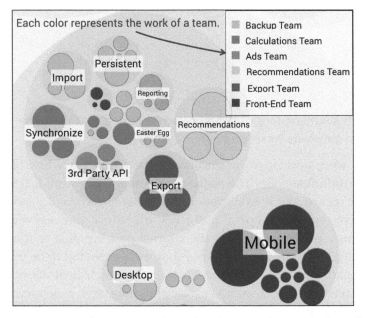

From the perspective of Conway's law the data in the preceding figure sure looks ideal. The team map, calculated from version-control data and discussed in detail in our next chapter, shows the operational boundaries of each team, and as you see there's a perfect separation between the responsibilities of each team, without any overlap. Thus, the coordination needs are limited to the contracts between the different components, which minimizes parallel work and interteam communication issues.

The flip side is the direct social costs of isolating teams with distinct areas of responsibility, and if we're unaware of these social costs they will translate into real costs in terms of both money and a dysfunctional culture. The most common social costs are *motivation losses* and *group conflicts*. Let's discuss them and see how we can minimize their impact.

Motivation Losses in Teams

A few years ago I worked with a team that was presented with a challenging task. During the past year the team had focused on making its work more predictable. It had learned to narrow down and prioritize tasks and to limit excess parallel development, and it had invested in a strong integration-test suite. It had been a bumpy ride, but life started to look bright until one day the team's sprint was halted and a rapid change of plans was ordered.

Suddenly the team had to start work on a feature completely unrelated to all other recent work, and a tight deadline was enforced. Since no one had the required domain expertise and the software lacked the proper building blocks, the team had to sacrifice both short- and long-term quality goals to meet the deadline, only to be surprised that the completed feature wasn't delivered to any customers. The reason that the feature suddenly gained importance and intense management focus was that someone had a bonus depending on it. The bonus goals were set two years earlier, before a single line of code had been written. The manager got his bonus, but the project suffered and was eventually canceled. It wasn't so much the accumulated technical debt, which could have been countered, but rather the motivational losses among the team members.

This story presents the dangers of making people feel like their contributions are dispensable, a factor that's known to encourage *social loafing*. Social loafing is a type of motivation loss that may occur when we feel that the success of our team depends little on our actual effort. We pretend to do our part of the work, when in reality we just try to look busy and hope our peers keep up the effort. It's a phenomenon that occurs for both simple motor tasks, like rope-pulling, as well as for cognitive tasks like template metaprogramming in C++.[5]

It doesn't take extreme situations like the previous story to get social loafing going in a team. If the goals of a particular project aren't clearly communicated or if arbitrary deadlines are enforced, people lose motivation in the task. Thus, as a leader you need to communicate *why* some specific task has to be done or why a particular deadline is important, which serves to increase the motivation for the person doing the job.

Social loafing is also related to the diffusion of responsibility that we discussed earlier in the sense that social loafing becomes a viable alternative only when you feel anonymous and your contributions aren't easily identifiable. Therefore, social loafing and the resulting process loss increases with group size, which

---

5. http://www.adamtornhill.com/articles/fizzbuzz.htm

is a phenomenon known as the *Ringelmann effect*.[6] Thus, part of the increased communication costs on a software project with excess staffing is likely to be Ringelmann-driven social loafing rather than true coordination needs.

Several factors can minimize the risk of social loafing:

- *Small groups*: In general, you want to strive for small teams of three or four people. Coordination losses increase with group size, and they increase in an accelerating manner. On a small team each contribution is also more recognized, which boosts motivation.

- *Evaluation*: Code reviews done right have positive motivational effects, as the reviews show that someone else cares about your contribution. Code reviews are, even if we rarely view them that way, a form of evaluation and social pressure, which are factors known to decrease social loafing.

- *Leadership by example*: If you're in a leadership position—which all senior developers are no matter what your business card says—you need to model the behaviors you want to see in others.

- *Visibility*: Recognize each person's contributions by presenting knowledge maps that show the main contributors behind each module, as the following figure illustrates. This information can be kept within each team.

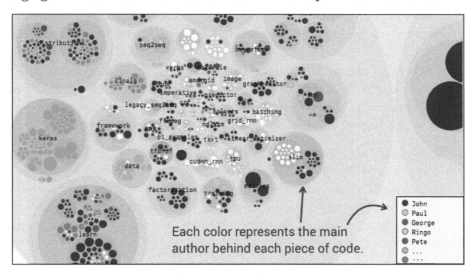

Each color represents the main author behind each piece of code.

John
Paul
George
Ringo
Pete
...
...

Note that visibility isn't about finding out if someone writes, or copy-pastes, enough lines of code each week. Instead the purpose is to instill a sense of pride, like, "Hey, look—this is the code I've written" along the lines of code

---

6. https://en.wikipedia.org/wiki/Ringelmann_effect

ownership and personal responsibility we discussed earlier. There's much to be gained by tapping into developers' intrinsic motivation.

Don't Turn Knowledge Maps into Performance Evaluations

The knowledge maps we talk about in this book aren't intended for performance evaluations, and the reason I advise against this is part ethical and part practical. In particular, once someone starts to evaluate contributors people adapt by optimizing for what's measured.

For example, if I'm evaluated by how many commits I push, I just increase my number of commits. Sure, those commits will no longer carry any meaning, but my statistics "improve." Worse, using this data for performance evaluation destroys the team dynamics. We become less likely to invest time in supporting our peers since we're busy optimizing for an arbitrary goal instead.

Us and Them: The Perils of Interteam Conflicts

When we fail to instill a culture of shared goals and broad knowledge boundaries, our organization is at risk of interteam conflicts. These conflicts don't have to be as dramatic as the term sounds, but are still a source of frustration and missed opportunities. Let's look at an example.

Today your team happened to break the nightly build as its comprehensive suite of long-running regression tests failed. You know that it was due to the stress of the looming deadline combined with some pure bad luck and an unstable build environment (someone should really fix that). Besides, maintaining all the legacy code you inherited isn't an easy task. However, when *they*—the members on the other team—break the build, you know equally well that it's because they are a bunch of careless cowboy coders whose code contributions have more in common with Italian food than the razor-sharp engineering marvels crafted by your team.

The distinction in this story between your group and an external group is known as the *fundamental attribution error* and has wrecked more software projects than even VB6.[7] The fundamental attribution error is a social bias that makes us attribute the same observable behavior to different factors depending on whether it concerns our group or another one.[8] In particular, we tend to overestimate personality factors as we explain the actions of others while we like to see situational forces as an explanation for our own wrongdoings.

---

7. https://en.wikipedia.org/wiki/Visual_Basic
8. https://en.wikipedia.org/wiki/Fundamental_attribution_error

Breaking the distinction between "us" and "them" is vital to reducing interteam conflicts, and that's why it's important to let all your teams share common and compelling goals. A goal also serves as motivator by communicating why a particular task is important and how it fits into the larger whole.

You also have to make sure that the people who work on different but related teams know each other on a personal level. Social psychology teaches us that one factor behind the fundamental attribution error is that we come to view members of other groups as having one personality. (See *Group Process, Group Decision, Group Action [BK03].*) This is true in real life as well as in software development any time we write off our peers as unprofessional and careless. As we start to know the individuals, we realize that they have distinct personalities and we may also start to understand the challenges and complexities of the code they work on. Perhaps we can even start to learn from them.

The ideas we discussed earlier on expanding knowledge borders such as sharing insights and encouraging developers to rotate teams all help with establishing relationships that reduce interteam conflicts. Several companies also form interteam communities dedicated to sharing technology knowledge, such as C#, Java, Python, or graph database modeling.

Coffee as an Organizational Tool

Years ago I worked for a development organization that had two separate teams. The different team members met each day at the coffee break. (Swedes like me are crazy about their coffee.) This break proved to be a great venue for informal conversations, a channel for sharing knowledge, and a way of getting to know each other. One day management banned that break, based on the idea that if we don't type on our laptops we don't work. Humans (yes, developers included) aren't machines, and this decision proved disastrous since it effectively killed interteam collaborations and knowledge sharing. No amount of meetings could make up for the loss of the informal coffee venue.

A common 15-minute coffee break is the cheapest team-building exercise you'll ever get, and we shouldn't underestimate the value of informal communication channels that help us notice new opportunities and work well together. As a nice bonus, getting to know your peers on other teams reduces the risk of social biases like the fundamental attribution error.

Combine Social and Technical Information

There's a fine line between having enough people to complete a large task and the point where critical parts of the code turn into coordination bottlenecks.

Conway's law provides us with guidance, and in this chapter you learned how to measure coordination needs between both individuals and teams. While we won't ever be able to put numbers on anything as complex as human interactions, we can still gather data that helps us ask the right questions.

Conway's law in isolation isn't enough, as team work is much more complex, and the main challenge is to combine code ownership where teams work relatively independently with shared and compelling goals rather than fostering artificial competition among the contributors. The social sciences have decades of experience for us to tap into, and we've discussed some of the most important factors, such as process loss and motivational issues, in this chapter.

It's also important to note that the social information we get from our version-control system may be biased. For example, you may be pair programming, yet only the person who does the commit gets recorded. This is a limitation in how traditional version control functions. A simple workaround is to include the names of both peers in your commit message and parse that information instead of Git's author field.

Another bias occurs when the same person is a member of several teams, which may be typical for a coach or mentor. If you don't account for that situation, your analysis may indicate more excess parallel work than you actually have. There are two solutions here. One is to exclude such persons from the analysis since they're expected to work on all parts anyway. Another approach is to introduce a separate team for them and analyze the work of that team in isolation.

In the next chapter we'll look more deeply at software architectures with respect to organizational factors. You'll also learn to connect social information to technical insights by combining knowledge analyses with technical data, which lets you identify dependencies between code that's owned by different teams.

Nothing's beautiful from every point of view.

➤ *Horace*

CHAPTER 8

Toward Modular Monoliths through the Social View of Code

Many of today's codebases are trapped in hard-to-maintain monolithic systems where the lure of a complete rewrite becomes more attractive with every development task that we painfully slide over to the Done column. However, a large-scale rewrite is always a strategic risk, and it will reset much of the existing team's understanding of the codebase. A worse but learned and understood design may trump its cleaner replacement.

In this chapter we discuss the pros and cons of rewrites, and we cover techniques that help us get situational awareness of existing architectures by evaluating both technical and social aspects. We use the resulting information to suggest new modules by identifying bounded contexts in existing code. Along the way you'll get to know architectural paradigms that represent use case–centric alternatives to traditional layered architectures, and you'll learn to evaluate when—and if—you need to migrate toward one of them. Let's start by dodging a bullet.

Dodge the Silver Bullet

Whatever architectural decisions we make, they're likely to be invalidated over time, simply because an organization isn't static. For example, I once worked with a company that had built a successful product based on a classic model-view-controller (MVC) architecture.[1] This was a sound decision as the company's framework of choice let it get new features out the door at a rapid pace and launch a successful business. Success frequently leads to a

---

1. https://en.wikipedia.org/wiki/Model%E2%80%93view%E2%80%93controller

combination of more money and new opportunities, which in this case meant that more people could be hired with the idea that additional product areas could be covered.

As the organization grew from the initial five to fifteen developers in the span of a year, the overall efficiency went down. MVC is a technical architecture, and when taken to the extreme, independent features get entangled in the same modules. This meant that the developers had to allocate an increasing amount of time to planning and coordinating changes, and soon the core people found themselves spending more time in meetings than in code.

A lot of effort also went into developing a comprehensive integration-test suite. While that test suite helped to prevent defects from slipping into production, it didn't really do anything to facilitate coordination. Quite the contrary, as it became yet another coordination bottleneck where the tests frequently broke due to conflicting changes. Taken together, the lead times from a feature request to the actual delivery increased dramatically, and the root cause of the problem was that the architecture failed to adapt to a changed situation.

The Trade-Off Between Architectural Refinements and Replacement Systems

Many organizations respond to similar situations by launching a project to develop a new system with an architecture that's better adapted to today's needs. This puts the organization in a difficult position, as it will face a set of potential problems:

- *Immediate legacy code*: Since the current system is the one in use, it has to continue to evolve and be maintained. However, the very act of declaring that a new system will be built effectively puts a legacy stamp on the existing codebase, even if the new system is little more than a twinkle in an architect's eye. The signal it sends is that refactoring efforts are wasted since the codebase will be replaced anyway.

- *Playing the catch-up game*: The new system will have to catch up to the continuous features and tweaks implemented as a response to user feedback on the old system, which turns the project into a moving target and implies stronger interproject coordination needs.

- *Division of efforts*: There will be fewer people working on the existing system, which admittedly isn't a bad thing in case the original codebase was overstaffed, but often it's the most experienced developers who get to move to the new code.

- *Motivation loss*: Let's face it: almost everyone wants to work on greenfield projects, and being stuck maintaining a legacy application while your colleagues get to work on your future product isn't particularly motivating.

However, the main risk with designing a replacement system is that we underestimate the true complexity of the system we're trying to replace. Unless we're intimately familiar with the existing codebase, we'll miss all implicit requirements, as code with a rich history hides lots of domain knowledge. All those odd-looking conditionals that are a pain to follow are often there for a reason, such as a bug fix or a specific customer request that got shoehorned into the existing code structure, as the following figure illustrates.

Code may be nasty, but still capture a wealth of domain knowledge:

```
msg_seq pick_first_msg(const std::vector<message>& available)
{
    message_ready = false;
                                            Our main customer in Brazil wants us
                                            to report this rare special case.
    if(!broken_links.empty()) {
        if (!available.empty() &&
            ALARM_MSG == messageTypeOf(available.first())) {
            write_warning("Alarm message lost due to broken link", available.first());
        }
        report_broken_link();
    }

    if(available.empty())
```

Code like this is far from a desirable solution, but it still represents requirements that are easy to miss when building the replacement system. The consequence is that the replacement system may build on flawed premises and fail to dimension itself for critical but hidden requirements.

Joe asks:
Should We Really Port Every Single Feature?

One advantage of building a replacement system is that it gives you an opportunity to revisit the existing feature set and strip out the features that have grown obsolete. As an example, I once worked on a real-time system with high availability demands, which meant the system had a failover solution where two instances run in parallel on separate hardware. In the previous version, much time had been spent on a feature that let a user trigger a failover by pushing a button.

That feature had been in all previous versions, but this time someone investigated the purpose of that functionality. It turned out to be an anachronism from the 1970s —two system generations back—when the hardware still contained relays that needed regular exercise. This meant that an obsolete feature had been ported between generations. By asking the right question, we were able to kill the feature and save lots of money in the new generation of the system.

In some situations the rewrite choice has already been made for you by the passage of time; for example, when you're stuck with obsolete technologies like 4GL languages that only compile to 32-bit native applications. A rewrite is also the right decision when the existing technology puts hard limitations on your system's performance, if it's no longer supported, or if it's hard to recruit and retain staff due to an unattractive programming language. (VB6, we're looking at you—again.)

Building a replacement system may be the right thing to do, but the consequences are way too easy to underestimate, and even when our response is an enthusiastic "Yes!" we should still invest efforts in improving our existing code. It's going to live for longer than we expect. The first step toward such improvements is to get situational awareness: how well does the current architecture support the way the system grows? On your own system you don't start from scratch, as your experience lets you form a set of hypotheses around what works and what doesn't, and from here you gather data to guide future change. Let's look at a common example.

Layered Architectures and the Cost of Consistency

If someone approaches you in a dark alley and asks, "Hey, wanna see a legacy codebase?", chances are they pull out a layered architecture. That's why we go to extra lengths to explore the pattern, which has been a popular strategy for structuring web and GUI applications over the past decade.

Layered architectures come with a set of trade-offs that impact maintainability in the sense that layers lead to increased coordination needs. To show how, we return to the concept of change coupling that we used in Chapter 3, *Coupling in Time: A Heuristic for the Concept of Surprise*, on page 35, as we identified surprising change patterns at the file level. Now we'll scale the analysis up to the architectural level.

When applied on the architectural level, change coupling lets us uncover change patterns between logical components, and these patterns reflect the programmer workflow that our architecture encourages. Let's start simple.

Change Patterns in Layered Architectures

The *MusicStore* codebase is a sample application used to test the general ASP.NET Core MVC framework.[2] MusicStore is a much simpler application than anything we come across in the wild, and thus a good starting point that lets us focus on the central principles common to all layered architectures without

---

2.   https://github.com/aspnet/MusicStore

spending much time on the domain. The following figure presents a hotspot view of the system, which gives us an overview of its main building blocks, and you can follow along interactively in the online results.[3]

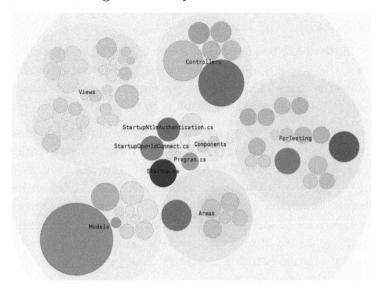

To analyze architectural change patterns we have to map the file names from our raw Git log to logical components, just like we did in the previous two chapters. The following figure recaps that text translation.

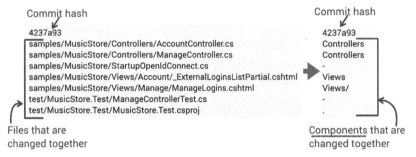

We could map every file in the codebase to a component, but let's keep the example simple and ignore all content except the models, views, and controllers. Here's what the change coupling between these layers in the Music-Store application looks like:

Layer 1	Layer 2	Degree of Coupling	Revisions
Controllers	Views	29%	100
Controllers	Models	27%	115

3.   https://codescene.io/projects/1561/jobs/4894/results/architecture/temporal-coupling

The change coupling results show that approximately every third commit has to touch multiple layers. This is an expected finding, given the purpose of layers, so let's discuss it in detail and see what it means to us.

A Separation of Concerns That Concern

The basic premise of any layered architecture is a separation of concerns—for example, that the views don't know anything about the database and the application logic is decoupled from the presentation details. At least, that's the theory. In reality, a layered world tends to be less rosy.

To start with, real implementations tend to use many more layers than the canonical three suggested by an MVC or MVP pattern.[4] These additional layers are driven by the complexity—both essential and accidental—of today's applications that require further separation between the different responsibilities of each component. As a consequence, today's layered architectures tend to introduce layers for services, abstract database access in repositories, and, of course, hide all native SQL in object-relational mappers. These additional layers cause our change patterns to extend across more logical components, as illustrated by the following figure.

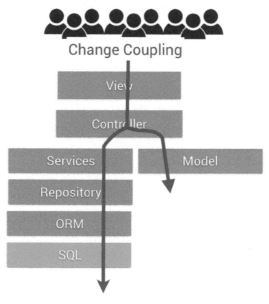

Layers divide our code along a technical axis, while the work we do is feature oriented. Our analysis of MusicStore shows the ramifications with a change coupling of approximately 30 percent between the layers. It's important to

---

4.   https://en.wikipedia.org/wiki/Model%E2%80%93view%E2%80%93presenter

note that this number is on the *lower* end compared to many proprietary codebases. In my day job I've analyzed dozens of layered architectures, and in general the degree of coupling goes from 30 percent in stable applications where most changes are bug fixes, to 70 percent in codebases that grow new features. Let's consider the impact.

If the majority of our commits cut through multiple layers, the promised benefit of separation works against us rather than supporting the changes we want to make to the system. We still have a separation of concerns for sure, but perhaps it's the wrong concerns we separate, as few changes are local. This puts us at risk of unexpected feature interactions and conflicting changes, which is a problem that gets worse with the scale of the development organization. With hierarchical layers, it's hard to define clear areas of responsibility for different teams.

Optimize for the Ordinary

 The abstraction acrobatics of multilayered architectures are often motivated by a possible future need to swap out one specific implementation for another, which may sound attractive at first. As we've seen in this chapter, that flexibility comes at a high cost, and it isn't a balanced trade-off. We optimize for a rare case at the expense of the everyday changes we make to the code. A supportive design is the other way around.

A layered architecture enforces the same change pattern on all end-user features in the codebase. It's a consistent design for sure, but that consistency doesn't serve us well with regard to maintenance. When adding a new feature, no matter how insignificant from a user's perspective, you need to visit every single layer for a predictable tweak to the code, often just passing on data from one level in the hierarchy to the next. It's mundane and time consuming.

All features aren't equal, and most layered codebases would benefit from acknowledging that and get the majority of the code expressed in a simpler and—yes, heresy—*less* structured form. Let's explore some alternatives.

Monolithic Alternatives: Use Case and Feature-Centric

Before we move on we need to clarify when consistency matters and when it's more of a hindrance. The distinction runs between the macro level of the system where we want consistency through high-level building blocks that carry meaning, and the micro level of individual features where we should be free to vary the design.

A well-known example of this principle is *microservices*, which we'll discuss in our next chapter. However, there's a vast amount of design space between monolithic applications and microservices, and we don't need to go full microservice to rescue a legacy codebase. The popularity of MVC—and its family of related, layered paradigms—means that many of us never get exposed to the alternatives, so let's take the opportunity to explore some other architectural patterns here.

Package by Components and Features

Package by component is a pattern captured by Simon Brown, an author and international speaker, that helps us slice intertwined layers into coarse-grained components.[5] The core idea is to make components an architectural building block that combines application logic and data-access logic, if needed. Presentation layers and APIs are then built on top of the components, as shown in the following figure.

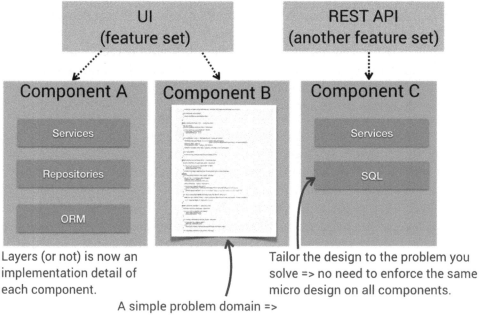

Simon Brown shows how each component can contain its own layers, but the strength of a component-oriented architecture is that you're free to choose. You may find that some features lend themselves to layers. Some may be

---

5.   http://www.codingthearchitecture.com/2015/03/08/package_by_component_and_architecturally_aligned_testing.html

natural to implement using *pipes and filters*,[6] while other features are so simple that they can be coded inside a single file—no need for design excess when it isn't called for. From a social point of view, components also provide natural operational boundaries for our development teams, which sets the stage for an efficient alignment of organization and architecture. Beautiful.

The *package by feature* pattern presents another architectural alternative that enables a high-level consistency without enforcing a specific technical design like traditional layers do.[7] Package by feature takes a domain-oriented approach where each user-facing feature becomes a high-level building block, as illustrated in the next figure.

Package by Component

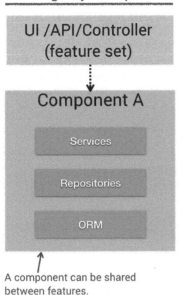

A component can be shared between features.

Package by Feature

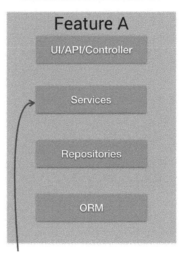

The interior of a feature cannot be shared without compromising the overall design by having complex dependencies.

Just like its component-based cousin, the *package by feature* pattern also makes it straightforward to align your architecture and organization. The main difference between the patterns is that the UI becomes part of each feature in package by feature, whereas it's a separate concern in package by component. The trade-off and main distinction from package by component is that it becomes harder to share code between different features. This could be solved by shared libraries, but there's no architecturally evident way of expressing that, and to let one feature access functionality that's built into another feature soon turns the design into a web of complex dependencies.

---

6.   http://www.enterpriseintegrationpatterns.com/patterns/messaging/PipesAndFilters.html

7.   http://www.javapractices.com/topic/TopicAction.do?Id=205

Use the Deletion Test

A good way to ensure that you can decouple different feature implementations is by trying to delete one. Just create a new branch in Git and remove a critical feature by deleting its code. If the application still builds and runs with a minimum of code tweaks, you can continue to sleep well at night. Chances are your team is going to be able to work independently in at least that part of the application.

These two patterns have different trade-offs, yet they are similar in structure and how they represent feature logic, so let's get some contrasting architectural inspiration by glimpsing at a radically different pattern. The architectural paradigm *data, context, and interaction* (DCI) provides a clear separation between the data/domain model (what the system is) and its features (what the system does). In short, DCI separates your data objects from the feature-specific behaviors, which are expressed in *object roles*, and different use cases express their context by combining specific object roles, as illustrated in the next figure.

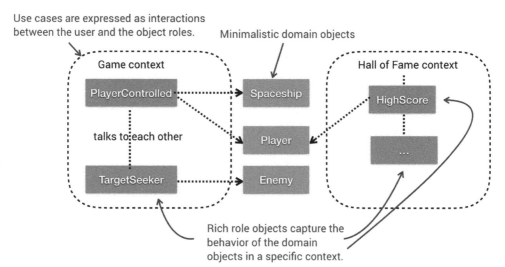

The novelty of the DCI pattern is its context-specific role objects, which give you a place for all those use case–specific details and tricky special cases that otherwise wreak havoc on your data model. Since DCI is a use case–centric pattern it enables independent developable parts with clear operational boundaries. The DCI pattern isn't as well known as the other architectures we've discussed, but it's a paradigm worth studying in more depth as a promising refactoring goal when modularizing legacy monoliths. (*Lean Architecture for Agile Software Development* [CB10] contains a detailed description of DCI and is a highly recommended read.)

As always, there's no simple choice between these patterns, and they all enable a more modular architecture oriented around the problem domain and suited to multiple teams. This means you need to study and prototype the different alternatives to find the paradigm that fits your situation and constraints.

Package by component is the easiest one to get you started, in particular if you migrate away from a layered architecture. A good starting point is to create a branch of your codebase and try to extract a component from the existing monolith. We rarely prototype refactorings, but since your new architectural style will impact the whole organization, the importance of spending time on rapid prototypes—based on the real code—can hardly be overstated. Let's get some behavioral data to guide us.

Discover Bounded Contexts Through Change Patterns

So far we've used change coupling to uncover potential problems, but the analysis has a broader use as well. Since a change coupling analysis highlights the change patterns of the developers working on the code, we can use the resulting information to suggest *bounded contexts*.

Bounded context is a pattern from *domain-driven design* (DDD) where multiple context-specific models are preferred over a global, shared data model. (See *Domain-Driven Design: Tackling Complexity in the Heart of Software [Eva03]* for an in-depth introduction.) Each such context-specific model—a bounded context—is tailored to express a particular domain concept based on where it is used. The pattern is best appreciated when you've experienced the opposite with a shared model for the whole application. Let's look at an example.

Some years ago I worked on a codebase for the medical domain, and one of the core domain models—Patient—was expressed as a class with tons of getters and setters. Some of these properties were related to the problem domain (for example, name), but many were specific to particular use cases in the application and thus bloated the class for other users. It wasn't obvious why the programmer behind a UI widget for editing patient data should be exposed to the Patient object's network transfer status. (Patient data was regularly transferred to a third-party system through a completely different subsystem.)

Use case–specific details are better expressed as separate bounded contexts, which makes for more cohesive models with lower cognitive overhead because all model properties become relevant to the context you work in, as the figure on page 152 illustrates.

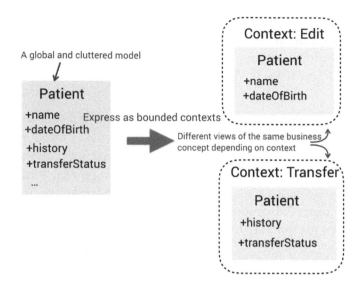

Designing context-specific models requires domain expertise, but you can use general techniques from social code analysis to discover code that's suitable to express as bounded contexts and drive your refactorings based on that information. Let's put change coupling to work to see how.

Look for Clusters of Cochanging Files

To discover candidates for bounded contexts we run a file-level analysis where we look for clusters of cochanging and hence logically related files. To illustrate the principle we analyze *nopCommerce*, which is a competent e-commerce shopping cart.[8]

nopCommerce is designed as a layered architecture based on the MVC pattern, with additional layers for services and persistence.[9] In our analysis we're interested in more recent change patterns since these are the ones that should drive a hypothetical new modularization. Thus, we start by exploring the change coupling between files changed over the past year, as shown in the figure on page 153. (You can view the analysis results online too.[10])

The figure shows that the evolution of News and Blog seem to be tied to each other on several levels. When the controllers and services for one of them change, the other follows in more than 80 percent of cases, and it isn't a fluke. It happened 15 to 20 times over a year. That's change coupling.

---

8. https://github.com/nopSolutions/nopCommerce
9. http://docs.nopcommerce.com/pages/viewpage.action?pageId=1442491
10. https://codescene.io/projects/1593/jobs/3920/results/code/temporal-coupling/by-commits

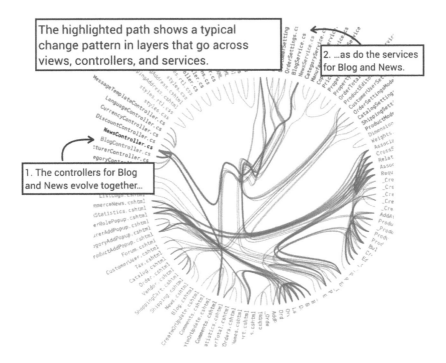

The highlighted path shows a typical change pattern in layers that go across views, controllers, and services.

2. ...as do the services for Blog and News.

1. The controllers for Blog and News evolve together...

To get more details we look for patterns on the method level, just like we did in *Minimize Your Investigative Efforts*, on page 40, when we X-rayed a change coupling cluster. Let's look at an example from the change coupling between NewsController.cs and BlogController.cs. As you see in the next figure, there's high code similarity between the methods responsible for Comments, the Edit functionality, and List methods responsible for fetching all stored news and blog entries.[11]

⇕ Coupled Functions	Coupling (%) ⊽	⇕ Average Revisions ⇕	Similarity (%)
BlogController.cs/Comments	31	43	92
NewsController.cs/Comments			
BlogController.cs/Edit	24	43	80
NewsController.cs/Edit			
BlogController.cs/List	21	43	92
NewsController.cs/List			

---

11. https://codescene.io/projects/1593/jobs/3920/results/code/temporal-coupling/by-commits/xray-result/details?file-name=nopCommerce/src/Presentation/Nop.Web/Administration/Controllers/NewsController.cs

This high degree of change coupling between similar methods—together with the change coupling between the corresponding service implementations—indicates that there may be a concept underlaying News and Blog that the design fails to capture. When you extract layered functionality into features or components, you use this data to drive the design. The following figure shows two possible variations.

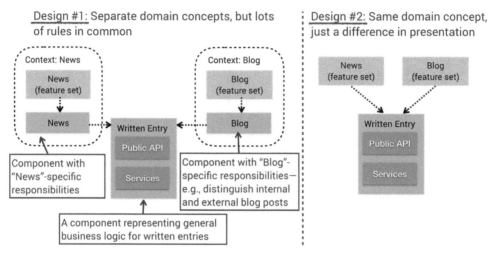

In your own codebase you're likely to be quite familiar with the domain concepts and thus have an easier way of modeling new components to iteratively replace the global layers. For example, it may also be the case that Comments is an orthogonal concept to Blog and News, and should be modeled as a distinct component.

Social code analysis—like any other tool set—won't make the decisions for you, but the techniques help you get on the right track by pointing out opportunities that are otherwise easily missed among large chunks of code spread out across different modules. The techniques are here to complement your expertise, not to replace it. The key is to know your own domain and make sure your architecture reflects it.

Finally, there are social views to consider in our architecture. If we look back at the preceding figure, design alternative #1 may look attractive, as it lets us share code between two features that were previously duplicated. However, as Eric Evans points out in *Domain-Driven Design: Tackling Complexity in the Heart of Software [Eva03]*, sharing code across bounded contexts is a hazard because different teams may be responsible for the Blog and News features, which may lead to blurred and conflicting changes to the shared context. To counter this we need to take a social perspective on our code and expand on the ideas we touched on in the previous chapters. Let's see how.

Breaking Up Monoliths: The Sequel

When breaking up a monolith, the database often remains a large monolithic piece —with a gravity that would make the black hole A0620-00 jealous—and all development tasks eventually end up there.[a] The consequence is that no matter how modular your application code is, your system is still at risk for independent feature interactions due to the database.

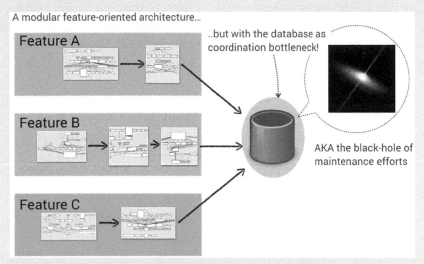

A modular feature-oriented architecture...

Feature A

..but with the database as coordination bottleneck!

Feature B

AKA the black-hole of maintenance efforts

Feature C

Your database schema has to evolve to a more modular design as well, which means taking transactional contexts into consideration. Database refactorings is a topic worthy of its own book, so check out *Refactoring Databases: Evolutionary Database Design [AS06]* in case you're in this situation. Note that you can still apply the ideas from this chapter since change coupling is a language-neutral analysis capable of highlighting dependencies between application code and SQL scripts, too.

---

a.   https://en.wikipedia.org/wiki/A0620-00

The Perils of Feature Teams

Last year I visited an organization that was in a situation all too familiar, as their features took much longer to implement than expected. But this wasn't just a case where estimates were used as proxies for management wishes, but a fundamental problem at conflict with the project's goals. This codebase was developed to replace a hard-to-maintain legacy application and the historic data from the development of the previous application served as a baseline for the project plan. The whole raison d'être of this project was to deliver a codebase that was cheaper to maintain, yet after two years of development, all numbers pointed in the opposite direction.

The slow pace of feature growth wasn't due to bad code quality, and the architecture couldn't be blamed either, as it revealed a modular component-based system with sane boundaries and dependencies. Odd. However, once we took a social view of the system a more worrisome architectural view arose. By applying the concept of knowledge maps on the team level—an idea that we touched on in the previous chapter—it became obvious that there weren't any clear operational boundaries between the teams. In the next figure, which shows the team contributions over the past three months, you see that it's hard to spot any patterns in the distribution of each team's work. Sure, some team may be a major contributor to some parts, but in general this does look chaotic.

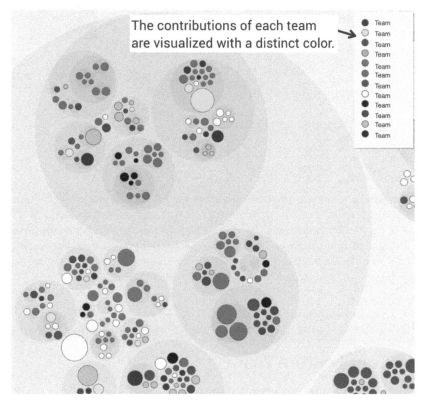

It turned out that the component-based architecture was created by a small team, and the pattern worked well during the initial development and proof of concept. As the project scaled up, management decided to introduce feature teams. Soon the development organization grew to include 12 teams, and in each iteration teams were assigned separate stories.

The consequence was that the organization had 12 different teams that needed to work across all components, and the code kept changing in parallel at a high rate as each team extended the existing components to build different features. Lots of time was spent in meetings and merging different feature branches, which often led to conflicts between both code and teams.

These organizational costs were direct in the sense of excessive coordination needs, but also indirect because they prevented synergies between different features, which in turn meant missed opportunities to simplify the solution domain.

The Big Win Is in the Problem Domain

 A deep understanding of the problem domain gives you a tool to simplify both architecture and code. Make sure you get to spend a day or two with your product's users. Such real-world education provides a different perspective, leads to deeper domain expertise, and builds informal networks between the technology and consumer side. It's invaluable.

The big advantage of team knowledge maps is that they visualize the otherwise-unseen social view of code, and make the problems rather than their symptoms visible to management. Even if you're aware of the problem, it's far from certain that nontechnical stakeholders will share your level of insight, which is why holistic visualizations play a key role in making change happen. A knowledge map in itself won't solve any problems, but it helps you ask the right questions.

We soon explore related situations and discuss the possible remedies, but let's first dive deeper into the analysis to make sure we understand what the data actually shows.

Build Team Knowledge Maps

Team knowledge maps are based on the amount of code contributed by each team within the analysis period. The reason we choose the number of contributed lines of code rather than a simple count of the number of commits or invoking git blame on each file is because knowledge goes deep. If I write a piece of code today and you choose to rewrite it tomorrow, that doesn't mean I have to start from scratch when working with that code again. Having solved a design problem and fleshed out the code builds knowledge of the problem domain that transcends the current structure of the code. By using the historic lines of contributed code, our metric reflects such knowledge retention.

Git lets us mine the number of added and deleted lines of code for each modified file through its --numstat option. We use the same algorithm as in *Analyze Operational Team Boundaries*, on page 129, to map individuals to teams. The only difference is that our input data is more detailed this time around, as shown in the figure on page 158.

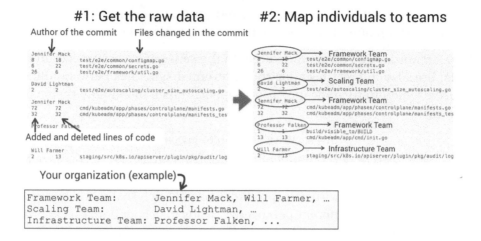

We use this data to operationalize our measure of knowledge by calculating a percentage of code added by each team to every file, as shown in the following table.

File	Team	Code Contributed
common/configmap.go	Framework Team	87%
common/configmap.go	Scaling Team	13%
log/backend.go	Scaling Team	100%
...	...	...

This data makes it easy to identify the team that has written most of the code for each file, and thus the team that has the main knowledge owners in that area. The algorithm is straightforward, although the Git data is harder to parse than in our previous analyses, and working implementations are provided in both *Measure Conway's Law*, on page 217, and CodeScene.[12]

Joe asks:
Why Can't I Get the Amount of Modified Code?

At first it looks limiting that Git only provides a count of added and deleted lines. However, if we attempt to calculate modified lines of code we soon find ourselves in a philosophical hole, faced with existential questions like "When is a line of code modified enough to be considered new?" and "What's the difference from a line that's merely modified?" Future research may provide definitive answers, but at the time of writing we need to work with the data we have.

12. https://codescene.io/docs/guides/social/knowledge-distribution.html#explore-your-team-knowledge-maps

Finally, you may have noted that we ignored the amount of deleted code in our calculation. The number of lines deleted does not effectively reflect a team's measure of knowledge, but the data could be used to show refactoring progress. For example, I recently worked with an organization that invested in cleaning up a legacy codebase that started to get out of hand, and we used a variation on the previous technique to highlight areas of code removal. Visualizing code deletion as progress could do much good for our industry.

Not All Teams Are Equal

Let's return to the perils of misaligned team boundaries now that we know how knowledge maps are built. The previous case study with an ill-advised feature-team adaptation is similar to the problems faced in the MVC-based project scaled from five to fifteen developers that we discussed in *Dodge the Silver Bullet*, on page 141. The architectural context is different, though, because a component- or feature-oriented architecture has natural team boundaries. But even in a feature-oriented context there's a cut-off point where the codebase can't afford more people working on it, as there will always be dependencies between different features, and more fine-grained components only accentuate that. As feature implementations start to ripple across team boundaries, your lead times increase one synchronization meeting after the other.

There's also a related organizational fallacy that I've come across in several companies, which is to have a separate maintenance team. The dangers with this approach are as follows:

- *Motivation loss*: As we saw in *Social Groups: The Flip Side to Conway's Law*, on page 134, low motivation is a common cause of process loss, and being stuck fixing bugs in a previous release is less fun than driving the future of the codebase.

- *Low in-group cohesion*: In an effective team, the members share a goal and work on related tasks, which are aspects that aren't achievable with a separate maintenance team, as their work is reactive and thus spread across unrelated bug fixes.

- *Broken feedback loops*: Each bug represents a learning opportunity for the implementing team, and if we never look back on our trail of defects but instead rush ahead feature by feature and leave the bugs to our peers on another team, we put ourselves outside this valuable feedback loop.

- *Blurred lines*: Code doesn't really care *why* it's changed, and in Part I we saw that there isn't a strong distinction between new features and what we traditionally call maintenance. Both are about making improvements to existing code, which means we run the risk of expensive coordination needs as the teams are likely to intersect in the codebase. In addition, this way of working is an invitation to diffusion of responsibility, as discussed in the previous chapter.

Most organizations notice the symptoms of those problems, and a common response is to implement a *gatekeeper mechanism* where all code has to be reviewed by a designated person, often called an architect. This approach adds an extra level of protection against destructive code changes and may even catch a bug or two, yet the traditional gatekeeper pattern comes with a number of drawbacks.

First of all, this pattern is reminiscent of the speedup in parallel computing captured in *Amdahl's law*, where the theoretical speedup is limited by the serial part of the program, as shown in the following figure.[13] In our case the gatekeeper acts as the serial part, which means your gatekeeping architect becomes a global lock that limits the throughput of the organization.

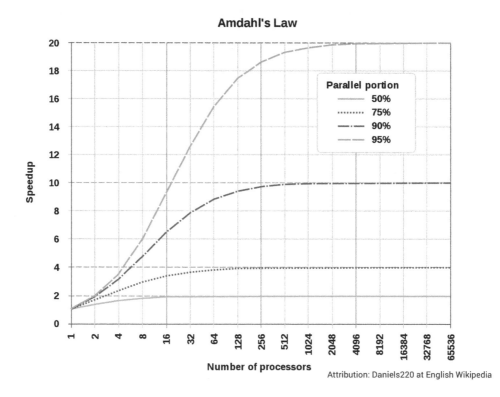

Attribution: Daniels220 at English Wikipedia

---

13. https://en.wikipedia.org/wiki/Amdahl%27s_law

An even more serious problem is that as your organization grows, code-reviewer fatigue becomes real, as there are just so many lines of code you can review each day. Beyond that point you're likely to slip, which results in increased lead times, bugs that pass undetected to production, and—in extreme cases—the risk of burnout.

A much better approach is to let each team act as gatekeeper of its own code, which is an idea we discussed in *Code Ownership Means Responsibility*, on page 126. Your teams will never become cross-functional if they depend on someone else to approve their code. This approach has the advantage that it doesn't rely on an individual, and if you combine it with a rotating scheme where your peers on other teams join in for a review, you limit the risk of sliding quality goals across teams.

Clean and Dirty Architectures

A specific architectural style isn't bad per se. Layers, DCI, and package by component all have their pros and cons. An architecture is good when it supports the changes we want to make to the system and, as we've seen, both the type of changes and the organization responsible for implementing them are likely to shift over time. This means that your architecture has to evolve and respond to changing circumstances, which inevitably means reworking the existing building blocks.

In this chapter we discussed the perils of a system rewrite and its consequences. From there we picked up the loose ends from Chapter 7, *Beyond Conway's Law*, on page 117, as we dissected layered architectures. As we saw, a layered architecture will always exhibit a conflict between the technical way the code is structured and the feature-oriented, end user–centric way the system evolves. As a consequence, neither feature nor component teams align well with layers. We also learned about alternative architectural patterns, how they contrast with layers, and how they fill an important role as large-scale refactoring goals to counter the siren song of a system rewrite.

Our primary analysis technique for architectures is change coupling. That's because when we work with a particular system for an extended period of time, we learn what works and what doesn't. With change coupling we tap into that learned behavior to highlight patterns that ripple across architectural boundaries. In this chapter we used that information as a guide to select candidates for high-level refactorings and tie the analysis results to the concept of bounded contexts. Although we demonstrated the idea on a layered architecture, the technique is more general and you can use it anytime you detect the need for better modular boundaries.

We have also ventured deeper into the social aspects of code, and learned that code ownership and team boundaries need visibility to drive our designs. The knowledge maps we introduced are built on rolling contributions to the actual code and are always up to date, which is in stark contrast to that Excel sheet on the Intranet that was last updated just before the ISO revision two years ago.

So far we've limited ourselves to code that's located within a single repository. Over the past decade many organizations have started to separate their subsystems into multiple Git repositories. This trend is partly driven by better version-control tools that make it practical, but also by the extended hype and drive toward microservices. In our next chapter we take such multirepository microservice codebases head-on. Follow along as we continue to combine technical and social analyses to uncover information we can't get from code alone.

Exercises

Doing high-level refactorings will never become easy, and like any other skill, we need to practice it. The following exercises give you an opportunity to experiment with the techniques on your own. You also get a chance to investigate a component-oriented architecture, which makes an interesting contrast to the change patterns we saw in layered codebases.

Detect Components Across Layers

- Repository: nopCommerce[14]
- Language: C#
- Domain: nopCommerce is an e-commerce shopping cart.
- Analysis snapshot: https://codescene.io/projects/1593/jobs/3920/results/code/temporal-coupling/by-commits

In this chapter we detected that News and Blog evolved together and thus may have a shared concept in common. Investigate the change coupling in nopCommerce and see if you can detect other examples on coevolving files that could serve as the basis for extracting them into a component.

Remember that you can get more information by comparing the implementations or taking the shortcut of running an X-Ray analysis. The answers in *Solutions: Modular Monoliths*, on page 230, provide one example, but there are other refactoring candidates too.

---

14. https://github.com/nopSolutions/nopCommerce

Investigate Change Patterns in Component-Based Codebases

- Repository: PhpSpreadsheet[15]

- Language: PHP

- Domain: PhpSpreadsheet is a PHP library used to read and write spreadsheet files such as Excel.

- Analysis snapshot: https://codescene.io/projects/1579/jobs/3839/results/code/temporal-coupling/by-commits

A component-based architecture needs to avoid tight coupling between different components because such dependencies would counter the potential benefits of the pattern. From this perspective PhpSpreadsheet serves as an interesting example, with most of its change coupling between files in the same package. Now look at the change coupling analysis linked above and try to detect a relationship that violates the dependency principle of independent components.

---

15. https://github.com/PHPOffice/PhpSpreadsheet

Many a small thing has been made large by the right kind of advertising.

> ≫ *Mark Twain*

CHAPTER 9

Systems of Systems: Analyzing Multiple Repositories and Microservices

The scale of today's systems has led many organizations to adapt microservice-like architectures. This implies that tomorrow's legacy codebases are going to be microservices and we should be prepared to address technical debt in a development context more complex than systems of the past.

From a 10,000-foot view there's nothing special to microservices with respect to the analysis techniques we have covered so far. In practice, however, microservices present their own set of challenges that exaggerate potential quality issues that we could have lived with in a monolithic system. Some of these issues are technical while others are social and cultural. In this chapter we start by adapting hotspots to a microservice context. From there we explore implicit dependencies between microservices by detecting change patterns across repository boundaries, and we wrap it all up by learning to measure technical sprawl in a polyglot codebase.

The techniques you learn in this chapter aren't limited to microservices, and they serve you well on any codebase split across multiple Git repositories.

Analyze Code in Multiple Repositories

The core idea behind microservices is to structure your system as a set of loosely coupled services, which—ideally—are independently deployable and execute in their own environment. Different services exchange information via a set of well-defined protocols, and the communication mechanism can be both synchronous, as in a blocking request-response, or asynchronous.

So far, this all sounds like a fairly technical view, but microservices also promise an architectural style that supports autonomous teams that can work independently on different services. Of course, such team independence isn't really a property of microservices themselves, but rather a result of any well-designed system oriented around use cases rather than technology.

This means that microservices—just like the monolithic patterns we discussed in the previous chapter—have to center around features and business capabilities. Any time you note systems where the services represent technical responsibilities like "persistence" or "validation," consider it a warning sign; Such systems won't deliver on the promised benefits of microservices but rather represent a distributed equivalent to hierarchical layers.

 Joe asks:

How Big Should a Microservice Be?

This is a heated question where flame wars have been fought and friendships have been ended, but it's also slightly misguided to reason about service size in terms of lines of code. Instead you want to focus on business capabilities. Each service should represent a single business capability—cohesion is key.

Detect Services with Low Cohesion

Microservices is a high-discipline architecture because as developers, there's a direct cost to introducing new design elements, and that cost grows as we climb the abstraction ladder. Creating a new function is quick, and we do that all the time. But extracting behavior into a new class or module is more rare, and introducing a new service as a response to a particular requirement is an even larger mental hurdle; it's so much easier and faster *in the short term* to just squeeze new behavior into an existing service and avoid the pains of tweaking the deployment pipeline, creating new test suites, and writing those API documents. This is the highway to legacy code.

A hotspot analysis serves as a useful heuristic to identify such low-cohesion services. Our architecturally significant building blocks are the services themselves, so we consider each service implementation a logical component and run the first hotspot analysis on that level as illustrated in the figure on page 167.

There are two strategies for defining the logical components in the analysis, and your choice depends on how the services are organized:

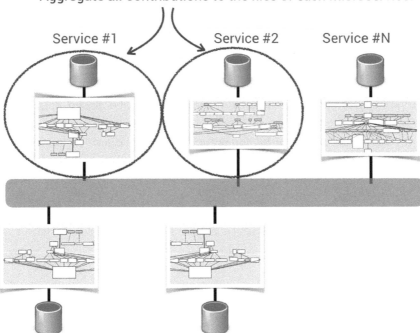

Aggregate all contributions to the files of each microservice.

1. *All services are in a single Git repository*: If your organization keeps its services in a single repository, you use the aggregation patterns from *A Language for Specifying Architectural Boundaries*, on page 97.

2. *The services are in separate Git repositories*: This strategy is the most common case, and the analysis is straightforward. We just need to aggregate the contributions per repository without the need to specify any aggregation patterns.

In the latter case, you can use the git rev-list command as shorthand to aggregate all contributions:

```
adam$ git rev-list --count HEAD
1922
```

The rev-list option lists all reachable commits and we instruct it to simply --count the total number, which amounts to 1922 commits in this example. We can also complement the data with a size dimension—for example, by using cloc as described in *A Brief Introduction to cloc*, on page 223—and iterate through each repository in the codebase to accumulate the results. Armed with that data, we're ready to reason about hotspots on the microservice level, as shown in the table on page 168.

Microservice	Change Frequency	Lines of Code
Recommendations	271	5,114
Diagnostics	269	3,440
Export	168	4,355
...	...	...

This hotspot analysis shows data from the evolution of a closed-source system, and we see that the top hotspot is the Recommendations service, with 5,000 lines of code. That's quite a lot for something advertised as "micro," so let's get some more information by generating an aggregated complexity trend for the service, just as we did in *Fight the Normalization of Deviance*, on page 107. The following figure shows the evolution of complexity in the Recommendations service.

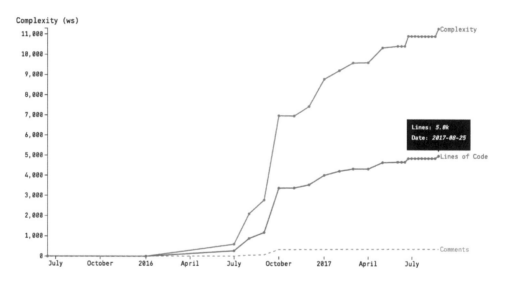

The complexity trend shows that the Recommendations service grew rapidly during the initial development in the second half of 2016, and it continues to grow in both complexity and lines of code.

This information helps us ask the right questions: does this service consisting of 5,000 lines of code with frequent changes really implement a single business capability or would it be better off when split into two or more distinct services? Remember, code changes for a reason, and a likely explanation for a high change rate is that the service attracts many commits because it has many reasons to do so—it has too many responsibilities.

Watch Out for Behavioral Magnets

A microservice system faces the question of how clients access the myriad services, and one answer is to introduce an *API gateway* that serves as a single entry point and routes calls to different services.[a]

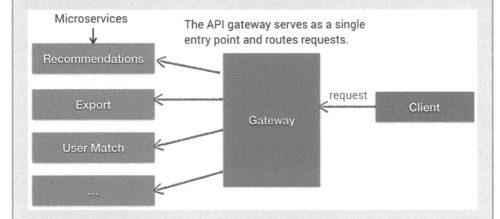

This works well as long as we avoid the temptation to stuff common behavior into the API gateway, which would soon turn it into a coordination bottleneck and single point of failure. So don't—it transforms your microservice architecture into a set of satellites gravitating around a new monolith.

a.   http://microservices.io/patterns/apigateway.html

React to Your Findings

There are several ways to react when you find an architectural hotspot. First, run a hotspot analysis on the file level because services with low cohesion often reveal complex implementations due to the intricate interplay between the different responsibilities. Use the file-level hotspots for exploring opportunities to refactor the service implementation just as we did in Chapter 2, *Identify Code with High Interest Rates*, on page 15. Not only will your service become easier to understand, but the refactoring steps themselves will help you build knowledge and detect concepts that should be separated into different services. (See *Reflective Practitioner: How Professionals Think in Action* [Sch83] for a deep discussion of how insights gained through experience help us make better decisions.)

Splitting a microservice into multiple services is similar to the monolithic case studies we discussed in the previous chapter. However, refactoring a service means we operate on a smaller slice of the codebase and it's typically easier to extract a new microservice from an existing one than it is to separate a monolith. Use the same change coupling techniques to identify bounded contexts, only this time the analyses drive the extraction of services rather than components.

Hotspots and change coupling analyses are all about gaining insights and collecting additional information to complement your existing knowledge about the system. Refactoring microservices—like software design in general—is, to a large extent, an intuitive and nondeterministic process. The analysis techniques let you remove a degree of uncertainty from that process by ensuring that your expertise is focused on where it's needed the most.

Compare Hotspots Across Repositories

Microservices take the idea of team autonomy to an extreme, which indeed limits coordination bottlenecks in the code itself. However, as Susan Fowler points out in *Production-Ready Microservices: Building Standardized Systems Across an Engineering Organization [Fow16]*, a microservice never exists in isolation and it interacts with services developed by other teams. Those are conflicting forces.

These forces put us at risk for incompatible changes and misunderstandings in the protocols between services, yet those are technical challenges that we can address by letting each team specify a regression suite for the microservices they consume. A much more challenging task is in the social field, where a microservice-oriented organization gets sensitive to interteam conflicts, which means you need to work actively with the techniques discussed in *Social Groups: The Flip Side to Conway's Law*, on page 134.

One such idea is to let people join in on code reviews of the teams whose microservices they consume. In practice it's quite challenging to switch context to another microservice, particularly with the added pressure of expecting to understand someone else's design well enough to deliver feedback. One technique that works well as a quick onboarding is a file-level hotspot analysis, so let's see how to pull that off over multiple repositories.

To analyze files in different repositories we have to provide some additional context, both as a mechanism for ordering the results and to differentiate between files with identical names (think README.md or Makefile). You introduce this context by prefixing each file with a *virtual root* based on the name of the file's Git repository, as shown in the figure on page 171.

The data mined from version control doesn't carry any context:

app/scripts/help/help.contents.ts
app/scripts/help/helpField.component.ts

⌐ Data from different repositories,
⌐ but no way to know :(

src/cli/command/NestableCommand.java
...

Prefix each file with the name of its repository:

(deck/)app/scripts/help/help.contents.ts
(deck/)app/scripts/help/helpField.component.ts
...

(halyard/)src/cli/command/NestableCommand.java
...

I'll demonstrate the technique on *Spinnaker*, which is a cloud-based continuous-delivery platform built as a set of microservices organized in 10 separate Git repositories.[1]

You generate your hotspots just like you did in *A Proxy for Interest Rate*, on page 17, and postprocess the results in a scripting language of your choice to prefix each file with its repository name. As an alternative, you embrace your inner command-line fu and glue it together with the sed command in a Git Bash shell.[2] Here's an example from the deck repository, which contains Spinnaker's UI code:[3]

```
adam$ git log --format=format: --name-only \
      | egrep -v '^$' \
      | sed -e 's/^/deck\//' \
      | sort | uniq -c | sort -r
1182 deck/gradle.properties
 238 deck/app/scripts/app.js
 209 deck/package.json
 148 deck/app/styles/main.less
 143 deck/app/scripts/modules/core/help/helpContents.js
 100 deck/app/index.html
...
```

After that you just keep generating one dataset for each repository in your codebase and concatenate the results. Let's have a look at the hotspots in Spinnaker that you see in the top figure on page 172, and you can also interact with the visualization through the online gallery.[4]

The top hotspot map does look cluttered, so a simple improvement is to filter away small files and those with low change frequencies from the results before visualizing them. The next figure on page 172 shows the same example on Spinnaker, but this time with filtered data.

---

1. https://www.spinnaker.io/reference/architecture/
2. https://www.gnu.org/software/sed/manual/sed.html
3. https://github.com/spinnaker/deck
4. https://codescene.io/projects/1650/jobs/4074/results/code/hotspots/system-map

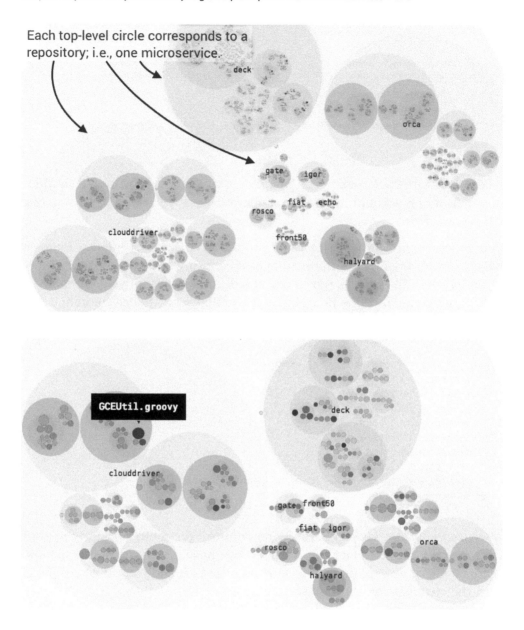

You use these file-level hotspots to guide code explorations of unfamiliar services, as the map helps you put code snippets into context, as shown in the figure on page 173.

Hotspots cast light on development silos and help make code reviews a collaborative activity by lowering the barrier to entry for members of other teams. Make it a strategic advantage.

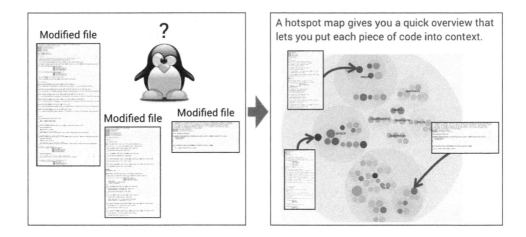

Communicate Across the Organization

The whole-system hotspot view also serves as an entry point to reason about the relative quality of different services. Hotspot data cannot give you a simple quality score—and it's doubtful if any automated metric could—but they let you detect modules that stand out. For example, in the preceding Spinnaker visualization, the hotspot GCEUtil.groovy is twice the size of the second-largest hotspot, and the generic name is a warning for low cohesion. as we discussed in *Signal Incompleteness with Names*, on page 62.

The technique is also useful to bridge the gap between the technical side of the organization and the business side; nontechnical managers struggle with traditional tech vocabulary, and hotspots turn our abstract world of code into a graspable concept.

As an example, let's say you've identified a number of services with low cohesion. The impact is hard to explain in nontechnical terms, but showing a visualization where one microservice is 10 times the size of the others is an intuitive and powerful demonstration. So the next time you find yourself in a discussion with a manager, bring up a hotspot map and benefit from the increased understanding that happens when you let them share a part of your world.

Track Change Patterns in Distributed Systems

If low cohesion is problematic, strong coupling is the cardinal sin that grinds microservice development to a halt. I experienced this the first time back in my days as a consultant working on a trading application. On my first day I got assigned what looked like a simple task, so I eagerly jumped into Emacs and started to write some code. Pretty soon I noticed that I lacked some data that were available in an adjacent subsystem, so I walked over to its team lead and asked for an extension to the API. "Sure," she said, "that's a simple tweak that we could do right away." So I went back to my desk and waited. And waited. It turned out that the "simple tweak" took a week, and over the next months I learned that this was the norm: no API change was ever quick.

However, the long lead times weren't due to slow development or a complex process, but rather were a consequence of the way the system and organization were structured. When one team did its "simple tweak" it had to request a change to another API owned by a different team. And that other team had to go to yet another team, that in turn had to convince the database administrators, which ostensibly is the place where change requests go to die. This meant that a simple code change rippled across organizational boundaries, as shown in the next figure.

Dependencies between systems developed by different teams...

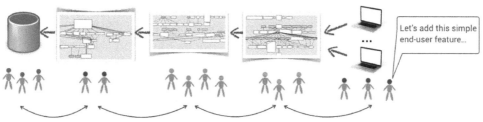

...translate to dependencies between people.

This wasn't a microservice architecture, but the same problem occurs any time we couple code that's under active development by different teams. The cost of future coordination is incurred. So let's look at the algorithm to uncover such change coupling across repositories.

Turn the Process on Distributed Monoliths

Ideally we would respond with a better-suited architecture or adapt the organization, but sometimes drastic measures aren't feasible. One workaround that patches the glitch is to turn the process on its head. Instead of having a user-facing subsystem initiate change requests from the next subsystem, put together a cross-organizational group with one representative from each team, including database expertise. Let the group meet as needed to discuss each new requirement, and once the group has a shared understanding, the database people initiate change. As soon as the database is prepared, the database people inform the group, who could then put their teams to work on the application changes in parallel. It's still expensive, but gives visibility to the problem and cuts the lead times in the process.

Use Logical Change Sets to Group Commits

So far we've limited change coupling to code referenced by the same commits. This won't work when code changes are made by different people contributing to the same feature, as their work will be done in distinct commits and Git won't be able to relate them to each other.

This means we need a higher-order concept, which we get by introducing *logical change sets*. A logical change set is a way to group different commits together. There are two ways of identifying logical change sets, and which one you choose depends on the data you have available:

- *Proximity in time and organization*: If the same modules are changed over and over again within a specific time window of, let's say, a day by the same developer or team, chances are that there's a logical dependency between those parts.

- *Task or ticket identifiers*: Many organizations add a task or ticket reference to their commit messages, as shown in the next figure, and those references let us group multiple commits into a logical change set.

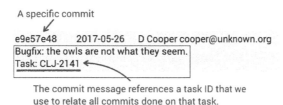

The commit message references a task ID that we use to relate all commits done on that task.

The ideal approach is to use ticket IDs since that minimizes the risk of false positives, and referencing a ticket in your commit messages has the additional benefit of providing traceability that lets you know *why* a specific change was made.[5] We'll look at a case study later in this chapter, but let's first cover the heuristic of time and organizational proximity with an example from Spinnaker.

Detect Implicit Dependencies Between Microservices

Just as we did for hotspots, we prefix each file in our version-control data with a virtual root and combine the raw data from all repositories in a single data set. In the simplest case we consider different commits part of the same logical change set if they are authored by the same person on the same day, and that algorithm is typically implemented using a sliding window.

In a large system this gives us lots of change coupling, so we need to prioritize the results. The concept of surprise works well here too, so let's focus on the

---

5.   http://www.yegor256.com/2015/06/08/deadly-sins-software-project.html#untraceable-changes

coupling that crosses service boundaries as such dependencies are contrary to the philosophy of autonomous microservices.

Here's the neat thing: by introducing a virtual root that specifies the name of each file's repository, it becomes straightforward to iterate through the data and keep the pairs of coupled files with different virtual roots. The next figure shows an example on such an analysis on Spinnaker, and you can follow along online too.[6]

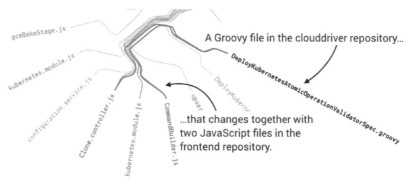

The preceding graph highlights a logical dependency between code for the user interface and the back-end service implementing the logic. Note that the information we uncover isn't visible in the code itself, as the coupled files are implemented in different languages and separated by HTTP, so there's no easy way to statically deduce the coupling, but behavioral code analysis does the trick. Magic!

Balance Monolithic UIs

The specific pattern of an implicit dependency between front-end and back-end code is common in microservice architectures. While we take great care to separate different responsibilities into distinct services, there's still—in most cases—a single UI visible to the end user where all our distributed wonders need to present themselves as a cohesive whole. A single UI is basically a technical partitioning that cuts across all business capabilities, which is at odds with team autonomy; the UI becomes the new monolith.

There are two primary ways to reduce the conflict:

- *Composite UI*: A modern user experience often requires interactions with several back-end services, and a *composite UI* acknowledges that by letting the microservices themselves compose the UI.[7] There are several variations

---

6. https://codescene.io/projects/1650/jobs/4074/results/code/temporal-coupling/between-repos
7. https://jimmybogard.com/composite-uis-for-microservices-a-primer/

on the pattern, but a common approach is to let the client code specify templates that are then populated by view models from the services.[8]

- *Back end for front end*: The *back end for front end* (BFF) pattern maintains a set of smaller monolithic UIs, but introduces a back-end service dedicated to each separate user experience, like one for mobile and one for web.[9] The BFF pattern has the nice side effect of providing a natural API layer for black-box tests of each microservice from a user perspective.

That said, there is a third alternative that's useful in contexts other than microservices, too. The CodeScene tool is always tested on its own code—it's only fair—and a while ago we noted a new change coupling between modules located in different repositories, as shown in the next figure.

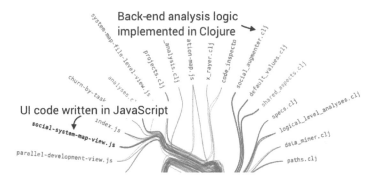

At first this was surprising since there's architectural distance between the two sides of the coupling, as shown in the following figure.

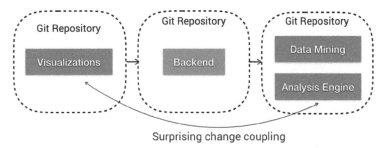

Surprising change coupling

To get some more information the team ran an X-Ray analysis on the cluster of cochanging files. Since the files of interest are in different repositories we need to group the files into logical change sets by their ticket references and

---

8. https://docs.microsoft.com/en-us/dotnet/standard/microservices-architecture/architect-microservice-container-applications/microservice-based-composite-ui-shape-layout
9. http://philcalcado.com/2015/09/18/the_back_end_for_front_end_pattern_bff.html

then look for cochanging functions within those change sets, resulting in a coupling graph like the one in the next figure.

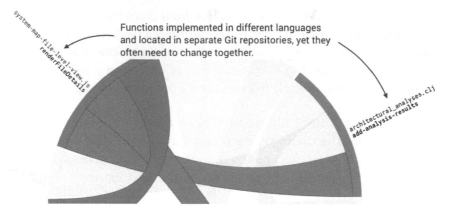

Since the X-Ray technique helped narrow down the functions of interest it was quick to inspect the code and detect that the back end generated a set of metrics that the front end presented. Each time a new metric was introduced in the analysis part, a predictable tweak had to be made in the UI—a classic producer-consumer relationship.

We could reduce the impact of the logical dependency by letting the back end provide some metadata that could drive the presentation. While that would solve this specific case, it would fail to address a more fundamental structural issue: the two parts are logically related, and therefore should be contained close to each other. Packaging the JavaScript files responsible for rendering the metrics together with the services that produce them solves the issue by reducing a systemwide implicit dependency to a local relationship within the same component. Sweet.

Detect Microservices Shotgun Surgery

In the last chapter we calculated change coupling between layers and components, and using the idea of logical change sets lets us do the same at the microservice level across Git repositories. In microservices, you want to watch out for change coupling across multiple services, as shown in the figure on page 179.

Such coupling is basically *shotgun surgery* on an architectural scale. (Shotgun surgery was introduced in *Refactoring: Improving the Design of Existing Code [FBBO99]* to describe changes that involve many small tweaks to different classes.) You want to change a single business capability and you end up having to modify five different services. That's expensive.

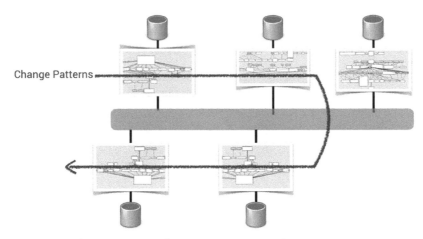

Change Patterns

There are several root causes for microservices shotgun surgery:

- The services share code that itself isn't stable from an evolutionary point of view.

- Protocol design is hard to get right. Thus some services turn into leaky abstractions and others start to depend on exposed implementation details.

- The same team is responsible for multiple services. Often in this case it becomes easier to send directed information between services that, logically, represent different concepts.

By making change coupling analysis a habit, you get an early warning that you can react to early and disarm the shotgun.

Express Higher-Level Concepts than Services

Some services aren't independent but form a natural hierarchy, and that's something I often see reflected in the change coupling analyses. Today's microservices lack an architectural concept that lets us express such groups of microservices as one logical unit. When you identify such services, organize them into the same Git repository to express the relatedness and benefit from easier code navigation within that business capability. Process boundaries alone don't make good components.

Optimize for Sociotechnical Congruence Across Boundaries

In larger organizations you want to take the analysis a step further and correlate the technical change coupling results to the social team analyses that we used in the previous chapters. Remember the system we discussed where a simple tweak took a week because the work rippled across organizational boundaries? Combining technical and social analyses lets you identify such patterns, and the next figure shows an example.

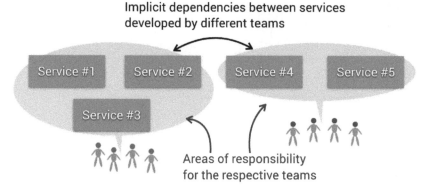

When you detect dependencies between code owned by different teams you have a number of options:

- *Live with it*: There's nothing wrong with accepting an interteam dependency as long as you ensure that the teams are close from an organizational perspective, as coordination costs increase rapidly otherwise.

- *Transfer ownership*: When possible, transfer the ownership of one of the affected services so that the parts that change together are owned by the same team.

- *Redefine the protocols*: As we discussed earlier, such coupling may be accidental if a service exposes implementation details, which is a technical problem that can be corrected.

- *Collapse the services*: Finally, inspect if the two services are logically the same and should be collapsed into a single service.

Whatever approach you choose, follow up with the same measures a few weeks later to ensure you get the desired effect. The shorter the communication paths, the better.

Measure Technical Sprawl

Four decades ago, Manny Lehman started documenting a series of observations on how software evolves, and his writings became known as *Lehman's laws*. (See *On Understanding Laws, Evolution, and Conservation in the Large-Program Life Cycle [Leh80]*.) One of the laws states the need for *conservation of familiarity*, which means that everyone involved in the life cycle of a system must maintain a working knowledge of the system's behavior and content.

The main reasons for diminishing knowledge of a system are high turnover of personnel and, as Lehman points out, excessive growth of the codebase. However, microservices present another challenge that may hinder both collaboration and knowledge sharing, so let's explore that.

Freedom Isn't Free

The trends and hype within the software industry follow a pattern: promising silver bullets are offered based on local success, only to be countered with warnings once an idea becomes popular enough for the discrepancy between expectations and actual outcome to be noted at scale. This happened to object-oriented programming, which once promised reusable Lego blocks of code, service-oriented architectures that guaranteed scalable enterprise systems, and NoSQL that apparently made it easy to deal with high volumes of unstructured data.

Just a couple of years ago microservices launched on the same trajectory, and one early selling point was that each team was free to choose its own technology and programming language. The consequences of unrestricted technology adoption became known as *technical sprawl.*

Technical sprawl comes in different forms, and the most obvious form is when our services use different libraries, frameworks, and infrastructures. This sprawl will slow down the development of the system and diminish our mastery of it. We avoid these dangers by standardizing our microservice ecosystem; *Production-Ready Microservices: Building Standardized Systems Across an Engineering Organization [Fow16]* comes with a good set of practical advice in this area.

Standardization has to go beyond tools and frameworks, and your teams also have to agree on a common structure and location for third-party dependencies. I've seen several microservice systems where each team chose its own structure, which led to slower onboarding without any obvious benefits. Consistency saves time.

Another aspect of technical sprawl arises when each team chooses its own programming language. It's all fun and games until your two productive Idris programmers leave to launch their startup, and they take your only kdb+ database expert with them.[10] [11]

---

10. https://www.idris-lang.org/

11. https://en.wikipedia.org/wiki/Kdb%2B

Sure, a good developer can learn the basics of any programming language in a week, but the mastery required to tweak and debug production code needs time and experience. While rewriting a service in another language is doable—at least as long as the service is truly micro—it has no value from a business perspective. It's a hard sell.

Technical sprawl also puts an accidental limit on knowledge boundaries since it becomes harder for an individual developer to keep up with the code in neighboring services.

Turn Prototyping into Play

We humans learn by doing, and prototyping different solutions gives you feedback to base decisions on. Unless you prototype a problem connected to a specific technology—for example, performance optimizations or scalability—use your prototypes as a learning vehicle. (Years ago I learned Common Lisp this way.) The strategy has the advantage of fueling the intrinsic motivation of developers and gives your organization a learning opportunity that you can't afford on production code. Besides, no manager will mistake that Common Lisp–based prototype as being production ready.

Measure Programming-Language Sprawl

Programming-language sprawl can be measured from a static snapshot of the code. The cloc tool that we used to count lines of code has built-in rules that recognize most programming languages. Let's try it on Orca, Spinnaker's orchestration engine:

```
adam$ cloc .
    1057 text files.
    1056 unique files.
      13 files ignored.
```

Language	files	blank	comment	code
Groovy	663	9136	10863	43993
Java	201	2382	3336	9726
Kotlin	108	1849	1892	9528
...			...	
Dockerfile	1	5	0	9
Slim	1	4	0	5
SUM:	1045	13506	16257	67004

Most of Orca is implemented in Groovy, but there are also significant portions in Java and Kotlin. We'll put this data to use later in this chapter, but for now we just pick the top language: Groovy.

Our next step is to repeat this process in each repository and then visualize it by associating each language with a distinct color, just as we did for teams earlier. The next figure shows the main programming languages for the services in Spinnaker, and the size of the circles represents the total amount of code.[12]

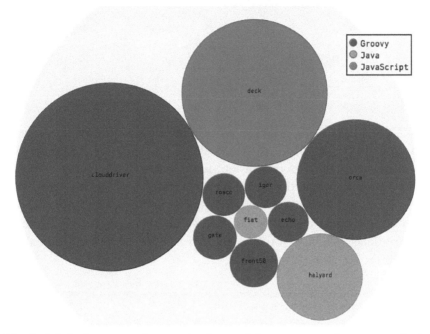

This kind of data becomes increasingly useful as your system grows in terms of services, and it's also a useful input to offboarding, as we discuss in the next chapter.

Calculate a Technical Sprawl Index

In a large system it's useful to detect services such as Orca that are implemented in multiple languages. Sometimes the choice to go polyglot is deliberate—for example, when front-end and back-end code are organized together—and sometimes such sprawl marks the transition to a new technology, like rewriting Java code in Kotlin or Scala. We could visualize the programming language of each file, as shown in the figure on page 184, but that makes it hard to identify trends and improvements.

---

12. https://codescene.io/projects/1650/jobs/4074/results/architecture/organization

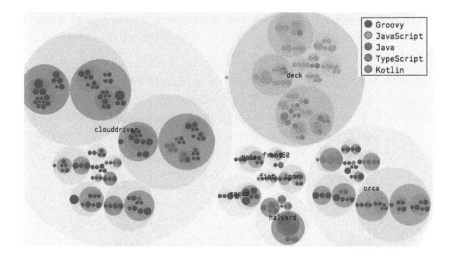

In *Rank Code by Diffusion*, on page 122, we introduced the fractal value metric that lets us detect how diffused the development efforts are between different programmers. The same formula lets us calculate a *technical sprawl index* that shows how diffused the implementation techniques are within a microservice or any other subsystem. A value of 0.0 means a single programming language, while the closer to 1.0 we get, the greater the sprawl. The next figure describes how you adapt the fractal value formula to calculate a normalized technical sprawl value.

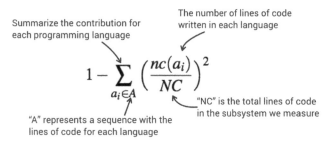

To generate the raw data we instruct cloc to deliver its output as CSV and save it as a machine-readable file:

```
adam$ cloc . --csv --quiet --report-file=orca_loc.csv
```

The resulting CSV file contains a code column—just as our previous cloc example did—that we feed into the preceding formula. The process is straightforward to piece together with a few lines of Python, but you could also open the CSV file in a spreadsheet application and do the calculation there.

Whatever strategy you choose, be sure to clean the data of common content, autogenerated XML files, or test data in JSON. For example, all Spinnaker repositories contain a Docker file and Markdown documentation, and we don't want such content to contribute to a higher sprawl index. Thus, we remove all those entries from our cloc output before the technical sprawl calculation.

The following figure shows an example based on the 2017 Spinnaker implementation, and we then speculate—wildly, without any insider insights—about 2018 just to illustrate how this technique lets you measure technical sprawl over time.

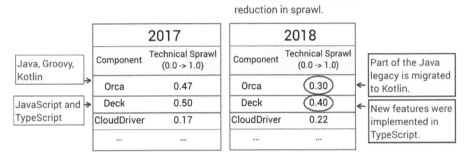

Use this information to strategically reduce technical sprawl, and measure frequently to ensure your strategic decisions are reflected in the code that gets produced.

When You Choose a Technology You Also Choose a Community

 Choosing a programming language is about more than solving business problems, which all Turing-complete languages are capable of. So study the community and culture around each language you consider. It'll influence what people you're able to hire—and retain—as well as define the core values of your architecture.

Distribution Won't Cure the Dependency Blues

In this chapter we discussed how behavioral code analysis helps us get tactical information on complex systems such as microservice architectures at scale. The same techniques are also useful as input to planning and as a way to reason about change, which is significantly harder in a microservice architecture. I first experienced that in the early 2000s as I worked on my first microservice system, so let me share a painful lesson.

Of course, back in the 2000s we didn't know we were doing microservices as the term hadn't yet been coined. Instead the architecture was the logical conclusion of applying the UNIX design philosophy on the scale of a distributed system. (See *Linux and the Unix Philosophy, 2nd Edition [Gan03]* for a great read and advice that's useful no matter what platform you target.)

The services in that system ranged from small implementations with about 100 lines of code to somewhat more complex services with about 3,000 lines, but none of them were hard to understand in isolation. This was a huge improvement over the previous legacy system, and the architecture was considered a success as it let other parts of the organization add smaller extensions in the shape of separate services.

However, even though the services were easy to understand, the system complexity was still there—only now it was distributed, too. As the system grew toward its second release, we noted that reasoning about the system behavior was difficult at best and much harder than it had been on the monolith we replaced. The communication between services was asynchronous through publish-subscribe middleware,[13] so each service was decoupled in code but the logical dependencies were still there. A change coupling analysis would have saved the team from lots of painful message tracing.

In complex systems a coupling analysis between logical change sets offers information that serves as a guide to code reading. Making it easier to reason about systems is where the big win is, so it pays off to ensure you have the information you need to uncover developer behavior. As we saw in this chapter, a ticket reference to each commit helps you spot dependencies that you can't detect in the code alone. The next time you plan to introduce a new feature, look at the change coupling of related services to foresee the impact of the suggested additions.

Now that we've analyzed a broad range of codebases such as layers, components, and microservices, we're prepared to generalize our knowledge to whatever architectural style our next project throws at us. For example, at the time of writing, *serverless architectures* and *function as a service* (FAAS) are gaining in popularity as a way to reduce server costs and, ideally, development costs.[14] That drive toward ever-smaller architectural building blocks makes it harder to maintain a holistic overview, and behavioral code analyses such as change coupling will fill an important gap there, too.

The techniques discussed so far are after-the-fact analyses, so what if we could catch potential problems early before they become an issue? That's up next as we look to detect early warnings on both the technical and organizational levels.

---

13. https://en.wikipedia.org/wiki/Publish%E2%80%93subscribe_pattern
14. https://martinfowler.com/articles/serverless.html

Exercises

We covered a lot of ground in this chapter as we focused both on gaining situational awareness of existing problems and on getting guidance that makes it easier to understand existing code. In the following exercises you get the opportunity to try a technique from each of those categories.

Support Code Reading and Change Planning

- Repositories: Spinnaker[15]
- Language: JavaScript and Groovy
- Domain: Spinnaker is a continuous-delivery platform.
- Analysis snapshot: https://codescene.io/projects/1650/jobs/4074/results/code/temporal-coupling/between-repos

A change coupling analysis lets you reason about suggested changes in the sense that you may detect implicit dependencies. By uncovering those dependencies you're able to plan ahead and avoid breaking existing behavior.

Let's pretend in this exercise that you want to do a change to the gceBakeStage.js module in the front end (the deck repository). What regression tests are likely to fail unless you update them?

Combine Technical and Social Views to Identify Communities

- Repositories: Spinnaker[16]
- Language: JavaScript and Groovy
- Domain: Spinnaker is a continuous-delivery platform.
- Analysis snapshot: https://codescene.io/projects/1650/jobs/4074/results/code/hotspots/system-map

When we discussed the need for sociotechnical congruence, we noted that code that changes together should be close from an organizational perspective. Normally we'd like to investigate it on the team level, but we could also start from individual authors and find social cliques whose work depends upon each other's code.

Start from the change coupling relationship you identified in the previous exercise and find the main authors behind each side of the change coupling. Are there any interpersonal dependencies you'd like to be aware of if you plan an organizational change?

---

15. https://github.com/spinnaker
16. https://github.com/spinnaker

Analyze Your Infrastructure

- Repositories: Git[17]
- Language: C and shell scripts
- Domain: Git is a distributed version-control system we know all too well.
- Analysis snapshot: https://codescene.io/projects/1664/jobs/4156/results/code/refactoring-targets

Many organizations invest in elaborate pipelines for continuous integration and deployment, which is a great thing that helps detect problems early and lets us manage increasingly larger systems. The necessary automation doesn't come for free, and I've seen several systems where infrastructure-related code—just like test code—isn't treated with the same care as the application code. (When was the last time you code-reviewed a build script?) The result is that the automation scripts become bottlenecks that make it harder to adapt to changed circumstances.

Git has an interesting architecture in the sense that its main domain concepts are visible in the top-level file names, as visible in a hotspot visualization.[18] The implementations in Git favor relatively large modules implemented in C, but none of that code is the top hotspot.

Look at the main hotspots and identify some potential technical debt that isn't in the application code. Investigate the complexity trend of that hotspot and think about possible refactorings.

---

17. https://github.com/git/git
18. https://codescene.io/projects/1664/jobs/4156/results/code/hotspots/system-map

Si vis pacem, para bellum.
➢ *Vegetius*

CHAPTER 10

An Extra Team Member: Predictive and Proactive Analyses

There's a common belief in our industry that technical debt sneaks into a codebase over time. However, recent research disagrees and suggests that many problematic code smells are introduced upon creation, and future evolution of the code merely continues to dig that hole deeper. This means we need a way to catch potential problems early, ideally before they enter our master branch. In this chapter we explore preventive and predictive uses of behavioral code analysis. Such analysis information becomes like an extra team member that helps us by pointing out areas of the code in need of our attention.

We start by detecting early warnings on code that evolves toward a future maintenance problem such as a growing hotspot, and look to predict code decay. This is information that's immediately actionable when combined with existing practices such as code reviews, and forms a natural part of any continuous integration pipeline.

From there we look deeper at the social data discussed in the previous chapters and see how it benefits onboarding tasks. We also combine the data with technical measures to simulate the impact and staffing needs during offboarding or job rotations. Let's get started by identifying a spectacular hotspot.

Detect Deviating Evolutionary Patterns

The largest hotspot I've ever come across is still around, and it's located in the prominent *.NET Core runtime.*[1] That codebase forms the basis for all .NET

---

1. https://github.com/dotnet/coreclr

applications by providing the byte code interpretation, memory management, addressing security, and much more. Let's take a quick look at it.

The following figure shows the hotspots that developed in the .NET Core codebase over time. As you see, most development activity has been in the just-in-time (JIT) compiler, where we find a whole cluster of hotspots.[2] We also see that there's a lone hotspot named gc.cpp, which represents the garbage collector in the .NET Core.

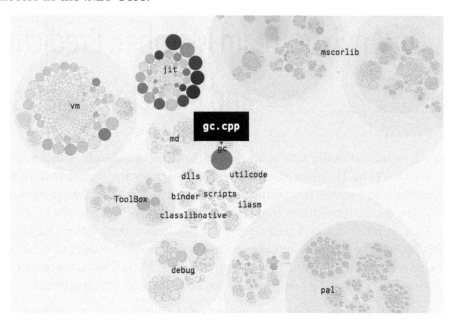

The hotspot gc.cpp may look rather innocent in the visualization, but that's only due to the scale of .NET Core. The runtime is a large codebase with close to four million lines of code, and gc.cpp is a big, big file, as shown in the next figure.

---

2. https://codescene.io/projects/1765/jobs/4433/results/code/hotspots/system-map

So what's inside the file? Is it a bird? Is it a plane? No, it's 37,000 lines of fear-inducing C++. An X-Ray of gc.cpp, as shown in the next figure, reveals that its functions are both large and complex.[3]

Remember, 15 is considered the cutoff point for very high complexity

⇕ Function	Change ▾ Frequency	Lines of ⇕ Code	Cyclomatic ⇕ Complexity
gc_heap::grow_brick_card_tables	28	354	33
GCHeap::Initialize	27	124	20
gc_heap::gc1	26	512	60
gc_heap::garbage_collect		415	56
gc_heap::plan_phase	21	1507	203
gc_heap::initialize_gc	19	204	37

Most functions are really large.

Working with the code has to be a challenge, in part because it models a complex domain, but also because all .NET users around the world rely on its correctness for their applications. A bug could be disastrous. There have been suggestions to refactor the code, but it's considered too risky and expensive to do so.[4]

While the size of gc.cpp is on the extreme edge of the scale, far too many organizations find themselves in similar situations where parts of the code cannot be refactored without significant risk. Thus it pays off to investigate ways of detecting code decay and future maintenance problems early. Let's see how.

When Code Turns Bad

How do we get to a single file with 37,000 lines of code whose functions have a cyclomatic complexity far beyond the pain point? In this case we can't tell for sure since only the last years of version control are available on GitHub, but a qualified guess is that the code has been tricky from the beginning. Let's see why that's the case and how you can avoid the same trap.

In a fascinating study, a team of researchers investigated 200 open source projects to find out *When and Why Your Code Starts to Smell Bad [TPBO15]*. The study identified cases of problematic code such as *Blob classes* that

---

3. https://codescene.io/projects/1765/jobs/4433/results/files/hotspots?file-name=coreclr/src/gc/gc.cpp
4. https://github.com/dotnet/coreclr/issues/408

represent units with too many responsibilities, classes with high cyclomatic complexity, tricky *spaghetti code*, and so on, and in all fairness gc.cpp ticks most of those boxes.

The researchers then backtracked each of those code problems to identify the commit that introduced the root cause. The surprising conclusion is that such problems are introduced already upon the creation of those classes! Really.

This finding should impact how we view code; it's easy to think that code starts out fine and then degrades over time. As we just saw, that's not what happens. The moment we get to a pull request, it may already be too late, as the pressure of a looming deadline makes it harder to reject an implementation. And even when we do reject a new piece of code, it has already become a cost sink.

That's why I recommend that you do your initial code walkthrough much earlier. Instead of waiting for the completion of a feature, make it a practice to present and discuss each implementation at one-third completion. Focus less on details and more on the overall structure, dependencies, and how well the design aligns with the problem domain. Of course, one-third completion is subjective, but it should be a point where the basic structure is in place, the problem is well understood, and the initial test suite exists. At this early stage, a rework of the design is still a viable alternative and catching potential problems here has a large payoff.

If you do one-third code walkthroughs—and you really should give it a try—start from the perspective of the test code. As we saw earlier in this book, there is often a difference in quality between test code and application code. Complicated test code is also an indication that something is not quite right in the design of the application code; if something is hard to test, it will be hard to use from a programmer's point of view, and thus a future maintenance issue.

Identify Steep Increases in Complexity

While we want to direct an eye toward new code, existing code may, of course, also turn bad as it evolves. When that happens, the affected code exhibits specific trends that differ from how clean code evolves. More specifically, the *weighted method complexity*—the sum of the complexity of every method in the class—increases much faster, and it's the first warning sign that the code will turn into a future Blob class. (See the research we discussed earlier, *When and Why Your Code Starts to Smell Bad [TPBO15]*, which also includes this finding.) Fortunately, behavioral code analysis can help us detect such code before it's even merged to the master branch. Let's look at an example.

The next figure shows the complexity trend of the file gdbjit.cpp, which is part of the debug functionality in .NET. As you see, there's been a steep increase in complexity over several weeks.[5]

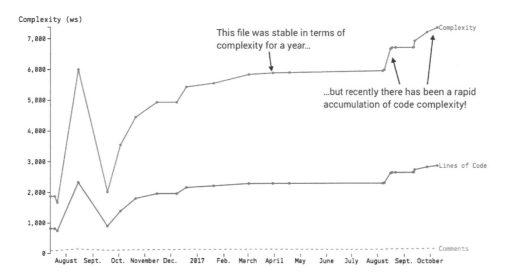

Given what we know about future maintenance problems, together with the fact that gdbjit.cpp already consists of more than 2,000 lines of code, this is a sign of trouble. If we could detect increasing trends like this automatically, we could run an analysis on each feature branch and react immediately to commits that introduce excess complexity.

To pull this off, we calculate the growth in complexity relative to a previous state and raise a warning each time an addition exceeds a given threshold. This threshold should be relative to the existing code because different organizations have different quality goals. In some codebases, large, monolithic files are the norm, while other teams prefer a more modular design with small and cohesive units. A complexity trend warning should be relative to the previous evolution of the file, which limits the number of false positives. As a rule of thumb, consider a 10 percent increase in code complexity a warning sign.

A simple start is to look at the delta of the last commit. However, in practice you need to take more revisions into account; otherwise you miss complexity

---

5. https://codescene.io/projects/1765/jobs/4433/results/code/hotspots/complexity-trend?name=coreclr/src/vm/
    gdbjit.cpp

> ### Joe asks:
> ## Wouldn't an Absolute and Universal Threshold Be Better?
>
> We could, of course, say that any class that has a weighted method complexity beyond 10, 100, or whatever, is too complex. The problem with an absolute threshold is that in many legacy codebases you would get a warning each time you touch a piece of code. Soon every developer is desensitized and the warnings lose their meaning. With a relative threshold you react to negative changes by using the current state of your code as a baseline. This gives you fewer—but more relevant—warnings. Remember, information should be actionable.

that's added gradually over several commits close in time. Two strategies let you achieve that:

1. *Use the commit at the branch point as a reference*: If you work on short-lived feature branches, use the state of the code as it looked when your branch diverged from the main line of development.

2. *Use a time window*: As an alternative that doesn't depend on branches, use the state of the code as it looked a month ago.

From here you scan the selected range of commits, calculate the complexity of the file in each state, and select the lowest complexity value as your point of reference. The reason for this extra step is to avoid another corner case where a file gets refactored but then grows again, as illustrated in the next figure.

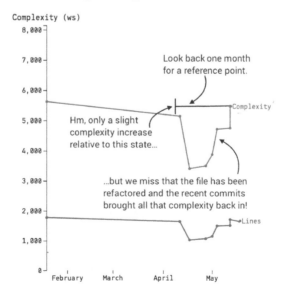

Finally, to avoid false positives you want to limit your complexity trend warnings to code that has grown beyond a particular size. For example, a new file that adds 20 lines of code to its previous 100 lines isn't likely to be of interest.

When you investigate your complexity trend warnings, you're likely to come across the following scenarios:

- *Misplaced behavior*: Rapid growth in complexity is a sign that the code keeps accumulating responsibilities. Often, those responsibilities would be better off when expressed as separate units, so use refactorings like *Extract Class*. (See *Refactoring: Improving the Design of Existing Code [FBBO99]*.)

- *Excess conditional logic*: Quite often new features or bug fixes are squeezed into an existing design with the use of if/else chains. Most nested conditionals indicate a missing abstraction, and refactoring the code to use polymorphism or list comprehensions, or even modeling the data as a sequence, erases special cases from the code.

- *The code is fine*: Yes, it happens, and in this case we're safe ignoring the warning.

Integrate Complexity Warnings into Your Workflow

The earlier we can act on a potential problem, the better. I recommend that you let your continuous integration pipeline scan each branch for complexity trend warnings. An alternative is to provide the functionality as a script that's run by a Git *pre-commit hook*.[6] All developers still have the option to bypass the check, but it has to be an active choice and as such provides an opportunity for reflection on whether that nested if statement really was the way to go.

Detect Future Hotspots

As we saw with gc.cpp, critical hotspots are likely to stick around, so we need to get them before the initial code-quality problems accelerate. When bad code is introduced, it is likely that it will soon require several modifications to smoke out defects, or it will keep attracting more commits because the code has too many responsibilities. This shows up as a shift in development focus.

---

6. https://git-scm.com/book/en/v2/Customizing-Git-Git-Hooks

We can detect such code by looking at files that climb rapidly in the hotspot ranking—that is, *rising hotspots*. To detect rising hotspots we perform two calculations:

- A hotspot analysis based on how the code looks right now
- Another hotspot analysis based on how the code looked in the past

The time spans differ based on size and amount of development activity in the codebase, but a rule of thumb is to look a few months into the past. We perform the analysis of past hotspots by instructing Git to only include commits that were --before="two months ago". The rest of the command pipeline is identical to what we used in earlier chapters. Here's what the complete command looks like:

```
adam$ git log --before="two months ago" --format=format: --name-only \
            | egrep -v '^$' | sort | uniq -c \
            | sort -r > two_months_ago.txt
```

We then generate one more file with the current hotspot ranking, simply by omitting the --before option, and redirect that output to another file. From here we compare the rankings of the individual hotspots to detect the ones that have climbed over the past two months, as shown in the next figure.

Hotspot ranking two months ago   Current hotspot ranking

```
121   44 src/vm/i386/cgenx86.cpp                    70   66 src/pal/src/thread/process.cpp
122   44 src/mscorlib/src/System/Threading/Thread.cs 71   66 src/jit/rationalize.cpp
123   44 src/gc/gcinterface.h                        72   65 src/jit/lsraarm.cpp
124   43 tests/x86_legacy_backend_issues.targets     73   65 src/inc/corinfo.h
125   43 tests/src/CLRTest.Execute.Bash.targets      74   64 src/jit/lsra.h
126   43 src/vm/stackwalk.cpp                         75   63 clr.coreclr.props
127   43 src/vm/gdbjit.cpp                            76   62 src/mscorlib/src/System/String.cs
128   43 src/vm/corhost.cpp                           77   60 src/pal/src/init/pal.cpp
129   43 src/mscorlib/src/System/Span...             78   60 src/mscorlib/src/System/TimeZoneInfo.cs
130   43 src/jit/lsraarm.cpp                                   ...t/lower.h
131   43 src/jit/ee_il_dll.cpp                                 .../prestub.cpp
132   43 src/jit/block.h                                       .../codeman.cpp
133   43 src/gc/gc.h                                 82   59 src/jit/inlinepolicy.cpp
```

The file lsraarm.cpp has climbed from position 130 to position 72.

In a system under active development, you want to automate this analysis in the form of a script. While the steps of such a script are straightforward, the challenge is to prioritize and limit the results. So start with a threshold where a hotspot needs to climb at least 10 steps on the ranking before considering it a rising hotspot. You can always tweak that value if the resulting data is too verbose.

Let's look at a real example by inspecting the rising hotspots in .NET Core, as shown in the figure on page 197 and in the online gallery.[7] These rising hotspots show a clear pattern where recent development efforts seem to focus on the just-in-time compilation support for the ARM CPU architecture, and most likely this reflects Microsoft's investment in porting .NET to Linux.

---

7. https://codescene.io/projects/1765/jobs/4433/results/warnings/rising-hotspots

All files that climbed at least 20 positions
on the hotspot ranking over the past two months

⇕ File Name	Frequency ⇕ Increase	New Hotspot ⇕ Rank	Old Hotspot ⇕ Rank
coreclr/src/jit/lsraarm.cpp	30	28	58
coreclr/src/jit/lsraarmarch.cpp	29	70	99
coreclr/src/jit/lsraxarch.cpp	55	93	148
coreclr/src/jit/lsraarm64.cpp	118	96	214

This finding raises an important point: just because some files start to attract many commits doesn't mean the code is a problem. Rather, this means significant development efforts are invested in a new part of the codebase. This is information we use to direct our attention in the form of a review, a code walkthrough, or a friendly dialog with the developers behind it. Our task is to confirm what we expect: that the code is up to par. Should that not be the case, then we need to invest in immediate refactorings to avoid future maintenance problems.

Clean Your Input Data

As we discussed earlier in Part II, the analysis results are easier to interpret if we clean out uninteresting content. The online results in this section reflect that, as noncode artifacts such as JSON and autogenerated Visual Studio project files have been removed. Thus, the rankings differ compared to the raw git commands used earlier, but the general principle behind rising hotspots is the same.

Catch the Absence of Change

The early-warning mechanisms that we've discussed so far help us detect deviating patterns in the evolution of a codebase. But problems may also be introduced by the *absence* of a change. For example, one microservice may produce a new event but the expected receiver doesn't implement code to handle it, or maybe we forget to add proper error handling in a higher layer as we let a lower layer raise a new type of exception.

Most examples of bugs by omission can be caught by proper tests, a decent type system, or a static analysis tool. However, those safety nets aren't able to cope with surprises of the kind we dealt with in Chapter 3, *Coupling in Time: A Heuristic for the Concept of Surprise*, on page 35. Copy-paste code where we forgot to update one of the clones? Too bad; the compiler won't help, and chances are slim that we remember to test for our omission.

To prevent these situations we use change coupling to our advantage. The technique won't deliver a complete guarantee of correctness, but it does help catch omissions. Let's demonstrate how.

If you did the exercises in Chapter 3, *Coupling in Time: A Heuristic for the Concept of Surprise*, on page 35, you've already come across the Roslyn codebase.[8] Roslyn is a compiler platform that also implements the C# and Visual Basic compilers. Since both compilers are bootstrapped, Roslyn contains an equal amount of Visual Basic and C# code, as shown in the next figure.[9]

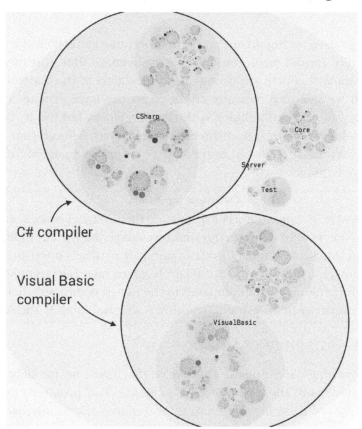

A corresponding change coupling analysis shows that there are strong logical dependencies across the language boundaries.[10] For example, the Visual Basic code in the file VisualBasicEESymbolProvider.vb changes together with the C# code in the CSharpEESymbolProvider.cs file in 100 percent of commits. This change coupling in Roslyn looks deliberate, and it's likely to be a design goal to

8.   https://github.com/dotnet/roslyn
9.   https://codescene.io/projects/1715/jobs/4299/results/code/hotspots/system-map
10.   https://codescene.io/projects/1715/jobs/4299/results/code/temporal-coupling/by-commits

maintain a similar structure in the two compilers. This means we can use our knowledge of such expected change patterns to verify the principle.

We do that by performing a change coupling analysis as part of a continuous integration pipeline, and then verify each commit against that baseline. Ideally, that check is implemented as a Git precommit hook, which means Git fires off a script that you provide.[11] Here's what's needed in that script:

1. Fetch the results of the last change coupling analysis and ignore everything below a (configurable) threshold, like 80 percent change coupling. The purpose of the threshold is again to avoid false positives.

2. Check each modified file in the pending commit against the last change coupling results, and look for omissions where an expected change coupling is absent from the pending commits set.

3. Inform the user and give her or him the option to cancel the commit. In a precommit hook, aborting a commit is as simple as returning a nonzero status from your script.

4. If all expected change couplings are present, the script runs to completion and reports success, and the developer doing the commit won't notice.

So if we have this mechanism in place and we make a mistake, we get a dialog like in the following session:

```
adam$ git status
On branch develop
Changes to be committed:
  (use "git reset HEAD <file>..." to unstage)

        modified:   CSharpEESymbolProvider.cs

adam$ git commit -m "PR #123: Correct error handling for missing symbols"
Pre-Commit Warning
==================
Previous modifications of CSharpEESymbolProvider.cs also
required a change to VisualBasicEESymbolProvider.vb

Are you sure you want to continue? (yes/no)
```

The final lines of output are examples from a precommit script. It's important to give the developer the choice to ignore the warning; otherwise we won't be able to refactor and break unwanted change coupling. That choice also has the nice side effect of being a self-learning algorithm; if we keep ignoring the warning, it will result in a lower change coupling over time, and eventually the coupling will go below the threshold and the warning will disappear.

---

11. https://git-scm.com/book/en/v2/Customizing-Git-Git-Hooks

This usage of change coupling concludes the technical analyses in this book. Used wisely, this technique fills the role of a *Minority Report* pre-cog, but for software (albeit with fewer car chases than the movie). Also note that you could apply the same early-warning technique on any level, such as between logical components, separate microservices, or on the level of functions. With that covered, we move on to take a quick glance at some proactive usages of social analyses.

Guide On- and Offboarding with Social Data

Earlier in the book we discussed that ease of communication has to be a key nonfunctional requirement for any software architecture. We also saw how principles like code ownership and broad knowledge boundaries help you minimize the risk of social biases and form part of an organizational design. These principles get even more important in organizations that are distributed across different departments or geographical sites (or both). Let's see why.

Identify the Experts

If you've ever worked in an organization that is located across multiple sites, you probably noted that distribution comes at a cost. What may be surprising is how significant that cost is. Research on the subject reports that distributed work items take an average of two and a half times longer to complete than tasks developed by a colocated team. (See the research in *An Empirical Study of Speed and Communication in Globally Distributed Software Development [HM03].*)

One of the challenges of communication is to find out who to communicate with, and this general problem gets harder with geographical distance. (See, for example, *Considering an Organization's Memory [AH99]* for a cognitive study on the challenges involved.) The previously mentioned research explains that in a distributed setting, the absence of informal discussions in the hallway makes it harder for distant colleagues to know who has expertise in different areas. In such organizations, knowledge maps gain importance.

In *Build Team Knowledge Maps*, on page 157, we saw how knowledge maps help us measure aspects like Conway's law by mapping individual contributions to organizational units. If we skip that step and retain the information about individual authors, we get a powerful communication tool that lets us locate the experts. It won't be perfect, as we still have to know which part of the application to look at, but if we get there, knowledge maps direct our communication efforts.

The next figure shows the current knowledge map of the authors behind the Kotlin programming language.[12] The knowledge map is focused on the front-end part of the Kotlin compiler, and you can interact with the visualization online.[13]

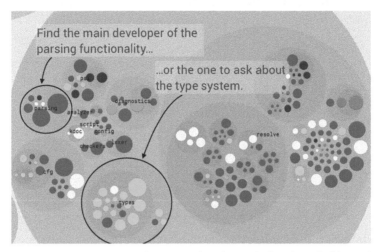

The knowledge map represents the main developer behind each file with a unique color. The main developer is measured as the person who has written most of the code, and thus is likely to be knowledgeable about that application area. For example, in the preceding figure we see that the lime green developer has implemented most of the types package, so if we want to learn more about that code, we look up the developer behind the color and initiate a conversation.

Of course, if you just look at a single file or function you don't need knowledge maps. A quick git blame points you to the person behind the code. The advantage of a knowledge map is it lets you detect clusters of code written by the same author, making it easier to identify the true domain expertise in a particular application area.

Collaborative Tools Are a Workaround, Not a Solution

Today's collaborative tools help a distributed team, but even the most elaborate tool cannot do much about time zone differences (at least not at the time of this writing). One effect of distributed, computer-linked groups is that *less* information gets exchanged; there's more to communication than words, and nonverbal communication tends to get lost. (Several studies have confirmed this; see, for example, the classic *The eyes have it: Minority influence in face-to-face and computer-mediated group discussion [MBMY97]*.) Additionally, chat groups are a noisy way to find experts, so with knowledge maps we can at least narrow down the number of people we need to ping.

---

12. https://github.com/JetBrains/kotlin
13. https://codescene.io/projects/1619/jobs/4004/results/social/knowledge/individuals

Power Laws Are Everywhere

We've already seen that hotspots work so well because the development activity in a codebase isn't uniform, but forms a power law distribution. We see a similar distribution when it comes to individual author contributions, as shown in the following figure with an example from Kotlin.

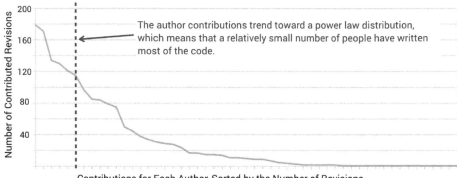

Contributions for Each Author, Sorted by the Number of Revisions

Kotlin is a popular open source project, which means that many contributors just provide one or two pull requests. However, the same power law curve seems to form in closed source codebases, where people are paid to work full-time. This means that in your own codebase, you're likely to see that a surprisingly small number of people have written most of the code. (You can have a look at your author distribution by typing the command git shortlog -s | sort -r.)

Typically, these main contributors are the ones who have been around for a long time and are intimately familiar with the codebase. What if one of them were to leave? We know it would hit the overall productivity of the organization as we'd get some *knowledge loss* in terms of code we may no longer understand. We may even have a good idea of what parts get abandoned, but it's often a guess. Let's see how we can put numbers on it.

Measure Upcoming Knowledge Loss

Since version-control data (our behavioral log) knows which developer has written each piece of code, we can use that information to estimate the impact if a developer leaves or gets transferred to another project. This analysis uses the same data as the knowledge maps; the only difference is that we form two virtual teams: one for people who actively work on the codebase, and one for people who are about to leave, as shown in the figure on page 203.

We introduce virtual teams because it's a more general solution that works even when we have groups of developers, such as a whole team that has worked closely together—perhaps mob programming—who move on to

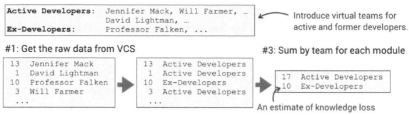

```
Active Developers:   Jennifer Mack, Will Farmer, …
                     David Lightman, …
Ex-Developers:       Professor Falken, ...
```
Introduce virtual teams for active and former developers.

#1: Get the raw data from VCS

```
13   Jennifer Mack
 1   David Lightman
10   Professor Falken
 3   Will Farmer
...
```

```
13   Active Developers
 1   Active Developers
10   Ex-Developers
 3   Active Developers
...
```

#3: Sum by team for each module

```
17   Active Developers
10   Ex-Developers
```
An estimate of knowledge loss

#2: Map individuals to virtual teams

another project.[14] The same algorithm works when you have a single developer that leaves, too. Let's look at a real-world example.

Over the past years the Scala contributors Paul Phillips and Simon Ochsenreither have made public announcements of their decisions to walk away as contributors.[15] [16] Both contributed to Scala for years, so this gives us an opportunity to see the impact when experienced developers leave. Let's look at the resulting knowledge loss in the Scala codebase, as shown in the next figure and in the online gallery.[17]

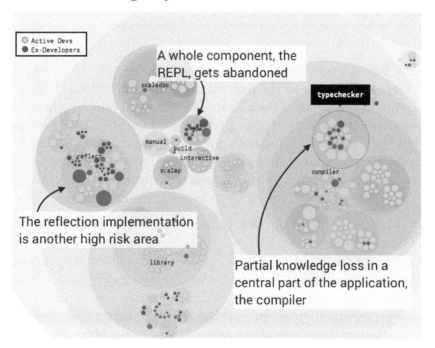

14. https://en.wikipedia.org/wiki/Mob_programming
15. https://www.youtube.com/watch?v=uiJycy6dFSQ
16. https://soc.github.io/six-years-of-scala-development/departure.html
17. https://codescene.io/projects/1822/jobs/4594/results/social/knowledge/individuals?aspect=loss

This knowledge-loss analysis highlights the areas of the system where most lines of code have been written by former contributors. In case of Scala, we see that as these two people leave, some areas of the codebase lose their main developer.

In an after-the-fact analysis like this, you use this information to reason about risk and to use as input to your planning process. In particular, look for components that are entirely in the heads of former contributors—like Scala's interactive prompt, the REPL package. If you know you plan extensions to it, make sure to schedule some additional time for learning because it is an increased risk to modify code we no longer understand.

React to Knowledge Loss

Last year I investigated a codebase under heavy development. That organization worked with several contractors, and two of the contractors had left just the day before I arrived. We used that information to measure and visualize the knowledge loss, and it turned out that an elaborate simulator used during the testing was written entirely by one of them. This was bad news, as the organization was depending on extensions to that simulator in the immediate future.

This story highlights the dangers of narrow knowledge boundaries and silo development. But it also shows that the analysis of knowledge loss is much more useful as a simulation than as an after-the-fact finding; onboarding is much more effective when the original developers are still present to communicate all the trade-offs and situational forces you can't see in the code or even in the version-control history. So when a developer resigns and has a notice period to work out, run this analysis to identify the parts of the system where your organization needs to focus to maintain knowledge.

You also need to classify your findings according to criticality. If we return to our Scala case study, we noted that the interactive prompt, the REPL, was abandoned. That will cost us, but on the positive side, many programming languages include an interactive prompt for evaluating expressions. Thus, the REPL knowledge loss may be low risk, as other developers are familiar with the domain even though they haven't written any code there. More troublesome are the Scala-specific aspects of the type system—a core strength and feature of the language—such as the typechecker and reflect internals. In your own system you want to look for such domain-specific, nontrivial areas of abandoned code.

Of course, you may find that someone else understands that code well enough to maintain it even though they haven't written it. That's good. If not, you need to use the knowledge-loss data for damage control, and other behavioral code analyses can help:

- *Hotspots*: A hotspot analysis on the recent development activity helps you identify critical parts of the code where potential knowledge loss is more severe.

- *Code age*: If an abandoned piece of code hasn't been touched for a long time, that area of the codebase is less critical than others. Chances are the original developer won't remember all the details anyway.

- *Technical sprawl*: While the largest risks are in the loss of domain knowledge, there's a technical dimension too, in case the only people who master a particular technology leave. Thus, you need to consider knowledge loss in the context of a technical-sprawl analysis, as well. In this case you want to take a higher-level view and perform the analysis on logical components, as shown in the next figure. The outcome of this analysis influences training, hiring, and rewrite decisions.

Check your upcoming knowledge loss...   ..against the technical requirements.

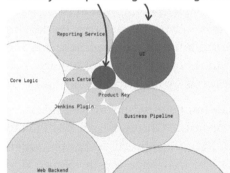 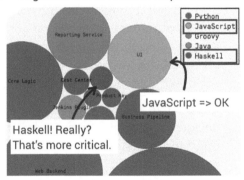

Broad knowledge boundaries, as we discussed earlier in the book, help mitigate offboarding issues. That said, no matter how much effort we put into knowledge sharing, some developers will still maintain a unique expertise and, as long as they're part of your organization, you benefit from their productivity. By simulating upcoming knowledge loss you get data to act upon, which helps you maintain a conservation of familiarity, as we discussed in *Measure Technical Sprawl*, on page 180.

Know the Biases and Workarounds for Behavioral Code Analysis

Most of the time our version-control history is an informational gold mine, but we might stumble across pyrite, too. No analysis is better than the data it operates on, and behavioral code analysis is no exception. So let's have a look at the pitfalls and biases so we know if—and how—they impact us.

First of all, you need a minimum amount of data before you can start to see clear patterns in a behavioral code analysis. I've (successfully) analyzed codebases with just a few weeks of development activity, and in general around 150 to 200 commits are enough for an initial analysis.

When you have an existing system, false positives often bias the data since hotspots are a relative measure. False positives also make the information harder to interpret; README.md and version.txt probably aren't maintenance bottlenecks. This means you need to clean your data by removing autogenerated code and noncode artifacts that aren't of interest to your analysis.

With the exception of false positives we can filter away, technical analyses like hotspots and complexity trends are much less sensitive to biases than the social analyses. Over the years I've run into a number of issues, and if you're aware of them, you can inspect your raw data and avoid the associated traps:

- *Incorrect author info*: A commit in Git will always be associated with an author, but it may not be the real author. This may happen in data that's migrated from an older version-control system where developers worked on long-lived branches that were then merged into the main branch, and the one doing the merge got the full credit in the version-control history. You see this if your noncoding build master turns up as a main contributor.

- *Copy-paste repositories*: A related bias happens when an organization decides to extract a component into a separate Git repository but fails to migrate its history. (Yes, you can—and should—preserve history when moving content between repositories.)[18] In that case the developer who commits the extracted code gets all the credit.

- *Misused squash commits*: Git lets you *squash commits*, effectively merging separate commits into one. This is useful on a smaller scale for a single developer, but disastrous when applied to work committed by several individuals. The resulting history erases both social information as well as change coupling data.

In any of the previous scenarios the resulting version-control data has to be treated with both care and skepticism when it comes to social information. When in doubt, ignore the social analyses and limit your investigative scope to technical concepts like hotspots.

---

18. http://gbayer.com/development/moving-files-from-one-git-repository-to-another-preserving-history/

The parallel development and knowledge analyses are also biased by practices such as pair programming and mob programming. In both of these cases, the individual author who committed a chunk of code wasn't alone behind the keyboard, and since Git—at least in its current version—lacks clairvoyant capabilities, the resulting data will be biased.

There are potential workarounds, like using the commit notes to tag all contributors and then mining author info from that field instead. However, in most cases it's not worth the additional complexity, as the individual-level metrics aren't actionable. Instead, focus on team-level metrics for parallel development and operational boundaries; pair programming or not, you want to make sure your organizational units carry meaning from an architectural perspective.

Your Code Is Still a Crime Scene

My previous book, *Your Code as a Crime Scene [Tor15]*, introduced concepts from forensic psychology as a means to understand the evolution of large-scale codebases. Forensics was a metaphor drawn from where it all started. Years ago I did a *geographical offender profile* on a series of burglaries in my hometown, Malmö, Sweden.[19] Such offender profiles look for patterns in the distribution of connected crime scenes, which are then used to focus investigations on the areas of interest. These forensic hotspots, as shown in the figure on page 208, are all about probabilities, just like the hotspots we detect in code.

At the same time I worked full-time as a software consultant on a project plagued by technical debt, and noted the parallels to forensics. Of course, I don't mean to imply that developers are burglars—save some clock cycles every now and then—but geographical offender profiling is about prioritizing based on human behavior and how humans interact with their environment. The environment of developers is code, and all their past behavior is preserved in version control, so what if we could uncover patterns in that behavior? The book you're reading right now descends directly from that thought.

However, a metaphor can only be stretched so far, and I didn't want the metaphor to distract from the real-world use cases of behavioral code analysis. Hence, the current book is void of forensics.

But I had a second reason for using the crime scene metaphor, and that reason remains important. Modern forensic psychology has evolved to use

---

19. https://en.wikipedia.org/wiki/Geographic_profiling

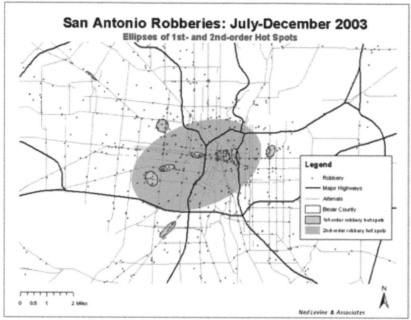

Figure by NedLevine

mathematical statistics as a tool to support actions and decisions. And here the software industry has a lot to learn, as far too many fateful technical and organizational decisions are based on little more than gut feelings, opinions, and the occasional biased group discussion.

The software industry has improved dramatically during the two decades I've been part of it, and there's no sign it will stop. But it's also an industry that keeps repeating avoidable mistakes by isolating its influences to technical fields. Large-scale software development has as much in common with the social sciences as with any engineering discipline. This means we could benefit from tapping into the vast body of research that social psychologists have produced over the past decades.

One of the implied goals of this book is to take mainstream software development one step closer to a point where decisions—both technical and organizational—are influenced by data and research from other fields. There are a lot of things we actually *know* about software development, and we've seen some of the studies behind that body of knowledge throughout this book. Some of the resulting findings and recommendations may well be controversial, and there's still a lot to discover and learn.

Behavioral code analysis doesn't offer any silver bullets, nor does it intend to replace anything. Instead the analyses are here to complement your existing expertise by focusing your attention on the parts of the system that need it the most. The ultimate goal is all about writing better software that's able to evolve with the pressure of new features, novel usages, and changed organizational circumstances. Writing code of that quality will never be easy, as software development is one of the hardest things we humans can put our brains to. We need all the support we can get, and I hope that *Software Design X-Rays* has inspired you to dive deeper into this fascinating field.

Exercises

In these final exercises you get an opportunity to look for early warnings of potential future quality problems. You also get to experiment with a proactive usage of the social analysis techniques as a way to facilitate communication, as well as to reason about offboarding risks.

Early Warnings in Legacy Code

- Repository: Tomcat[20]

- Language: Java

- Domain: Apache Tomcat is a servlet container that implements several Java EE specifications.

- Analysis snapshot: https://codescene.io/projects/1713/jobs/4294/results

Apache Tomcat has a rich history and the code continues to evolve, which makes it a great case study for detecting early warnings due to new features. One of Tomcat's classes, java/org/apache/tomcat/util/net/AbstractEndpoint.java, had been around for eight years before it suddenly started to accumulate complexity. The class is still small, around 700 lines, so if this turns out to be a real problem, now is a great time to counter it.

Start by investigating the complexity trend of java/org/apache/tomcat/util/net/ AbstractEndpoint.java. Continue with an X-Ray and see if you can find any areas that could benefit from focused refactorings. Bonus points are awarded if you, using the Git history,[21] track down the new code and focus your investigative efforts there. (In reality, you'd deliver the possible feedback as part of the pull request.)

---

20. https://github.com/apache/tomcat
21. https://github.com/SoftwareDesignXRays/tomcat

Find the Experts

- Repository: Kubernetes[22]

- Language: Go

- Domain: Kubernetes is a tool to manage containerized applications—for example, Docker.

- Analysis snapshot: https://codescene.io/projects/1823/jobs/4598/results/social/knowledge/individuals

As we discussed distributed teams we saw that tasks often take longer to complete as we struggle to find the experts. It takes time to learn who does what, and that learning curve gets longer when we're located at multiple sites.

Pretend for a moment your team works on Kubernetes and looks to complete a particular feature. After an initial investigation you realize you need to modify the staging/src/k8s.io/apiextensions-apiserver package and probably the staging/src/k8s.io/client-go code too. Who should you discuss your changes with? Have a look at the knowledge map and see if you can identify the main developers.

Offboarding: What If?

- Repositories: Clojure[23], Git[24]

- Language: Clojure, Java, C, and shell scripts

- Domain: Clojure is a Lisp dialect for the JVM, and Git is git.

- Analysis snapshot, Clojure: https://codescene.io/projects/1824/jobs/4597/results/social/knowledge/individuals?aspect=loss

- Analysis snapshot, Git: https://codescene.io/projects/1664/jobs/4156/results/social/knowledge/individuals?aspect=loss

We've seen how we can measure the impact when a developer leaves, and now we get a chance to simulate the same effect with proactive use of a knowledge-loss analysis.

In this exercise you get to investigate two popular open source projects and see what happens if their creators leave. Simulate what happens if Git's inventor, Linus Torvalds, leaves and compare it to the effect on Clojure if Rich Hickey abandons the codebase.

---

22. https://github.com/kubernetes/kubernetes
23. https://github.com/clojure/clojure
24. https://github.com/git/git

The demand to give up the illusions about one's condition
is the demand to give up a condition that needs illusions.
➤ *Sigmund Freud*

The Hazards of Productivity and Performance Metrics

Knowledge maps facilitate communication across an organization because they help you find the people that carry the history of your codebase and product in their heads. Often their stories complement the analysis results and help you put your findings into context. However, using the same data for performance evaluations is dangerous, so let's look into that topic as a cautionary tale.

Adaptive Behavior and the Destruction of a Data Source

Over the past years I've been asked if the social analyses presented in this book could be used to evaluate the performance of individual programmers. My short answer is no, and—when I get the chance to elaborate—my longer answer is "No, because it will hurt more than it will help."

The reason I advise against this is part ethical, part juridical, and to a large degree practical. Some of the statistics you're able to collect with the techniques in this book may be considered sensitive from a legal perspective, a topic that varies among different jurisdictions and company policies.

From a practical point of view, once someone starts to evaluate contributors, people adapt by optimizing for what's being measured. For example, if I'm evaluated on how many commits I do, I'll increase my number of commits. My commits will no longer carry any meaning, but my statistics "improve." As Heraclitus said, we cannot step into the same river twice, and his ancient wisdom would hit us with full force the next time we try to apply the analyses; the nature of the thing we try to measure would have changed for the worse.

This means we destroy a valuable collaboration tool and bias our hotspots and change coupling measures in the process. Painful.

An even worse aspect of such performance evaluations is that they're likely to ruin the team dynamics. Again, if we're measured by how many commits or lines of code we produce, we're less likely to invest time in supporting our peers and we end up with local optimizations that hurt the overall productivity. And even when we do manage to get a sensible performance metric, we still can't use it for job-performance evaluation. Let's see why.

The Situation Is Invisible in Code

A quick look at a knowledge map reveals the main developer in a codebase, as illustrated by the next figure. Could we use that to identify the top performers?

This strategy will be just as destructive as measuring the number of commits, as all incentives for true improvements are gone. Replace a large chunk of code with a library? No—negative performance. Delete dead code? No—negative performance. Check in those large code-generated blobs? Yes—positive performance.

Some of the best developers I've worked with are able to produce more value with less code. A while ago I was part of a project where a small team of developers replaced 30,000 lines of code with a brilliant implementation based on domain-specific languages. The size of that new solution? 1,500 lines of code. That won't happen if you measure productivity as lines produced.

Alright, so we can't use lines of code as a productivity metric. But perhaps we can get a decent performance evaluation by looking at deeper quality attributes? Let's see what happens.

We can create a simple quality metric by identifying the modules with the most defects. However, an after-the-fact analysis may contain contributions from both the programmer introducing the bug as well as the one who fixed it, so we need to be smart here; instead of looking at corrected code, we rewind history and look at the contributions leading up to the defect. That is, we identify the programmers who have introduced the most defects, as illustrated in the next figure.

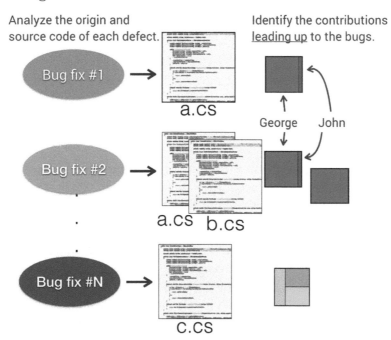

That figure shows the fractal figures of the developers who have contributed the most defect-dense code, and so far it's not looking good for George. From here it's a small step to calculate individual statistics on bugs per line of code, as shown in the figure on page 214.

A quick look at this data lets us know that Ringo isn't performing at the level of the others. Easy. Well, without more context the preceding analysis is seriously flawed. What if

- Ringo's code is the only part of the system that has been tested?

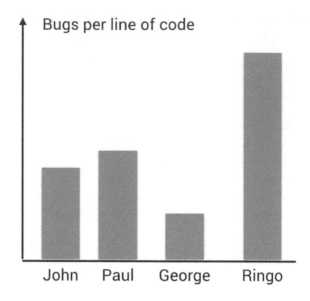

- George works on the simplest parts of the system while Ringo does the heavy lifting?

- Ringo was ordered to write a "throwaway" prototype that got included in production anyway?

As you see, trying to measure the quality and performance of developers without taking situational forces into account is flawed at best. The only way to make a fair assessment is to share the context of the developers, and that requires involving yourself in the development process. There's no way around it.

To summarize, misusing behavioral code analyses for performance evaluations will lead to changed developer behavior. Sure, the quality metrics we discussed are harder to game than the simpler quantitative measures of lines of code or number of commits. That doesn't mean those metrics are safe; instead the team dynamics turn into negotiations and blame games, like the classic "No, this is not a defect." People may also become less inclined to pursue tricky problems as they put themselves at risk for failures and thus negative evaluations. At the end of the line, productivity suffers.

Code Maat: An Open Source Analysis Engine

Code Maat is an open source command-line tool used to mine and analyze data from version-control systems. Code Maat is implemented in Clojure, and you get the code at GitHub.[1] The GitHub page contains up-to-date documentation, so please refer to it for a complete manual. In this appendix we just focus on how you get the tool and how it works.

Run Code Maat

At the time of writing, you need to install a Java runtime, at least version 1.8. You can test which Java version you have by typing java -version.

You can build Code Maat directly from source. Code Maat's GitHub page, linked in the footnotes on this page, contains instructions on how to build an executable JAR file using the build tools from the Clojure ecosystem.

You can also get a prebuilt executable JAR file of the latest version of Code Maat. Just download Code Maat from my homepage.[2]

Data Mining with Code Maat

Code Maat operates on the level of log files generated from any of several version-control systems (including Subversion, TFS, Git, and others), and the GitHub page contains detailed instructions on how to generate the input data to the tool.

---

1. https://github.com/adamtornhill/code-maat
2. http://adamtornhill.com/code/maatdistro.htm

Once you have a log file you feed it to Code Maat, which parses the log file and then performs any of the file- or architectural-level analyses discussed in this book. You specify the type of analysis via a command-line argument. Here's an example of a change coupling analysis, specified through the -a coupling argument, and using one of the supported Git formats where the version-control log is stored in the file vcs_log.txt:

```
adam$ java -jar code-maat-standalone.jar -c git2 -l maat.log -a coupling
entity,coupled,degree,average-revs
analysis/effort.clj,analysis/effort_test.clj,100,5
analysis/churn.clj,analysis/churn_test.clj,89,15
parsers/git.clj,parsers/git_test.clj,80,24
...
```

As you see in the preceding output, the analysis results are delivered as CSV, which you can redirect to a file. Since pure text is the universal interface it allows you to postprocess that data or visualize it as discussed later in this appendix.

I recommend that you run Code Maat in a Git Bash shell if you're on Windows, as illustrated in the next figure. If you use alternative shells, you may have to specify an encoding option to Code Maat, as the tool expects its input to be *UTF-8*. Refer to the documentation on the GitHub page for examples.

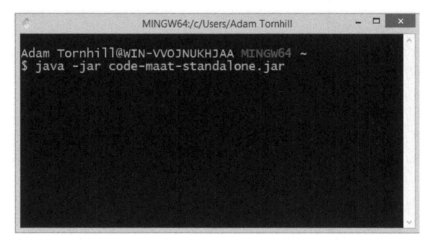

Run Architectural Analyses

Code Maat is input agnostic, so the analysis algorithms are identical no matter if they operate on files or logical components. To analyze logical components, you need to specify a transformation file that maps file names to a logical component. You specify those transformation rules as regular expressions in a text file. The syntax uses an ASCII arrow to map the regular expression to a component name—for example, ^some/path/to/a/folder => My Component.

You can specify multiple rules in the same text file and use the full power of regular expressions. Here's an example:

```
^src\/((?!.*Test.*).).*$ => Code
^src\/.*Test.*$          => Unit Tests
```

The first rule specifies a transformation that maps any file, located under the src folder, that does *not* contain the token Test to the logical component Code. The second rule matches all files that contain the token Test in their name to a Unit Tests component.

You instruct Code Maat to use your transformations by saving them to a file and pointing to it via the --group option. For example, let's say you saved your transformations in a file named code_vs_test.txt. To run a hotspot analysis on those logical components you'd type the following command:

```
adam$ java -jar code-maat-standalone.jar -c git2 \
          -l git.log -a revisions --group code_vs_test.txt
```

Measure Conway's Law

By default, all social analyses in Code Maat are performed on the level of individual authors. After all, that's the information that's available in the Git log. To run the analyses on a team level, you need to provide a file that defines which team each individual author belongs to.

That team-definition file has to be in CSV format, with two columns: author and team. Here's an example of an organization with two teams, Analysis and Hardware:

```
author,team
Ada Lovelace,Analysis
Charles Babbage,Hardware
Luigi Federico Menabrea,Analysis
```

Once you've defined your teams, you run Code Maat with the --team-map-file that specifies the path to your team-definition file. Note that any author who isn't included in the team mapping is kept as is. This has the advantage that any omissions in the mapping are detected quickly.

Visualizations

Code Maat itself doesn't contain any visualizations. Visualization is an orthogonal concept to the analyses, and keeping the visualizations as separate concerns gives you the power to experiment with different representations. There are several options, so let's look at some popular alternatives.

The simplest approach is to just import the generated CSV file in a spreadsheet program such as OpenOffice or Excel to generate charts. Alternatively, if you have access to business intelligence analysis software like Tableau or Qlik, you can use that to explore and visualize your data.

A more hands-on option is to use the D3 library, which comes with support for a rich set of visualizations. The examples you've seen throughout this book are to a large extent built upon the D3 libraries. The D3 examples contain plenty of code to get you started.[3]

Several of the D3 examples operate directly on CSV data, in which case the Code Maat output can be used directly. Other visualizations, most prominently the enclosure diagrams we used for hotspots, require their input data in JSON since it allows for a hierarchical representation.

A set of Python scripts in one of my GitHub repositories illustrates such transformations.[4] For example, to generate a hierarchical JSON representation of hotspots, we'd do the following:

1. Calculate the change frequencies using Code Maat via its revisions analysis.

2. Count the lines of code for each file (for example, by using cloc as discussed in *A Brief Introduction to cloc*, on page 223) and save the data as CSV.

3. Use the script maat-scripts/transform/csv_as_enclosure_json.py to generate the required JSON. Run the script like python csv_as_enclosure_json.py -h to get a usage description.

Please note that the scripts are for the Python 2.X version of the language, although they should be simple to port to Python 3.

Finally, writing and experimenting with your own visualizations is a fun area that provides a good learning experience. I tend to prefer the *Processing* language and environment.[5] Processing is an environment for creative coding and sketches, and while I never quite manage to write maintainable programs in it, it's a lot of fun, and fun is a much-underestimated driver of software design.

---

3. https://github.com/d3/d3/wiki/Gallery
4. https://github.com/adamtornhill/maat-scripts
5. https://processing.org/

Have a look at the referenced tree-map implementation to see an example of Processing code used to visualize hotspots, as shown in the next figure.[6] You could, of course, also use that Processing code directly to visualize your own hotspots.

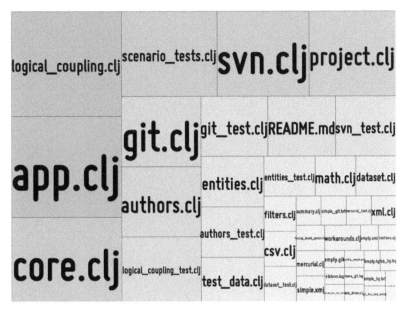

6.   https://github.com/adamtornhill/MetricsTreeMap

Data Mining with Git, cloc, and CodeScene

This appendix contains a brief summary of the data mining commands used throughout the book. There's also a brief introduction to cloc as a proxy for complexity metrics, and a quick look at the planned support for exporting analysis data from CodeScene.

Behavioral Code Analysis with Git

This section summarizes the most important Git commands. Please note that the trailing backslash, \, is used to break the lines so that they appear readable in the text, and you want to omit those backslashes and join the lines together when you enter the commands.

Detect Hotspots

Here we ask Git to deliver a list of all modified files in every commit. We then remove empty lines—a side effect of the Git command—with the egrep command. The command then counts the frequency of the resulting file names and delivers the results sorted in descending order:

```
adam$ git log --format=format: --name-only | egrep -v '^$' | sort \
                        | uniq -c | sort -r
```

You limit the analysis period by specifying the --after option—for example, as --after=2016-01-01 to only get modifications since January 1, 2016.

In large codebases, you may want to run the analyses on each subsystem. You do that by specifying the path to the root folder of each subsystem. For example, the following command limits the data mining to the code under Linux's drivers/gpu folder:

```
adam$ git log --format=format: --name-only --after=2016-01-01 \
    -- drivers/gpu/ | sort | uniq -c | sort -r
```

Use git rev-list --count HEAD to aggregate all contributions and calculate hotspots on the level of logical components. You can run the same command on individual folders too, in case they align with the logical components in your codebase. Here's an example:

```
adam$ git rev-list --count HEAD -- src/application/engine/
55
```

The X-Ray functionality is typically built using language-specific parsers, but you can get a working version for free with some Git magic. In that case you specify the -L option, which instructs Git to fetch each historic revision based on the range of lines of code that make up a function. Here's an example on Linux to X-Ray the intel_crtc_page_flip function in the drivers/gpu/drm/i915/intel_display.c hotspot:

```
adam$ git log -L:intel_crtc_page_flip:drivers/gpu/drm/i915/intel_display.c
```

Note that the command will take quite some time to complete on large files. The command outputs the complete state of the code as it looked in each revision. This comes in handy if you want to calculate complexity trends. If you just want to get a proxy for the technical debt interest rate, then you can count the change frequency of the hotspot function by means of command-line tools. Here's an example from a Bash shell where grep filters out each commit hash, wc -l counts them, and the --after option limits the amount of data to a recent development period:

```
adam$ git log -L:intel_crtc_page_flip:drivers/gpu/drm/i915/intel_display.c \
        --after=2017-01-01 | grep 'commit ' | wc -l
    5
```

Explore Git's Command-Line Options

 Git wasn't designed for data mining, so we often need to postprocess its output. This becomes less painful if we learn the different command-line options offered by the Git commands. Often, finding the right combination of options can dramatically simplify the postprocessing by delegating the heavy lifting to Git itself. The Git reference manual is a behavioral data miner's best friend.[1]

---

1. https://git-scm.com/docs

Get Author Summaries

The command git shortlog -s gives you a list of all contributing authors, including a count of their number of commits. You can run this command on a specific folder, too, by specifying a path with a double dash, as shown in the next example:

```
adam$ git shortlog -s -- src/application/engine/
   943  John
    11  Paul
   280  George
    20  Ringo
```

This data serves as the basis for quick knowledge maps and as a first hint at a possible knowledge loss during offboarding.

Just as in earlier examples, you limit the data-mining depth to a specific time period with the --after option. This is useful to get information on the recent amount of parallel development in a component. In that case you summarize the number of unique authors by piping the output to the wc -l utility (available in a Bash shell), as shown in the next example:

```
adam$ git shortlog -s --after=2016-09-19 -- drivers/gpu/drm/i915/ | wc -l
55
```

Get the Age of Your Code

Code age is calculated in two steps: first we fetch a list of all files in the repository with the git ls-files command, then we request the modification date of each file using a variation of git log, as shown in the next example:

```
adam$  git log -1 --format="%ad" --date=short \
  -- activerecord/lib/active_record/base.rb
2016-06-09
```

A Brief Introduction to cloc

cloc is used to calculate the number of lines of code and its GitHub page contains detailed documentation on the tool.[2] This section shows only the basic commands used to augment a change-frequency analysis with a lines-of-code dimension.

To get a summary of the content of your repository, move inside your repository and run cloc with the --quiet option:

---

2. https://github.com/AlDanial/cloc

```
adam$ cloc . --quiet
--------------------------------------------------------------------
Language            files          blank        comment           code
--------------------------------------------------------------------
JavaScript           8208         122901         130552         655610
HTML                  243           1533             35          21836
...                   ...            ...            ...            ...
Dockerfile              2              7              4             22
Lisp                    1              0              0              6
--------------------------------------------------------------------
SUM:                12966         179726         138584        1145430
--------------------------------------------------------------------
```

You generate machine-readable CSV by adding the --csv option. This is the recommended approach since it makes it easier to postprocess the results by means of scripts or command-line tools.

To get the lines of code for each individual file you use the --by-file option. Here's an example where the line count of each file is delivered as CSV:

```
adam$ cloc ./ --by-file --csv --quiet
Java,./src/jvm/clojure/lang/Compiler.java,1000,651,7302
Clojure,./src/clj/clojure/core.clj,855,70,6844
Java,./src/jvm/clojure/lang/Numbers.java,676,1569,1911
Markdown,./changes.md,574,0,1860
...
```

Just add the --report-file option to instruct cloc to save the data to a file:

```
adam$ cloc ./ --by-file --csv --quiet --report-file=lines_by_file.csv
```

cloc offers several options that help you filter and clean your data. The one I use all the time is --exclude-dir, which lets you exclude folders with third-party code or autogenerated content:

```
adam$ cloc ./ --by-file --csv --quiet --exclude-dir=node_modules
```

Take Care on Windows

 If you're on Windows you want to specify the --unix flag to get the cloc file names in the same UNIX path format as the data from Git.

Export Analysis Data from CodeScene

At the time of writing (winter 2018), the CodeScene APIs aren't public yet, but they're likely to be if you pick up this book in the future. So let's have a brief discussion on those future possibilities and what you could do once the CodeScene APIs are available.

CodeScene automates most of the analyses in this book and provides some additional analyses—for example, risk classifications and machine learning–based prioritization algorithms. One of the goals with CodeScene is to make all that data available so that you can build your own analyses on top of it, or maybe complement it with other types of metrics.

In the final chapter of the book we looked at some proactive usages of behavioral code analysis. This is a field that has a lot to offer, in particular when we integrate the data into our IDEs and code editors. For example, we saw how a change coupling analysis could help detect omissions in *Catch the Absence of Change*, on page 197. The same data could be used to solve a much harder problem: reading code. Wouldn't it be great if the next time you looked at an unfamiliar piece of code, you got a friendly message that said, "Hey, other developers who read the code in this file also looked at the backup_procedures.sql in the database and the regular_scheduling.js file in the front-end repository."? Using existing analysis data would allow you to build that.

Hints and Solutions to the Exercises

The exercises in the book let you try the techniques on real-world codebases. In this appendix we walk through each of those exercises and look at their solutions. Since this is about software design, there may be several answers to some of the design problems, and in that case the solutions point out that there are alternatives.

Solutions: Identify Code with High Interest Rates

Here are the solutions to the exercises in Chapter 2, *Identify Code with High Interest Rates*, on page 15.

Find Refactoring Candidates in Docker

From the perspective of test automation, the code that drives the test execution from the command line has evolved into two hotspots: integration-cli/docker_cli_build_test.go and integration-cli/docker_cli_run_test.go. Their complexity trends show a steep upward drift and, combined with the pure size of the files, these hotspots make great refactoring candidates.

Follow Up on Improvements to Rails

The historic hotspots activerecord/lib/active_record/base.rb and activerecord/lib/active_record/associations.rb both show a dramatic reduction in size and code complexity in the years 2011 and 2012. Today they are small units that only specify some common declarations. As such, it's misleading when they show up as hotspots. This finding has a number of implications:

- It illustrates why the hotspot criteria need a complexity dimension in addition to change frequencies.

- It shows complexity trends are useful to show the effect of refactorings too.

As for the bonus points promised in the exercise, a code-age dimension works well to down-prioritize historic hotspots in the ranking. In case some hotspot hasn't been worked on recently–as indicated by its code age–we could down-prioritize its importance. Well done!

Solutions: Coupling in Time

Here are the solutions to the exercises in Chapter 3, *Coupling in Time: A Heuristic for the Concept of Surprise*, on page 35.

Learn from the Change Patterns in a Codebase

There's a strong degree of change coupling between the test cases for the Visual Basic and C# compilers, where files with the same name but located in different folders and implemented in different programming languages are changed together. If you join the project, you use this information so that you can plan changes to both parts of the code; the compiler won't be able to detect the omission of a test.

We also note that the change coupling between the test suites is deliberate. Last year I had the opportunity to ask some of the lead developers on Roslyn about that change coupling, and they explained that earlier in the project they found a number of command line parsing issues. Thus they decided to add the same tests for both compilers even when a bug was identified in only one of them.

Detect Omissions with Internal Change Coupling

Functions with duplicated code make it hard to distinguish between context-specific conditions and true omissions that lead to bugs. In the function fully_connected there's a type check on the input argument num_outputs that's missing in convolution2d_transpose. In addition, the conditional check if not normalizer_params: in fully_connected is written in a different form in convolution2d_transpose. It's a minor style variation, but small inconsistencies add up.

Kill the Clones

Both LinkTagHelper.cs and ScriptTagHelper.cs contain a Process, and the code similarity between the two implementations is 92 percent. If you look at the code you see that the only differences are that the variable names and—this is rare—the comments have been updated. (So, this is more like copy-paste with a gold plating.) Since the methods model the same process and the same business concept, you could extract that common knowledge into a module of its own and break the change coupling.

Solutions: The Principles of Code Age

Here are the solutions to the exercises in Chapter 5, *The Principles of Code Age*, on page 73.

Cores All the Way Down

TensorFlow's core/lib/core has low package cohesion and could be separated into smaller and more cohesive packages. The threadpool module would go into a concurrency package, while the arena and refcount modules are related to managing heap memory and could be contained together in a new allocation package.

Deep Mining: The Median Age of Code

To calculate a median value, we need to get the age of each individual line of code. This sounds like a job for git blame. We could even add the --porcelain option to make it easier to consume the output.

Solutions: Spot Your System's Tipping Point

Here are the solutions to the exercises in Chapter 6, *Spot Your System's Tipping Point*, on page 93.

Prioritize Hotspots in CPU Architectures

The main suspect in the arch subsystem is arch/x86/kvm/vmx.c. The file contains 8,500 lines of code, and several of its functions are quite excessive in terms of complexity. Another refactoring candidate with slightly lower change frequency but equal complexity is arch/x86/kvm/x86.c.

Get a Quick Win

There's plenty of structural duplication within the file erts/emulator/beam/erl_process.c. Fortunately, the functions with the most duplication are relatively small. That means you can either look to live with the duplication by organizing the clones according to proximity, or start to address the top couples.

As a starting point, two central functions, sched_dirty_cpu_thread_func and sched_dirty_io_thread_func, are closely related and differ only in details. That suggests an abstraction waiting to get out—perhaps sched_dirty_thread—that can encapsulate the commonalities and leave the two original functions to parameterize with the few parameters that vary.

Supervise Your Unit-Test Practices

The task was to detect if the unit tests are actively maintained, or if there are signs of worry. Interestingly, the trends of the logical components reveal that we have both cases here; until mid 2016 there was a clear disparity, as application code was being added without any corresponding growth in tests. In addition, we see that there's an imbalance between the amount of application code and test code. This changed in 2016; the maintainers seem to have invested in adding a more comprehensive test suite. In such cases you want to continue to supervise the trends and ensure that the tests are being kept up to date to support the evolution of the code.

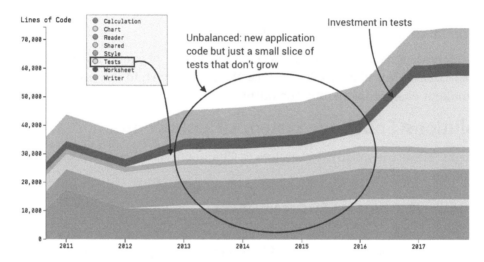

Solutions: Modular Monoliths

Here are the solutions to the exercises in Chapter 8, *Toward Modular Monoliths through the Social View of Code*, on page 141.

Detect Components Across Layers

There are several answers to this exercise, which indicates that there should be opportunities to reconsider the current class boundaries by extracting and representing a new set of abstractions. Just to give one specific example, have a look at the CategoryController.cs and the ManufacturerController.cs, which change together in 88 percent of commits. As you see in the top figure on page 231, an X-Ray reveals that they have a similar concept for pop-up adds, and that concept could be expressed in its own component and context.[1]

---

1. https://codescene.io/projects/1593/jobs/3920/results/code/temporal-coupling/by-commits/xray-result/details?file-name=nopCommerce/src/Presentation/Nop.Web/Administration/Controllers/ManufacturerController.cs

⇕ Coupled Functions	⤓ Coupling (%)	⇕ Commits	⇕ Similarity (%)
src/Presentation/Nop.Web/Administration/Controllers/CategoryController.cs/ProductAddPopup	26	91	92
src/Presentation/Nop.Web/Administration/Controllers/ManufacturerController.cs/ProductAddPopup			
src/Presentation/Nop.Web/Administration/Controllers/CategoryController.cs/Edit	16	91	79
src/Presentation/Nop.Web/Administration/Controllers/ManufacturerController.cs/Edit			
src/Presentation/Nop.Web/Administration/Controllers/CategoryController.cs/ProductAddPopupList	14	91	98
src/Presentation/Nop.Web/Administration/Controllers/ManufacturerController.cs/ProductAddPopupList			
src/Presentation/Nop.Web/Administration/Controllers/CategoryController.cs/Create	13	91	80
src/Presentation/Nop.Web/Administration/Controllers/ManufacturerController.cs/Create			

A missing abstraction

Investigate Change Patterns in Component-Based Codebases

The different packages have high cohesion in the sense that most change coupling relationships are limited to files within the same package. This implies that the modular boundaries hold up well during the evolution of the codebase. The one exception is the change coupling between the two Worksheet.php files, where one implements the Xls format and the other implements the Xlsx format.

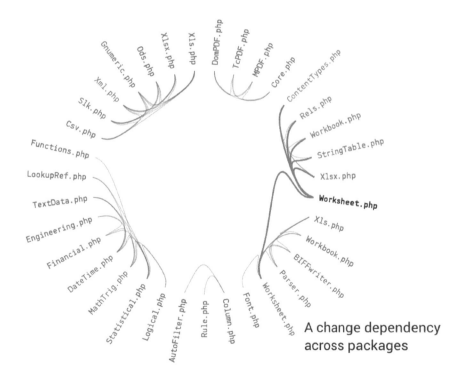

A change dependency across packages

Solutions: Systems of Systems

Here are the solutions to the exercises in Chapter 9, *Systems of Systems: Analyzing Multiple Repositories and Microservices*, on page 165.

Support Code Reading and Change Planning

The file gceBakeStage.js in the front end has a change coupling to the automated test BakeHandlerSpec.groovy in another repository (rosco). Use such change coupling information to explore the related module from the perspective of the planned changes.

Combine Technical and Social Views to Identify Communities

The code in gceBakeStage.js is mainly developed by the author *chrisb* while the change-coupled file BakeHandlerSpec.groovy is developed by *duftler*. This kind of information serves as a communication aid for developers in different parts of the organization.

Analyze Your Infrastructure

The top hotspot in Git is the Makefile, which consists of 2,500 lines of code. If you look at its complexity trend, you see that there was a reduction in size back in 2013. However, the recent trend shows that the Makefile keeps accumulating responsibilities. In part that's because the file isn't limited to build dependencies, but rather contains several parts of the process too. As an example, have a look at the lines of code linked in the footnote on this page; they specify rules that apply only in a specific context.[2]

A Makefile could be the target of splinter refactoring too, which would help us clarify roles and responsibilities in the same way as what the Git architecture does for the application code.

Solutions: An Extra Team Member

Here are the solutions to the exercises in Chapter 10, *An Extra Team Member: Predictive and Proactive Analyses*, on page 189.

Early Warnings in Legacy Code

The top hotspots at the function level, unlockAccept and addSslHostConfig, are both rather complex. One way to counter the complexity accumulation would be

---

2. https://github.com/SoftwareDesignXRays/git/blob/59c0ea183ad1c5c2b3790caa5046e4ecfa839247/Makefile#L2241

to introduce chunks as discussed in *Turn Hotspot Methods into Brain-Friendly Chunks*, on page 67.

The recent changes in AbstractEndpoint.java seems to have been an extension of addSslHostConfig that gives the method the additional responsibility of replacing an existing host configuration. This also introduces some control coupling, as shown in the next code snippet:

```
public void addSslHostConfig(
        SSLHostConfig sslHostConfig,
        boolean replace)
      throws IllegalArgumentException {
  // ...snip...
  if (replace) { // <--- control coupling
      SSLHostConfig previous = sslHostConfigs.put(key, sslHostConfig);
      //...snip...
```

One alternative is to separate the responsibility of the replace behavior into its own method if the distinction is important.

Find the Experts

There are multiple contributors to both of those packages, but there's also a clear main developer for each of them. In client-go, Chao Xu has contributed most of the code, and the alias deads2k has written most of the apiextensions-apiserver. If this were a corporate project, those two people would be the first to discuss the suggested extensions with.

Offboarding: What If?

Yes, the last exercise in the book was close to a trick question because Linus Torvalds turned over the maintenance of Git to Junio Hamano in 2005.[3] As a consequence, there are few remaining parts where Linus is the main developer. One such module is date.c, which models a stable problem domain. More Git-specific parts include merge-tree.c and diff-tree.c, and none of them are hotspots.

In contrast, Rich Hickey still maintains the Clojure project, and if he'd leave it would be ... hmm, *challenging*. The figure on page 234 compares the knowledge loss for Git with the simulated knowledge loss for Clojure.

---

3. https://en.wikipedia.org/wiki/Junio_Hamano

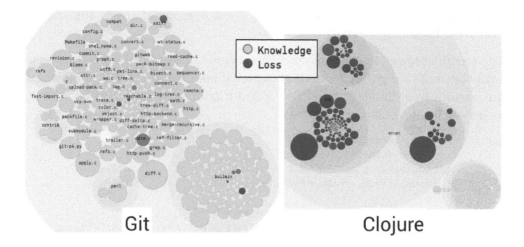

Of course, knowledge loss is about more than abandoned code—for example, loss of vision, experience, and project history. Since we cannot measure those aspects, the analysis remains an approximation.

Bibliography

[AH99]   M.S. Ackerman and C. Halverson. Considering an Organization's Memory. *Proceedings, Computer Supported Cooperative Work Conference.* 39-48, 1999.

[AS06]   S.W. Ambler and P.J. Sadalage. *Refactoring Databases: Evolutionary Database Design.* Addison-Wesley, Boston, MA, 2006.

[Bak95]   B. Baker. On Finding Duplication and Near-Duplication in Large Software Systems. *Proceedings of the Second Working Conference on Reverse Engineering.* 86-95, 1995.

[Bec07]   K. Beck. *Implementation Patterns.* Addison-Wesley, Boston, MA, 2007.

[BG05]   N Braisby and A Gellatly. *Cognitive Psychology.* Oxford University Press, New York, NY, 2005.

[BK03]   R.S. Baron and N.L. Kerr. *Group Process, Group Decision, Group Action.* Open University Press, Berkshire, United Kingdom, 2003.

[BNMG11]   C. Bird, N. Nagappan, B. Murphy, H. Gall, and P. Devanbu. Don't Touch My Code! Examining the Effects of Ownership on Software Quality. *Proceedings of the 19th ACM SIGSOFT symposium and the 13th European conference on foundations of software engineering.* 4-14, 2011.

[BOW11]   R.M. Bell, T.J. Ostrand, and E.J. Weyuker. *Does Measuring Code Change Improve Fault Prediction?.* ACM Press, New York, NY, USA, 2011.

[Bra95]   S Brand. *How Buildings Learn: What Happens After They're Built.* Penguin, New York, NY, 1995.

[Bro86]   Frederick Brooks. No Silver Bullet—Essence and Accident in Software Engineering. *Proceedings of the IFIP Tenth World Computing Conference.* 1986.

[Bro95]   Frederick P. Brooks Jr. *The Mythical Man-Month: Essays on Software Engineering.* Addison-Wesley, Boston, MA, Anniversary, 1995.

[CB10]   J.O. Coplien and G Bjørnvig. *Lean Architecture for Agile Software Development.* John Wiley & Sons, New York, NY, 2010.

[CB16]   L.J. Colfer and C.Y. Baldwin. The Mirroring Hypothesis: Theory, Evidence, and Exceptions. *Ind Corp Change.* 25:709–738, 2016.

[CE78]   R.C. Cass and J.J. Edney. The commons dilemma: A simulation testing the effects of resource visibility and territorial division. *Human Ecology.* 6, 1978.

[CH13]   M. Cataldo and J.D. Herbsleb. Coordination Breakdowns and Their Impact on Development Productivity and Software Failures. *IEEE Transactions on Software Engineering.* 39, 2013.

[Con68]   M.E. Conway. How do committees invent?. *Datamation.* 4:28–31, 1968.

[DB02]   F. Detienne and F. Bott. *Software Design: Cognitive Aspects.* Springer, New York, NY, USA, 2002.

[DLG05]   M. D'Ambros, M. Lanza, and H Gall. Fractal Figures: Visualizing Development Effort for CVS Entities. *Visualizing Software for Understanding and Analysis, 2005. VISSOFT 2005. 3rd IEEE International Workshop on.* 1–6, 2005.

[Ebb85]   H. Ebbinghaus. *Über das Gedächtnis. Untersuchungen zur experimentellen Psychologie..* Duncker & Humblot, Leipzig, Germany, 1985.

[Eva03]   Eric Evans. *Domain-Driven Design: Tackling Complexity in the Heart of Software.* Addison-Wesley Longman, Boston, MA, First, 2003.

[FBBO99]   Martin Fowler, Kent Beck, John Brant, William Opdyke, and Don Roberts. *Refactoring: Improving the Design of Existing Code.* Addison-Wesley, Boston, MA, 1999.

[Fea04]   Michael Feathers. *Working Effectively with Legacy Code.* Prentice Hall, Englewood Cliffs, NJ, 2004.

[Fel14]   F. Feldt. Do System Test Cases Grow Old?. *Proceedings of the 2014 IEEE International Conference on Software Testing, Verification, and Validation.* 343-352, 2014.

[Fow16]   S.J. Fowler. *Production-Ready Microservices: Building Standardized Systems Across an Engineering Organization.* O'Reilly & Associates, Inc., Sebastopol, CA, 2016.

[FP09]   Steve Freeman and Nat Pryce. *Growing Object-Oriented Software, Guided by Tests.* Addison-Wesley Longman, Boston, MA, 2009.

[Gan03]   M. Gancarz. *Linux and the Unix Philosophy, 2nd Edition*. Digital Press, Woburn, MA, 2003.

[GHC15]   M. Greiler, K. Herzig, and J. Czerwonka. Code ownership and software quality: a replication study. *Proceedings of the 12th Working Conference on Mining Software Repositories*. 2015.

[GKMS00]   T. L. Graves, A. F. Karr, J. S. Marron, and H Siy. Predicting fault incidence using software change history. *Software Engineering, IEEE Transactions on*. 26[7], 2000.

[HGH08]   A. Hindle, M.W. Godfrey, and R.C. Holt. *Reading Beside the Lines: Indentation as a Proxy for Complexity Metrics. Program Comprehension, 2008. ICPC 2008. The 16th IEEE International Conference on*. IEEE Computer Society Press, Washington, DC, 2008.

[HM03]   J.D. Herbsleb and A. Mockus. An Empirical Study of Speed and Communication in Globally Distributed Software Development. *IEEE Transactions On Software Engineering*. 29, 2003.

[HT00]   Andrew Hunt and David Thomas. *The Pragmatic Programmer: From Journeyman to Master*. Addison-Wesley, Boston, MA, 2000.

[KR87]   R.M. Karp and M. O. Rabin. Efficient randomized pattern-matching algorithms. *IBM Journal of Research and Development*. 31(2):249–260, 1987.

[Leh80]   M. M. Lehman. On Understanding Laws, Evolution, and Conservation in the Large-Program Life Cycle. *Journal of Systems and Software*. 1:213–221, 1980.

[Mar17]   R.C. Martin. *Clean Architecture: A Craftsman's Guide to Software Structure and Design*. Prentice Hall, Englewood Cliffs, NJ, 2017.

[MBMY97]   P.L. McLeod, R.S. Baron, M.W. Marti, and K. Yoon. The eyes have it: Minority influence in face-to-face and computer-mediated group discussion. *Journal of Applied Psychology*. 82:706–718, 1997.

[MLM96]   J. Mayrand, C. Leblanc, and E. Merlo. Experiment on the Automatic Detection of Function Clones in a Software System Using Metrics. *Proceedings of the 12th International Conference on Software Maintenance*. 244-253, 1996.

[MPS08]   R. Moser, W. Pedrycz, and G. Succi. A Comparative Analysis of the Efficiency of Change Metrics and Static Code Attributes for Defect Prediction. *Proceedings of the 30th international conference on Software engineering*. 181–190, 2008.

[MW09]   A. Meneely and L. Williams. Secure open source collaboration: an empirical study of Linus' law. *Proceedings of the 16th ACM conference on computer and communications security.* 453–462, 2009.

[NMB08]   N. Nagappan, B. Murphy, and V. Basili. The Influence of Organizational Structure on Software Quality. *International Conference on Software Engineering, Proceedings.* 521–530, 2008.

[OV14]   A. Olsson and R. Voss. *Git Version Control Cookbook.* Packt Publishing, Birmingham, UK, 2014.

[OW10]   A. Oram and G. Wilson. *Making Software: What Really Works, and Why We Believe It.* O'Reilly & Associates, Inc., Sebastopol, CA, 2010.

[Par94]   D. Parnas. Software Aging. *ICSE '94 Proceedings of the 16th international conference on Software engineering.* 279–287, 1994.

[SABB17] D. Spadini, M. Aniche, M. Bruntink, and A. Bacchelli. To Mock or Not To Mock? An Empirical Study on Mocking Practices. *Unknown - Fix it!.* 2017.

[Sch83]   D.A. Schön. *Reflective Practitioner: How Professionals Think in Action.* Basic Books, New York, NY, 1983.

[SSS14]   G. Suryanarayana, G. Samarthyam, and T. Sharma. *Refactoring for Software Design Smells: Managing Technical Debt.* Morgan Kaufmann, Massachusetts, USA, 2014.

[Ste72]   I.D. Steiner. *Group Process and Productivity.* Academic Press, New York, NY, USA, 1972.

[TBPD15] M. Tufano, G. Bavota, D. Poshyvanyk, M. Di Penta, R. Oliveto, and A. De Lucia. An Empirical Study on Developer Related Factors Characterizing Fix-Inducing Commits. *Journal of Software: Evolution and Process.* 2015.

[Tor15]   Adam Tornhill. *Your Code as a Crime Scene.* The Pragmatic Bookshelf, Raleigh, NC, 2015.

[TPBO15] M. Tufano, F. Palomba, G. Bavota, R. Oliveto, M. Di Penta, A. De Lucia, and D. Poshyvanyk. When and Why Your Code Starts to Smell Bad. *Proceedings of the 37th International Conference on Software Engineering.* 2015.

[Vau97]   D. Vaughan. *The Challenger Launch Decision: Risky Technology, Culture, and Deviance at NASA.* University of Chicago Press, Chicago, IL, 1997.

[ZWDZ04] T. Zimmermann, P. Weißgerber, S. Diehl, and A. Zeller. Mining Version Histories to Guide Software Changes. *Proceedings of International Conference on Software Engineering (ICSE).* 2004.

Index

Thank you!

How did you enjoy this book? Please let us know. Take a moment and email us at support@pragprog.com with your feedback. Tell us your story and you could win free ebooks. Please use the subject line "Book Feedback."

Ready for your next great Pragmatic Bookshelf book? Come on over to https://pragprog.com and use the coupon code BUYANOTHER2018 to save 30% on your next ebook.

Void where prohibited, restricted, or otherwise unwelcome. Do not use ebooks near water. If rash persists, see a doctor. Doesn't apply to *The Pragmatic Programmer* ebook because it's older than the Pragmatic Bookshelf itself. Side effects may include increased knowledge and skill, increased marketability, and deep satisfaction. Increase dosage regularly.

And thank you for your continued support,

Andy Hunt, Publisher

SAVE 30%!
Use coupon code
BUYANOTHER2018

Better by Design

From architecture and design to deployment in the harsh realities of the real world, make your software better by design.

Design It!

Don't engineer by coincidence—design it like you mean it! Grounded by fundamentals and filled with practical design methods, this is the perfect introduction to software architecture for programmers who are ready to grow their design skills. Ask the right stakeholders the right questions, explore design options, share your design decisions, and facilitate collaborative workshops that are fast, effective, and fun. Become a better programmer, leader, and designer. Use your new skills to lead your team in implementing software with the right capabilities—and develop awesome software!

Michael Keeling
(358 pages) ISBN: 9781680502091. $41.95
https://pragprog.com/book/mkdsa

Release It! Second Edition

A single dramatic software failure can cost a company millions of dollars—but can be avoided with simple changes to design and architecture. This new edition of the best-selling industry standard shows you how to create systems that run longer, with fewer failures, and recover better when bad things happen. New coverage includes DevOps, microservices, and cloud-native architecture. Stability antipatterns have grown to include systemic problems in large-scale systems. This is a must-have pragmatic guide to engineering for production systems.

Michael Nygard
(376 pages) ISBN: 9781680502398. $47.95
https://pragprog.com/book/mnee2

Learn Why, Then Learn How

Get started on your Elixir journey today.

Adopting Elixir

Adoption is more than programming. Elixir is an exciting new language, but to successfully get your application from start to finish, you're going to need to know more than just the language. You need the case studies and strategies in this book. Learn the best practices for the whole life of your application, from design and team-building, to managing stakeholders, to deployment and monitoring. Go beyond the syntax and the tools to learn the techniques you need to develop your Elixir application from concept to production.

Ben Marx, José Valim, Bruce Tate
(225 pages) ISBN: 9781680502527. $42.95
https://pragprog.com/book/tvmelixir

Programming Elixir ≥ 1.6

This book is *the* introduction to Elixir for experienced programmers, completely updated for Elixir 1.6 and beyond. Explore functional programming without the academic overtones (tell me about monads just one more time). Create concurrent applications, but get them right without all the locking and consistency headaches. Meet Elixir, a modern, functional, concurrent language built on the rock-solid Erlang VM. Elixir's pragmatic syntax and built-in support for metaprogramming will make you productive and keep you interested for the long haul. Maybe the time is right for the Next Big Thing. Maybe it's Elixir.

Dave Thomas
(398 pages) ISBN: 9781680502992. $47.95
https://pragprog.com/book/elixir16

A Better Web with Phoenix and Elm

Elixir and Phoenix on the server side with Elm on the front end gets you the best of both worlds in both worlds!

Functional Web Development with Elixir, OTP, and Phoenix

Elixir and Phoenix are generating tremendous excitement as an unbeatable platform for building modern web applications. For decades OTP has helped developers create incredibly robust, scalable applications with unparalleled uptime. Make the most of them as you build a stateful web app with Elixir, OTP, and Phoenix. Model domain entities without an ORM or a database. Manage server state and keep your code clean with OTP Behaviours. Layer on a Phoenix web interface without coupling it to the business logic. Open doors to powerful new techniques that will get you thinking about web development in fundamentally new ways.

Lance Halvorsen
(218 pages) ISBN: 9781680502435. $45.95
https://pragprog.com/book/lhelph

Programming Elm

Elm brings the safety and stability of functional programing to front-end development, making it one of the most popular new languages. Elm's functional nature and static typing means that run-time errors are nearly impossible, and it compiles to JavaScript for easy web deployment. This book helps you take advantage of this new language in your web site development. Learn how the Elm Architecture will help you create fast applications. Discover how to integrate Elm with JavaScript so you can update legacy applications. See how Elm tooling makes deployment quicker and easier.

Jeremy Fairbank
(250 pages) ISBN: 9781680502855. $40.95
https://pragprog.com/book/jfelm

Pragmatic Programming

We'll show you how to be more pragmatic and effective, for new code and old.

Your Code as a Crime Scene

Jack the Ripper and legacy codebases have more in common than you'd think. Inspired by forensic psychology methods, this book teaches you strategies to predict the future of your codebase, assess refactoring direction, and understand how your team influences the design. With its unique blend of forensic psychology and code analysis, this book arms you with the strategies you need, no matter what programming language you use.

Adam Tornhill
(218 pages) ISBN: 9781680500387. $36
https://pragprog.com/book/atcrime

The Nature of Software Development

You need to get value from your software project. You need it "free, now, and perfect." We can't get you there, but we can help you get to "cheaper, sooner, and better." This book leads you from the desire for value down to the specific activities that help good Agile projects deliver better software sooner, and at a lower cost. Using simple sketches and a few words, the author invites you to follow his path of learning and understanding from a half century of software development and from his engagement with Agile methods from their very beginning.

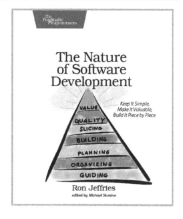

Ron Jeffries
(176 pages) ISBN: 9781941222379. $24
https://pragprog.com/book/rjnsd

The Pragmatic Bookshelf

The Pragmatic Bookshelf features books written by developers for developers. The titles continue the well-known Pragmatic Programmer style and continue to garner awards and rave reviews. As development gets more and more difficult, the Pragmatic Programmers will be there with more titles and products to help you stay on top of your game.

Visit Us Online

This Book's Home Page
https://pragprog.com/book/atevol
Source code from this book, errata, and other resources. Come give us feedback, too!

Register for Updates
https://pragprog.com/updates
Be notified when updates and new books become available.

Join the Community
https://pragprog.com/community
Read our weblogs, join our online discussions, participate in our mailing list, interact with our wiki, and benefit from the experience of other Pragmatic Programmers.

New and Noteworthy
https://pragprog.com/news
Check out the latest pragmatic developments, new titles and other offerings.

Save on the eBook

Save on the eBook versions of this title. Owning the paper version of this book entitles you to purchase the electronic versions at a terrific discount.

PDFs are great for carrying around on your laptop—they are hyperlinked, have color, and are fully searchable. Most titles are also available for the iPhone and iPod touch, Amazon Kindle, and other popular e-book readers.

Buy now at *https://pragprog.com/coupon*

Contact Us

Online Orders:	*https://pragprog.com/catalog*
Customer Service:	*support@pragprog.com*
International Rights:	*translations@pragprog.com*
Academic Use:	*academic@pragprog.com*
Write for Us:	*http://write-for-us.pragprog.com*
Or Call:	+1 800-699-7764

Milton Keynes UK
Ingram Content Group UK Ltd.
UKHW052109231023
431173UK00001B/3